Thanksgiving

Revisiting New England: The New Regionalism

SERIES EDITORS

Siobhan Senier, University of New Hampshire
Darren Ranco, Dartmouth College
Adam Sweeting, Boston University
David H. Watters, University of New Hampshire

This series presents fresh discussions of the distinctiveness of New England culture. The editors seek manuscripts examining the history of New England regionalism; the way its culture came to represent American national culture; the interaction between that "official" New England culture and the people who lived in the region; and local, subregional, or even biographical subjects as microcosms that explicitly open up and consider larger issues. The series welcomes new theoretical and historical perspectives, and is designed to cross disciplinary boundaries and appeal to a wide audience.

For a complete list of books available in this series, please visit: www.upne.com

THANKSGIVING

The Biography of an American Holiday

James W. Baker

Foreword by Peter J. Gomes

University of New Hampshire Press
Durham, New Hampshire

PUBLISHED BY UNIVERSITY PRESS OF NEW ENGLAND
HANOVER AND LONDON

University of New Hampshire Press
Published by University Press of New England
One Court Street, Lebanon NH 03766
© 2009 by University of New Hampshire Press
Printed in the United States of America

A Book Club Edition

This book is for Peg and Lucie

Contents

Foreword
Thanksgiving in America

Peter J. Gomes

HARVARD UNIVERSITY

FORMER PRESIDENT, THE PILGRIM SOCIETY

One of the most enduring and endearing of American images is the Thanksgiving holiday family dinner. The turkey, cranberry sauce, and the array of pies have attained nearly iconic status, and Norman Rockwell has provided a *Saturday Evening Post* fantasy of ordinary gratitude from which no one can escape and to which everyone aspires. Not for nothing is this the most heavily traveled day in the American calendar. Christmas has its struggles between its secular and religious meanings. Easter has retained much of its Christian overtones, and the Fourth of July survives as a holiday of summer that may or may not have something to do with the origins of the American Republic. But Thanksgiving has a unique claim on the American psyche. Part of the reason has to do with the fact that this holiday, above all others, is bound up with our sense of the mythic past. The Fourth of July is certainly American, and goes with the founding of the Republic and the Declaration of Independence. But Thanksgiving, as we always remind ourselves in New England, is older than the Republic. And while in America we cultivate the new and unprecedented, because by comparison to other cultures we have so little of it, we venerate the past. And it is not a small thing to claim a past that precedes the nation and which seems founded on such homely virtues as family, food, and friendship. Thanksgiving does not suggest conflict or conquest: there are no military or local patriotic issues to be addressed, and the religious element can be as modest as local custom and family tradition permit. Thus, Thanksgiving becomes the American holiday that embraces all that we value without stressing any of the things that make a public holiday problematic.

Thanksgiving is a big deal in America because we Americans believe it to be our unique holiday, hardly found in this form anywhere else on earth. And wherever on earth Thanksgiving is celebrated, it is invariably associated with America and its founding virtues and values. At the heart of the mythic enterprise, of course, are to be found the Pilgrim fathers and mothers of Plymouth who, despite various claims to the contrary, are regarded as the founders of the feast. Hardly a schoolroom in America can get through the month of November without some depiction of the Pilgrims and their Indian neighbors feasting and playing together in the New England autumn. Even the ubiquitous football games, professional and amateur, while significant, are secondary icons on a day when the urgencies of the moment require an obligatory act of piety toward the past.

Growing up in Plymouth, Massachusetts, I became very aware at an early age of my hometown's special claim on this holiday. But even in Plymouth not many people knew a great deal about the Pilgrims or Plimoth Plantation. Some may have heard of the good ship *Mayflower,* and families may even have visited the fabled Plymouth Rock and been terribly disappointed at its modest size. "Speak for yourself, John," the famous line of Priscilla Mullins to John Alden, when he went to propose marriage to her in behalf of Captain Myles Standish, owes such currency as it enjoys to Henry Wadsworth Longfellow's once very popular poem *The Courtship of Miles Standish.* There remains much to be known and learned about the Pilgrims of Plymouth, but what most people know is that "they" had something to do with the "First Thanksgiving." And that is enough to earn the Pilgrims a permanent place in the American pantheon.

What Longfellow and poets considerably less accomplished than he did for the Pilgrims in words, Currier and Ives did for the even more vital imagery of print and engraving and for the place of the Pilgrims' great adventure, New England. "Over the river and through the woods to grandmother's house we go" suggests a rural New England landscape, fitted up for the feast of family and the occasion of Thanksgiving. And although Thanksgiving is celebrated in California, and Hawaii, and Arizona, the picture in people's heads is of that idealized New England scene where the generations gather around the hearth, huddled against the snow outside and renewed by generational proximity within.

Half a century ago, Thanksgiving in Plymouth, as in most of New England, meant family. Most people either hosted their family or went to the trouble of traveling home to their family, there to eat the festal meal and to deal as needs be with the relatives and the claims of family. So private a holiday was this in my youth that I recall the Plymouth Chamber of Commerce having to persuade a local restaurant to stay open to serve the small number of tourists who wanted to be where it all began. This was no easy task, as any sensible person expected not to work on Thanksgiving, because there were duties to be done at home. And so, each year, somebody would have to be persuaded to provide for the strangers who, contrary to nature, were not at home but touring. I remember, as a child, thinking it odd that anyone should be anywhere but home on Thanksgiving Day. It was for many years the quietest day of the year.

This is hardly the case today, as Plymouth is filled with tourists who are in fact encouraged to come early and stay late. Part of this has to do with America's insatiable wanderlust and curiosity about its own past, a past in which Plymouth continues to play such a vital role. But part of it also has to do with the effective marketing of the day and the place as a destination, a stop that spares the modern family the troubles of home, and can be understood as both diverting and educational. For many, of course, Thanksgiving is the beginning of the Christmas shopping season, and if those commercial considerations can be combined with a little bit of cultural piety, then why not come to the place where, since childhood, we were told "it all began"?

But is this really all there is to know about Thanksgiving? Is this holiday what it seems to be, and is there a backstory behind the front story? James W. Baker takes up these questions in what is sure to become the standard text on Thanksgiving. In this extraordinary book, Baker separates fact from fiction, tells us what the Pilgrims did and did not have to do with the holiday, and traces the cultural development of the holiday in the hearts and minds of Americans. Baker has spent his life on this subject, both as a native Plymouthean and as a professional historian. He writes with the eye of both a novelist and an anthropologist, and his grasp of the elements of popular culture over nearly four hundred years of the American experience is compelling and impressive. No detail is too small for him to notice. He writes of Thanksgiving in popular songs, movies, and television shows, and notices how the Pilgrims and cranberry sauce have been marketed successfully by Madison Avenue pitchmen and their predecessors. He is particularly adept in the discussion of how a local phenomenon gets "sold" to a national audience over long years and how the locals live with the ambiguous success of "their" holiday. On Thanksgiving Day, he asks in the words of the angry American Indians who since 1970 have kept what they call "a Day of Mourning," what do Native Americans have to be thankful for? The Pilgrims survived, flourished, and were appropriately grateful for their survival, which came at the cost of the extinction of the indigenous culture. Does not this fact rain upon our cultural parade on Thanksgiving Day?

And there is more. What happens to Thanksgiving Day when the Pilgrim fathers and mothers cease to be "the spiritual ancestors of all Americans," in the felicitous words of American historian Samuel Eliot Morison, and become, in our increasing consciousness of our pluralist origins, just some more English immigrants whose descendants wrote most of the books on the subject many of us used to read? Can Thanksgiving as we have come to know it survive the "browning" of America? Is the common myth strong enough still to hold us together, or will the feast fail of its own weight, becoming little more than a cliché and the celebration of the dysfunctional American family?

Then there are those who claim that the "First Thanksgiving" isn't: partisans in Virginia, Spanish America, and in the upper reaches of Maine all make credible claims to Thanksgiving observances that precede those of Plymouth. How do we access these claims, and what are we to do with them? New England has long since ceased to be the cultural capital of America. Can a holiday so intently identified with New England survive the unavoidable eclipse of its birthplace?

James W. Baker has taken on a major subject here and treats it magisterially: there is no other book like this extant, and all future discussions of America will depend on this one. Specialist and generalist alike will be rewarded in reading this: there is something here for everyone. But perhaps of greatest importance is the fact that for the first time in modern times we have a significant book by a significant author attending to the fascinating analysis of arguably America's most significant holiday. To Thanksgiving, this book is now as indispensable as the turkey, the cranberry sauce, and the football.

Acknowledgments

I would like to thank those generous friends and colleagues who encouraged me in undertaking this work. My old friend Rev. Peter Gomes first read and enthused about the completed manuscript, and then graciously supplied a foreword couched in his inimitable mellifluous phrases. Carolyn and Len Travers also read the work in production, offering valuable comments and, in Len's case, publication of a preview of the ideas developed here in the *Encyclopedia of American Holidays and National Days* (Greenwood Press, 2006). Alicia Crane Williams, my longtime employer and colleague, also read and offered useful editorial comments. Lisa and Bernie Sampson were the first to see how this project was going, offering encouragement and comment. Die Hoxie, Marie Pelletier, and Karin Goldstein, who remain my valued colleagues and friends at Plimoth Plantation, supplied necessary materials toward the development of the project. John Keenum and Jonathan Lane welcomed me at the American Antiquarian Society and provided an invaluable introduction of the available historical resources of their institution. Nat Philbrick and Tony Horwitz took the time to read and comment from the perspective of far grander historical authorship. John Galluzzo acted as a voluntary agent and encouraged the completion of my earlier publications. Lee Regan and Bev Ness, in the Reference Department of Plymouth Public Library, added valuable assistance in tracking down elusive details. Finally, I especially thank Jerry Kaplan, my old friend and anarchist colleague at Harvard University Press, my brother Tony Baker (who supplied technical expertise in the matter of photography), and most of all my accomplished and enthusiastic wife and fellow museum professional, Peggy Baker, without whom the publication of this "real book-type book" could never have happened.

Introduction

A Thanksgiving Detective Story

These historical myths grow up silently. Some of them reign for centuries. Modern research has exposed many of ancient lineage and long acceptance, has torn away the
mask and revealed them in their true character. Yet the historical myth rarely dies.
No exposure seems able to kill it. Expelled from every book of authority, from every
dictionary and encyclopedia, it will still live on among the great mass of humanity. The
reason for this tenacity of life is not far to seek. The myth, or the tradition, as it is sometimes called, has necessarily a touch of the imagination, and imagination is almost
always more fascinating than truth. The historical myth, indeed, would not exist at all
if it did not profess to tell something which people for one reason or another, like to believe, and which appeals strongly to some emotion or passion, and so to human nature.
— Henry Cabot Lodge, "An American Myth"

Thanksgiving Day! What a wealth of sentiment is evoked by this all-
American holiday. The multitude of familiar images that spring to
mind would require an American Dickens to do them justice: In-
trepid, be-buckled Pilgrims and their dignified Indian neighbors sit down
to dinner in the serenity of an eternally golden autumn afternoon. Radiant,
white-painted New England churches welcome cheerful congregations
from local neighborhoods and the rural farmsteads that have supplied the
bounty of the harvest. Shocks of corn and heaps of pumpkins dot the fields
and fill the barns as the strutting monarch of the farmyard, the fattened
Thanksgiving turkey, marches unaware of his imminent fate. Generations
converge on old family homesteads where wrinkled grandparents welcome
the returning members of their clan. High school and college football
teams defend their honor just as preceding generations did, under crisp
blue fall skies sensuously spiced with a faint aroma of burning leaves. Pies
are drawn steaming from ovens in stoves on which bubbling pots foretell

the coming feast. All of these traditional scenes are recognized by genera-tions of Americans as embodying the essence of Thanksgiving.

But above all, there is the celebrated origin of the holiday in that fabled outdoor feast to which the Pilgrims of Plymouth Colony welcomed their Native American neighbors back when it all began in 1621.

Despite disagreements over details, such as whether the Pilgrims or the Wampanoag Indians deserve the greater honor for the event, or if turkey was on the original bill of fare, the universal consensus is that the mythi-cal Plymouth event was the historical birth of the American Thanksgiving holiday. The accepted narrative incorporating that event (i.e., the "Pil-grim Story," of which Thanksgiving is the denouement) goes something like this:

In the autumn of 1620, a tiny, crowded ship called the *Mayflower* left Plymouth, England. On board were 102 passengers—a mixed company of pious Separatists and profane "Strangers" thrown together by fate (and their troublesome financial backers) on a perilous voyage to find new homes in the wilderness of British North America, or "Virginia," as the entire territory was then known. The Separatists (sometimes identified as "The Pilgrims" proper, although this word is more commonly used to indicate the entire group of passengers) were English religious dissidents who had fled their homeland years before in the face of royal persecu-tion to live in the safety of the tolerant Netherlands. However, poverty, the threatened loss of their English identity and the possible resumption of war between Holland and Spain induced them to emigrate once again, this time to England's American territory. There they hoped to find a place where they could live unmolested and worship as they chose. The "Strangers," on the other hand, simply sought a better life in a new world where land ownership and prosperity were more achievable than in tradi-tion- and class-bound England. Armed with a Virginia Company patent or charter legalizing their new colony, the *Mayflower* passengers set sail across the treacherous North Atlantic ocean.

After a dangerous, frightening, and thoroughly uncomfortable 66-day voyage cooped up in the dark, dank, and smelly bowels of the *Mayflower*, they were immeasurably relieved to sight land on November 9. Following a fruitless attempt to continue on to their original destination at the mouth of the Hudson River, they decided to stay where they had ended up, in New England. They anchored in Cape Cod harbor (now Provincetown harbor) on November 11, 1620. As they were now outside of the legal boundaries of their charter, some of the Strangers asserted that they were no longer obliged to live under the dominion of the "Saints" (as the Separatists commonly referred to themselves), but could strike out on their own. Fortunately, cooler heads prevailed, and the men of the party signed a momentous document called the Mayflower Compact that not only saved the colony by requiring all to live together under a government of their own making, but also introduced democratic principles of government to America and in time inspired the United States Constitution.

Following a month of exploration on Cape Cod, which included a brief, bloodless foray with the Indian inhabitants themselves as well as the discovery of vacant Indian homes, providential corn supplies (which they took but later paid back with interest), and graves, an exploring party arrived at what is now Plymouth. It was a dark and stormy December night of wind and sleet as the little shallop (a coastal craft brought over in pieces on the *Mayflower* and reconstructed on Cape Cod) approached the entrance to Plymouth harbor. Although both sail and rudder were lost in the storm, the boat entered the harbor and safely anchored. Its passengers found themselves on an island in the morning, and there they spent the weekend before crossing over to the mainland on Monday, December 11 (or December 21, by the New Style or Gregorian calendar), when they made the climactic landing on Plymouth Rock.[1] The *Mayflower* crossed Massachusetts Bay a week later, and on Christmas Day (which the Separatists did not believe in), work began on the new village.

There followed the terrible First Winter, during which all but a few persons suffered from exposure and disease, and half the *Mayflower's* passengers and crew died. Nevertheless they persevered, and when spring came planted their first crops and built homes and storehouses. On March 16, a lone Indian entered the settlement and astonished the colonists by greeting them in English. This was Samoset, a Native Sagamore from Maine, who had learned the language from English fishermen who made annual voyages to the Maine coast each year. On March 22, he introduced them to another Native man, Squanto, who had once lived at Patuxet, the site of the new Plymouth settlement, before being kidnapped by an English sea captain and sold into slavery in Spain. Remarkably, Squanto had escaped and made his way to London, from where he returned to America as a scout for the Newfoundland Company. When he finally reached his old home, he found it abandoned—the result of a plague that had decimated the coastal population of southeastern New England. He, too, spoke English, and became the little colony's translator, as well as its instructor in planting corn and finding local resources. That same day, the "great Sagamore" Massasoit arrived with his retinue of sixty men and, with the help of the English-speaking Native men, entered into a treaty of peace with the colonists that would last more than fifty years.

The following autumn, the all-important corn harvest that would insure Plymouth Colony's survival proved successful, although some of the English crops were a disappointment. In honor of this 1621 harvest, Edward

Winslow noted that Governor William Bradford sent four men out to hunt wildfowl "so that we might after a special manner rejoice together after we had gathered the fruit of our labors." They brought back enough fowl to feed the community a week, including "many of the Indians [who came] amongst us, and among the rest their greatest king Massasoit, with some ninety men." They hosted their guests for three days of feasting, to which the Indians contributed five deer. This ecumenical outdoor harvest feast and November celebration was America's "First Thanksgiving"; it was later adopted by other New England colonies in memory of that momentous event.

The holiday remained a regional observance until 1789, when George Washington declared the first nationwide Thanksgiving for the new United States (an earlier Thanksgiving for the thirteen colonies had been declared by the Continental Congress in 1777). The custom of national Thanksgivings lapsed after 1815, until Abraham Lincoln, urged on by Sarah Josepha Hale (editor of *Godey's Lady's Book* and a fervent advocate for a national Thanksgiving holiday), declared a traditional November Thanksgiving in 1863. Since that time, the holiday the Pilgrims established has been celebrated without fail each fall, and the memory of that First Thanksgiving has been indelibly colored by the famous images of colonists and Native neighbors sitting down to dine in autumnal splendor, surrounded with the bounty of the harvest.

This is the basic Thanksgiving story as most of us remember it from grade school. But although at least partially accurate, it only represents the tip of the iceberg when it comes to what Thanksgiving means to us today.

Where I come from, Thanksgiving is an unavoidable fact of life. Despite (or perhaps because of) growing up in Plymouth, Massachusetts, many young Plymoutheans such as me never gave the history of the Thanksgiving holiday much thought. Tradition asserted that the holiday originated there with the Pilgrims and their Indian neighbors, and that was that. We engaged in the same family gatherings and time-honored Thanksgiving turkey dinners as other Americans. The ubiquitous, mass-produced images of buckle-hatted Pilgrims, generic Indians, turkeys, pumpkins, and cornstalks that hung in Plymouth classrooms were the same as those found in schools and homes across the nation. Like schoolchildren throughout America we accepted this as gospel, and besides, it lent the historically famous, declining industrial town we lived in a touch of glamour each autumn. The Pilgrims were, or had been, real enough—it was only later that this crowning glory was seen to be, like the town itself, more modest in reality.

Of course, there was considerable fuss made about the holiday each year in "the town where Thanksgiving began," but it was more for the accommodation of holiday visitors than for us townsfolk. Older Plymouth-eans have fond memories of the holiday morning circuit they made as youngsters to take advantage of the free cider and donuts provided by the town for distribution to the public at the historic houses. We participated in the annual Pilgrim Progress march to the windy eminence of Burial Hill on gray November afternoons, posed in tableaux illustrating the Pil-grim Story on the stage of Memorial Hall, and on occasion distributed free "Pilgrim hats" at Pilgrim Hall Museum when official Plymouth made an extra effort to gratify holiday guests. Yet most Plymcoutheans were reluc-tant to interrupt their private holiday arrangements to attend to the needs of tourists, and avoided the downtown area on Thanksgiving, despite ef-forts to involve them in the new public interfaith service in First Church. While we had our dinner at home or with grandparents, a few specially designated local restaurants served endless turkey dinners to crowds of eager visitors, and the Town of Plymouth even hosted a Thanksgiving feast in Memorial Hall. Such holiday activities were a grudgingly acknowledged part of life in the Old Colony town.

After Plimoth Plantation opened the Pilgrim Village in 1958, its an-nual Thanksgiving observation became the central attraction for modern pilgrims seeking the "First Thanksgiving" spirit. Plimoth Plantation, the new, open-air re-creation of the original Pilgrim settlement, was the larg-est and most popular Pilgrim attraction in town. As Thanksgiving was the ultimate Pilgrim event, the holiday became the museum's climactic close of the tourist season. Pilgrim Progresses were still put on each year, but the mulled cider, tableaux, free hats, and other public accommodations faded away. An "authoritative" version of the traditional story intended for schools was included in *Plymouth Colony: The First Year*, a film made at Plimoth Plantation in 1960. It faithfully re-created the standard scenes of outdoor cooking, the arrival of the "Indians" (high school boys in loin-cloths and body makeup, carrying a taxidermized deer), and the famous dinner after the manner of popular illustrations in children's books with an odd, picturesque admixture of raw and cooked foods. I worked for the Plantation aboard the museum's *Mayflower II* during undergraduate summers and off-season weekends from 1963 to 1966, but the ship was on the downtown Plymouth waterfront several miles away from the Pilgrim Village. I missed the gala Pilgrim Village celebrations, but the importance of the conventional Thanksgiving story for the museum was inescapable.

When I returned to Plimoth Plantation as its research librarian in 1975, I found that the institutional engagement with Thanksgiving had undergone a revolution. The years between my summer employment and my return wrought drastic changes throughout American society, and Plimoth Plantation had been deeply involved in the intellectual turbulence of the times. The old verities of the Pilgrim story had been attacked by a new cohort of museum professionals eager to debunk the cozy sentiments of preceding generations. The museum's earlier Thanksgiving observation had been arraigned on two counts—the false identification of the 1621 celebration as a Puritan day of thanksgiving and praise, and its negative symbolic significance for modern Native Americans.

The Plantation had always recognized that the famous "First Thanksgiving" was not quite a true Calvinist Thanksgiving. An authentic New England Thanksgiving was an officially declared weekday event marked by a day of religious meetings and pious gratitude for God's favorable providence (and celebratory dinners as well). The 1621 festivities, on the other hand, with their recreations, heathen guests, three-day duration, and no mention of church far more closely resembled a secular English harvest celebration. However, this anomaly had always been considered insignificant in the face of the 1621 event's traditional identification as the *fons et origo* of our modern holiday.

Such equivocation became unacceptable in the late 1960s. Not only was the 1621 event determinedly redefined as a secular harvest festival, but also its public observance at the Plantation was shifted from November to Columbus Day weekend in 1973, closer to the Michaelmas (September 29) season when such events had traditionally been held in England. Special Thanksgiving Day activities were abolished, and the day itself was given over to unexceptional seasonal work demonstrating November preparations for winter. It was in many ways a daring decision to reinterpret the history of the holiday, as it might well have had a drastic effect on the Plantation's critical Thanksgiving Day attendance. The change did upset some traditionalists, but most visitors continued to flock to the Pilgrim Village on the holiday as they always had. In fact, the new Columbus Day "Harvest Festival" became a popular tradition in its own right, so that there were two revenue-maximizing events where before there had been only one.

Another influence on the Plantation's reinterpretation of Thanksgiving was the Native American protests that came to surround the Thanksgiving holiday. Thanksgiving is the only American holiday in which the American Indian has been accorded a substantial if supporting role, but the image of the Plymouth colonists and their Wampanoag neighbors sitting down to a feast in irenic harmony on a golden autumn afternoon was not one some Native peoples felt comfortable with. This sentimental impression of the "First Thanksgiving" was protested in Boston and Plymouth on Thanksgiving in 1969 by a group of American Indian students, not so much for its historical inaccuracy—the events had actually occurred more or less in the manner commonly described—but in recognition that the pretty picture obscured later momentous conflicts between the Indians and the English colonists.

The following year, on the 350th anniversary of the landing at Plymouth, the committee in charge of the anniversary celebration withdrew an invitation to Frank James, a Wampanoag teacher from Cape Cod, who had planned to deliver a thoughtful but critical dissent to the general congratulatory tenor of the anniversary celebration. In response Mr. James organized a protest on Thanksgiving 1970, which attracted sympathizers from numerous Native communities, including members of the radical American Indian Movement, freshly energized by the recent occupation of Alcatraz Island in San Francisco Bay. In the spirit of the times, the protest included various melodramatic scenes such as an assault on *Mayflower II* during which the English flag was torn down, the manikin representing the Pilgrim ship's master thrown into the harbor, and nearby Plymouth Rock "buried" with sand. Plimoth Plantation invited the Native Americans to a turkey dinner, but on arrival the protesters overturned the tables and bore away the cooked turkeys. The protest, called "the Day of Mourning," was subsequently institutionalized by the United American Indians of New England as an annual event. A new Thanksgiving tradition was born.

The refusal of the protesters to accept the Plantation's hospitality only heightened the museum's desire to reach out to the Native community. A quasi-independent "Indian Program" was established in 1973 that employed Native individuals in the new "Summer Camp" exhibit, and respected local leaders in the Wampanoag community were asked to become advisers to the program. It was impossible in light of these changes to continue with the old Thanksgiving festivities, and the shift in interpretation to a "harvest festival" was accordingly instituted. A press release was issued to explain this change, outlining the historical justification for the radical revision of the program in 1973.

This press release was the one I was given so that I might answer public inquiries about the Thanksgiving holiday, a time-consuming responsibility that fell to the Research Department each autumn. The points made in the release seemed compelling, although I thought one or two small corrections might be made. For example, the release stated that the first national Thanksgiving had been declared by Washington in 1789, but this overlooked the Thanksgiving declared by the Continental Congress in 1777. Plimoth Plantation was ready to relinquish the "First Thanksgiving" title for 1621 (if not 1623), but it was opposed to other, even less credible, claims. It seemed a small point to us, but the question of "the true first Thanksgiving" seemed to loom large in the public mind, and there were a number of rival claimants to the title. The media were similarly fascinated and eagerly sought out these claims to earlier Thanksgivings in order to challenge Plymouth—whether or not they had any true historical significance.

There were, we found, numerous pretenders to the title of the "First Thanksgiving." For example, Dr. Michael Gannon of the University of Florida cited a thanksgiving service held for Ponce de León's expedition on April 3, 1513. The Texas Society of the Daughters of the American Colonies had erected a marker on the Palo Duro commemorating an alleged thanksgiving proclaimed by Fr. Juan de Padilla for Coronado's troops on May 23, 1541. Similar examples had been extracted from historical records for 1564 (Florida), 1565 (Florida), 1578 (Newfoundland), 1598 (Texas), 1607 (Virginia), 1607 (Maine), 1610 (Virginia), and 1619 (Virginia). Each was technically a "thanksgiving," and each occurred before Plymouth Colony was founded in 1620, but these claims were essentially irrelevant, as each was an isolated instance that had no connection with, or influence on, the future American holiday.

The alternative "firsts" were usually instances from the Catholic or Anglican liturgical tradition giving special thanks to God for some act of providence, during a Sunday mass or service rather than a separate day set aside in the Calvinist manner. They might also have been thanksgiving services celebrated on the day of a safe arrival, such as Adelantado Menéndez De Avilés' arrival in Florida on Saturday, September 8, 1565, or Captain John Woodleaf's arrival at the Berkeley Plantation on Saturday, December 4, 1619. Neither the Menéndez event, which even included a dinner for members of the local Seloy tribe, nor the Berkeley service, which was supposed to be held each anniversary of the arrival that day in Virginia, were Sabbath-day events. Moreover, the one-shot Florida service was of little interest to historians of early America, and the Berkeley tradition was stillborn due to the massacre of the colonists in 1622. The existence of this purported annual thanksgiving had been forgotten until rediscovered by Virginia partisan Lyon G. Tyler in 1931.[2] In 1958, John J. Wicker, Jr., established the "Virginia Thanksgiving Festival" for the first Sunday in November.

Historically, none of these had any influence over the evolution of our modern holiday. The American holiday's true origin was the New England Calvinist Thanksgiving. Never coupled with a Sabbath meeting, the Puritan observances were special days set aside during the week for thanksgiving and praise in response to God's providence. Not surprisingly, the glamour of chronological precedence—evidence of a deep-rooted "Guinness Book of World Records" mind-set among the public—overshadowed the question of historical significance, and we were obliged to respond to such claims every year.

My associate Carolyn Freeman Travers and I revised the press release and incorporated it in *The Thanksgiving Primer*, a booklet that included more information on Thanksgiving, the Pilgrims, their church services, cuisine, dress and myths associated with their popular image. I supplied an analysis of the probable origins of the modern holiday, observing that it appeared to be a synthesis of three independent traditions: the Calvinist day of Thanksgiving, the customary English harvest festival, and Forefathers' Day, an earlier holiday celebrating the Pilgrims' landing on Plymouth Rock on December 22, whose observation had faded away when Thanksgiving monopolized the Pilgrim story after 1900.[3]

Despite our efforts, the conventional misconceptions and popular stereotypes associated with Thanksgiving continued unabated among the general public. Americans still learned about the Pilgrims and Thanksgiving in grade school, where traditional images and stories were uncritically accepted — or if they were questioned, it was often only to favor the Indians over the Pilgrims, with the basic 1621 narrative modified to suit. Most adults felt that Thanksgiving history was for kids, and not worth serious consideration. Consequently, almost all available books on the subject were (and still are) aimed at children. When they concentrated on the colorful 1621 event, some authors conscientiously adopted the Plantation's strictures on period costume, foodways, activities, and Native involvement, always with the popular conviction that Thanksgiving began with the Plymouth harvest festival. The few scholarly works on the subject such as William DeLoss Love's *Fast and Thanksgiving Days of New England* (1895), the Lintons' *We Gather Together* (1949), and Appelbaum's *Thanksgiving* (1984) accepted the modern importance accorded Plymouth and harvest observances, although De Loss Love did so somewhat diffidently in the face of his own evidence.[4]

The first doubts I had about the common assumption that there was an unbroken linear tradition between the Pilgrims' harvest festival and the modern Thanksgiving holiday occurred in 1985 during Plimoth Plantation's mounting of Aye, Call It Holy Ground, an exhibit on the popular Victorian images of the Pilgrims. We had no trouble finding Victorian visual representations of the voyage of the *Mayflower*, the landing on Plymouth Rock, the "courtship of Miles Standish," and similar tropes, but we were unable to locate a suitable nineteenth-century painting, or even a big *Harper's Weekly* engraving, illustrating the famous "First Thanksgiving" in all its familiar outdoor autumnal splendor. The best-known depictions by Jennie Brownescombe (figure 1), J.L.G. Ferris, and Percy Moran all dated to after 1900. The closest we got at the time was a *Harper's* engraving from 1870 depicting the Pilgrims gathered indoors around a table with Indian guests standing grimly behind them, which was not quite the depiction we

1. Jennie A. Brownscombe, *The First Thanksgiving at Plymouth* (1914). (Courtesy of Pilgrim Hall, Plymouth, Mass.) The classic representation of Plymouth's "First Thanksgiving."

had in mind. There was another early "Pilgrim and Indian" Thanksgiving image in addition to the *Harper's* print that we did not discover until much later. Plimoth Plantation curator Karin Goldstein located *The First Thanksgiving*, a painting by Edwin White (1817–1877) that may be earlier than the *Harper's* engraving, but it does not seem to ever have been reproduced or published and therefore had no particular cultural influence. The White *Thanksgiving* has a Pilgrim family seated indoors with a single Indian standing behind them, more like a silent butler than a guest.

I was surprised, not only by the absence of the very famous outdoor autumn scene in Victorian art, but also by an unexpectedly popular motif of violence between the colonists and the Indians, which appeared to be a common theme in nineteenth-century depictions of colonial Thanksgivings—quite in contrast to irenic representations of the 1621 dinner. An early example of these violent images, which appeared in *Frank Leslie's Illustrated* (1869), was titled *Thanksgiving Day in New England Two Hundred Years Ago* (figure 2). It showed a Puritan family's Thanksgiving dinner interrupted by a hail of arrows from an unseen enemy. Other examples involving generic Puritan-era colonists and hostile Indians ranged in quality from full-page engravings in *Harper's* and *Leslie's* to humorous and irreverent cartoons in the old *Life* magazine (1883–1936). The hail of arrows from an invisible adversary was a recurrent theme, there even being examples by Norman Rockwell showing a fleeing boy carrying a turkey or a bewildered Pilgrim huntsman amid arrows from offstage. This

2. *Thanksgiving Day in New England Two Hundred Years Ago*, from *Frank Leslie's Illustrated Newspaper*, November 27, 1869, p. 180. An early example of the pervasive motif of Native-colonial violence in nineteenth-century depictions of historical Thanksgivings.

convention of colonial violence appeared to have been far more resonant in the nineteenth century than the peaceful Thanksgiving gatherings of the Brownescombe variety. Presumably the contemporary frontier wars following the Civil War had made it difficult for Victorian artists and their audience to relate to any historical image of peaceful relations between the colonists and their Indian neighbors. The now-familiar outdoor dinners significantly appeared only after overt violence out west was over. Also, few images specifically referenced the 1621 Plymouth event at all, which seemed odd. One of the few identifiable "Pilgrim" (as opposed to generic colonial) representations from this period presented a contest between a Pilgrim musketeer and an Indian bowman in *Harper's Weekly* (1894). They were shooting at a target made up of a stuffed scarecrow with colonial shirt and breeches, hardly the peaceful aspect celebrated in later art.

Since the description of the famous 1621 harvest by Edward Winslow in *Mourt's Relation*—from which the modern conception of the holiday is drawn—was first published in 1622 (figure 3), it was surprising that the nineteenth-century artists would ignore the peaceful implications of the passage that so impressed their successors:

Our harvest being gotten in, our governor sent four men on fowling, that so we might after a special manner rejoice together after we had gathered the fruit of our labors. They four in one day killed as much fowl as, with a little help beside, served the company almost a week. At which time, among other recreations, we

NEW-ENGLAND, &c.

them in the blossome; our harvest being gotten in, our Governour sent foure men on fowling, that so we might after a more speciall manner reioyce together, after we had gathered the fruit of our labours; they foure in one day killed as much fowle, as with a little helpe beside, served the Company almost a weeke, at which time amongst other Recreations, we exercised our Armes, many of the *Indians* coming amongst vs, and amongst the rest their greatest King *Massaoyt*, with some nintie men, whom for three dayes we entertained and feasted. and they went out and killed fiue Deere, which they brought to the Plantation and bestowed on our Governour, and vpon the Captaine, and others. And although it be not alwayes so plentifull, as it was at this time with vs, yet by the goodnesse of God, we are so farre from want, that we often wish you partakers of our plentie. Wee haue found the *Indians* very faithfull in their Covenant of Peace with vs; very louing and readie to pleasure vs: we often goe to them, and they come to vs; some of vs haue bin

3. Facsimile from *A Relation or Iournall of the beginning and proceedings of the English Plantation settled at Plimoth in New England* [*Mourt's Relation*], 1622, p. 61, describing the 1621 harvest event.

exercised our arms, many of the Indians coming amongst us, and among the rest their greatest king Massasoit, with some ninety men, whom for three days we entertained and feasted, and they went out and killed five deer, which they brought to the plantation and bestowed upon our governor, and upon the captain, and others. And although it be not always so plentiful as it was at this time with us, yet by the goodness of God, we are so far from want that we often wish you partakers of our plenty.[5]

I undertook a search in early sources to see just when the current emphasis had begun, and found that no account of the Pilgrims published before the 1840s made any reference to either a Thanksgiving or a harvest celebration in 1621. Eventually I discovered why this was the case. Although *Mourt's Relation* had been published in 1622, the original booklet had, not surprisingly, become rare, so that by the eighteenth century there were apparently no surviving copies in New England. Scholars relied on an abridged version included in Samuel Purchas' *Hakluytus Posthumus or Purchas His Pilgrimes* (1625), which was reprinted by the Massachusetts Historical Society in 1802.[6] The Purchas version omitted the Winslow letter; so the 1621 event had been entirely forgotten! It was not until a copy of the original pamphlet was discovered in Philadelphia in 1820 that the famous harvest account was rediscovered. The previously missing information had no immediate effect, presumably because the Massachusetts Historical Society, rather than printing the text in full in 1822, extracted the missing phrases and paragraphs and arranged them with directions as to where they could be inserted into the abridged Purchas version, a singularly awkward manner of proceeding.

The first republication of the full text of *Mourt's Relation* appeared in 1841 in Rev. Alexander Young's *Chronicles of the Pilgrim Fathers*.[7] Significantly, Young added a footnote to the description of the 1621 event stating, "This was the first Thanksgiving, the harvest festival of New England." This is the earliest identification of the 1621 event as a Thanksgiving. The 1621 festival may have been nothing like a Puritan Thanksgiving, but by the time Young wrote, the New England holiday had lost much of its old Puritan providential significance. Apparently the 1621 event looked very much like a contemporary Thanksgiving to the liberal Unitarian clergyman, hence the identification. Young's judgment that the Pilgrim celebration and harvest was the "first Thanksgiving . . . of New England" was slow to attract public attention, despite the support of Dr. George B. Cheever in his edition of the *Mourt's Relation* text published in 1848. After all, the Thanksgiving holiday had developed a substantial historical tradition quite independent of the Pilgrims, emphasizing contemporary New England family reunions, dinners, balls, pumpkins, and turkeys. Early winter scenes rather than harvest motifs dominated Thanksgiving imagery, as in the sleigh ride "over the river and through the wood" in Lydia Maria Child's famous Thanksgiving poem (1844) or the popular Currier and Ives lithographic winter scene of George Durrie's *Home for Thanksgiving* (1867). In fact, rather than being the autumnal icons they are today, the Pilgrims themselves were most often depicted in snowy landscapes because of their arrival in Plymouth Harbor in the winter of 1620, which was associated with the then widely observed holiday of Forefathers' Day commemorating the annual anniversary of the landing at Plymouth Rock on December 22.

Having solved the mystery of the "missing link" between the 1621 event and the modern holiday, the challenge was to discover how the American Thanksgiving holiday actually evolved over the intervening centuries. What was the true history of America's Thanksgiving Day?

New England's Puritan Holy Days

The 1621 "First Thanksgiving" was referred to from time to time after 1841, but it did not begin to dislodge the holiday's traditional locus in post-Revolutionary New England tradition until the turn of the twentieth century. There was, for example, no mention of the colonists in presidential proclamations until 1905, when Theodore Roosevelt mentioned the "first settlers" as initiating the holiday. The Pilgrims were not invoked by *name* before Franklin Roosevelt did so in 1939, long after the "First Thanksgiving" had become firmly fixed in popular culture (President Hoover had noted the "custom dating from the garnering of the first harvest by our forefathers in the New World" in 1931). Instead of the historical commemoration of the "First Thanksgiving," providential blessings and "time-honored custom" were offered as the reason for declaring the holiday each year. Similarly, the massive numbers of Thanksgiving postcards published in the early twentieth century include no examples of colonists and Indians seated around a harvest table, until 1920 (and then only in a single example). Indians and Pilgrims were featured separately or in generic Puritan Thanksgiving settings (including a few humorous "violent" examples), but not in unified feasts. Thanksgiving's colonial Puritan origin was widely acknowledged, but the 1621 First Thanksgiving received little popular attention.

Young and Cheever had set the process in motion in the 1840s, yet the Pilgrim Thanksgiving did not begin to capture public attention until the end of the nineteenth century. Why then? The case for the Plymouth "First Thanksgiving" was first made in detail by Rev. Increase N. Tarbox in "Our New England Thanksgiving, Historically Considered" (*New Englander*, March 1879), but it took a best seller to really move things forward. The "tipping point" appears to have been the popular novelization of the Pilgrims' first years in Plymouth, Jane G. Austin's *Standish of Standish* (1889).

4. W. L. Taylor, *The First Thanksgiving Dinner, with Portraits of the Pilgrim Fathers*, from *Ladies Home Journal*, November 1897. The first depiction of the 1621 harvest celebration as an outdoor dinner with the Pilgrims and their Wampanoag neighbors, as described by Jane G. Austin in her novel *Standish of Standish* (1889).

It was an immediate success, going through at least twenty-eight printings as well as a dramatization in 1919. In *Standish of Standish*, Austin presents a fictionalized, sentimental account of the "First Thanksgiving" centered on an *outdoor* feast. Although it was only one incident among many in the novel, Austin's account appears to have brought about a new awareness of the First Thanksgiving theme.[1] In the November 1897 issue of the *Ladies Home Journal*, Clifford Howard drew heavily on Austin's fictional account for an ostensibly historical description of the First Thanksgiving. Accompanying Howard's article was an illustration, *The First Thanksgiving Dinner, with Portraits of the Pilgrim Fathers*, by W. L. Taylor (figure 4): around several tables, the Pilgrim men and their Indian guests (demeaningly portrayed as crude savages) are being served by Pilgrim women, who can also be seen in the background cooking over a fire in front of their log cabins. This appears to be the first of the now-familiar depictions that we sought for the 1985 Plimoth Plantation exhibit. Taylor's illustration was quickly reproduced by Plymouth souvenir publisher A. S. Burbank in his *Pilgrim Plymouth Illustrated* (1900) and in the Ohio Printing Company's *Thanksgiving Souvenir* (first issue ca. 1903) that was sold to teachers for distribution to their pupils for many years. The linking of the Pilgrims and Thanksgiving would not achieve full iconic status until after World War II, but all the familiar elements were now in place.

In addition to explaining the puzzling absence of the famous Thanksgiving scene in Victorian art, the addition of the Pilgrims at a relatively late date also explains why the harvest theme remained a minor element in Thanksgiving sermons, stories, and art before the Civil War. The old New England holiday had over time become a late November occasion — hardly a time of harvest in that region. It had also been the Puritan stand-in for Christmas (a holiday they rejected as noncanonical and pagan), an early winter time for feasting and pious hope before the long, dreary months of cold and privation to follow. At Thanksgiving, all the blessings of the year, including but in no way limited to successful harvests, were totted up, and God was given thanks for the entire preceding year, just as his merciful providence was beseeched each spring on the annual Fast Day, Thanksgiving's vernal opposite number. Far from having maintained a continuous association with the Plymouth colonists since colonial times, the American Thanksgiving holiday had evolved quite an independent body of historical associations and symbols.

The decay of the old Calvinist worldview in the nineteenth century's liberal evangelical climate transformed both of the Puritan providential holy days — Thanksgiving and Fast Day. The solemn presentiments of the traditional spring day of fasting and humility lost their social significance, and Fast Day was eventually superseded in Massachusetts and Maine by a secular commemoration of "Patriots' Day." Simultaneously, Thanksgiving's original providential basis calcified into pious rote pronouncements of America's achievements in trade, industry, and agriculture. The antebellum revival of Christmas relieved Thanksgiving of its role as a substitute winter holiday, leaving it free to embrace Winslow's rewarding story of the Pilgrims and their 1621 harvest party, with its turkey dinner and Indian guests, so that it gradually shed its early winter associations. This was far more agreeable to modern taste than Calvinist obsessions with God's will. Symbolically, it was an entirely satisfactory outcome, as everyone "knew" that Thanksgiving had originated in Puritan New England and that Puritan New England had its origin in little Plymouth Colony. The discovery of a Pilgrim First Thanksgiving gave the holiday a commemorative status it had previously lacked. In framing Winslow's account as an etiologic tale, the Pilgrim story came to explain and define the holiday through an account of its alleged origin.

Rev. Young's footnote brought about the creation of a modern myth — our familiar "First Thanksgiving" and everything that goes with it. Scenes of cornfields ripe with pumpkins and beautiful New England autumn foliage superseded Thanksgiving's previous winter landscapes, and the Pilgrims became the harvest's iconic representatives. By virtue of its new associations, writers were led to believe that the true origins of America's Thanksgiving lay in logical but imaginary Thanksgiving precedents such as the Jewish Sukkoth or Feast of Tabernacles, the English Harvest Home (which was enjoying its own mythical apotheosis at this time), and Native American customs. The minutiae of what exactly happened in 1621 became terribly important as the actual history of the holiday was buried beneath newly invented tradition.

Nevertheless, the American Thanksgiving's real origin lay in Puritanism's quarrel with extrabiblical ecclesiastical holy days and the two occasions on which they honored God's providence in a special manner—Fast days and Thanksgiving days. Therefore, instead of initiating this study of the holiday as so many have done, by seeking insight in the myths incorporating the Plymouth colonists or harvest customs, we shall begin at the holiday's theological roots.

It is quite correct to identify Thanksgiving with New England. The American holiday originated in the Puritan communities of the Northeast, and spread from there across the nation. Memories of early winter celebrations and family reunions around the festive table as well as the crisp late-fall days in field and orchard were treasured by generations of expatriate Yankees and shared with their new neighbors. To appreciate the true origin of the holiday, however, we must look across the Atlantic. Thanksgiving may have developed most fully in the New World, but it was not born in America. It came from England as a part of the mental baggage of the Puritan colonists. Thanksgiving's origins were rooted in the early Puritan practices of fasting and "prophesying," and the holiday—with its dour twin, Fast Day—was fully mature before the English settlers stepped onto Plymouth Rock.

Thanksgiving days began in the turmoil of the English Reformation as the Puritans sought to eradicate the lingering traces of Catholicism in the Anglican Church. One of the many complaints the leaders of the Reformation had about medieval Christianity was the inordinate number of holidays that had been introduced over the centuries. Until Henry VIII began the work of reform, there were, including Sundays, 147 religious holidays in England each year. They included not only the Christological cycle of Christmas, Easter, Whitsuntide, and the feasts of the Virgin but also an ever-increasing number of saints' days. This might not seem like a problem at first glance. The prospect of that many days off work might even seem a positive virtue to modern observers—until it is realized that all these were *unpaid* holidays with mandatory church attendance under the threat of a fine. No work was allowed, even at crucial times of the agricultural year such as harvest. Not only could people earn nothing during their holidays, but also the traditional celebrations were costly in food and drink, decorations for churches, processions, and the like. The medieval world of wakes, guild celebrations, church ales, and bride ales (an "ale" being a sort of drinking party celebrating an event or acting as a fund-raiser in support of some cause) had become more of a burden than a blessing. These festivals also contributed to the beery buffoonery, bawdiness, idleness, and profanity of a susceptible portion of the populace. It was pragmatism as well as piety that influenced the reformers to put an end to holidays that threatened people's livelihoods, stopped craft production, endangered the food supply, and encouraged drunkenness and violent behavior.

Henry VIII's 1536 reforms reduced the number of holidays to the Sabbaths and a more manageable 27 festival days a year. The old "evens" or evenings preceding holidays were transformed into times of fasting rather than carousing. In addition, the harvest season of July 1 through September 29 was set aside as a time when work took precedence over church and tavern alike. This solved the practical problems while leaving plenty of time for religious and social needs. However, the growing numbers of Puritans were not satisfied. They questioned the fundamental justification for the holidays, declaring them to be "Popish inventions" that were not only unsupported by scripture but of obvious pagan origin.

The Puritan faction first demanded that the number of festivals be reduced to the primary celebrations of Christ's life and the Sabbath, and no more. When this did not happen, the reformers became more radical after the example of John Calvin of Geneva, who had gradually arrived at the opinion that only Sabbaths were permissible. Reformers sought to abolish all the remaining old holidays including Christmas and Easter. However, there was another influence at work that would eventually modify this extreme constraint.

In the mid–sixteenth century, the Puritans introduced a new religious practice that they called "prophesying." Such "prophecies" had nothing to do with foretelling the future but referred rather to the "speaking of prophets" in the sense that Saint Paul intended in 1 Corinthians 14, where enlightened men might expounded on scripture for the edification and encouragement of their congregations. At first, this occurred only at times when religious leaders gathered at a central location such as a market town for private spiritual conferences that including prophesying, preaching, and theological discussion. These conferences or exercises, which might last several days, were prepared for by fasting and often closed with a public sermon, followed by dinner at an inn. A variation on the practice of "prophesying," in which laymen rose to offer their opinions on scriptural topics, quickly became popular, and it was sometimes included in Puritan church services (especially among Separatist congregations). Soon secondary weekly meetings apart from the Sunday service were instituted for the public discussion of religious issues in Puritan parishes, which became the precedent for the "Lecture Days" of colonial New England. However, such unofficial religious behavior became a matter of concern to the leaders of the English Church, and in 1576 Queen Elizabeth put a ban on the practice.

There also arose a custom among the Reformed churches of declaring special days in response to God's providence whenever unexpected disasters or special benefits to society occurred. The Church of England declared such days on a national basis from time to time so that appropriate observations might be held in each parish or, as was customary, people from several parishes might gather at an officially sanctioned central assembly. The assembly was treated to pertinent sermons, communion, and admonitions to wrongdoers, whereupon the entire company might close the day with an evening community meal (Fast days officially extended from afternoon to afternoon, so an evening meal on the day itself was quite acceptable). In addition to the nationwide observances, Fast and Thanksgiving days might be observed by individual congregations or even by private families depending on the nature of the providential event. The Puritans, forbidden to meet and exercise their prophesying in their earlier manner, quickly seized on this practice as a basis for similar gatherings. Fasting became a regular practice, not only in response to providence, but also as preparation for any important decision or momentous occurrence. As good Protestants they wanted to avoid the "empty practice" or mechanical observance of the Roman Church, in which corporal abstinence might not be accompanied by earnest spiritual activity; so not only abstinence and prayers but also psalms, preaching, and even "prophesy" soon slipped into the mix.

Official fasts were declared whenever it was felt that God had visited some unusually threatening or dangerous "judgment" on his people. Similarly, thanksgivings were announced to celebrate some impressive "mercy" awarded by God to his grateful flock. Consequently, fasts were held in response to drought in 1611, floods in 1613, and the plague in 1604 and 1625, whereas thanksgivings were declared for the victory over the Spanish Armada in 1588 and for Queen Anne's safe deliverance in 1605. These special observances were normally included as part of the usual church services on Sunday, Wednesday, or Friday, and had appropriate services in the *Book of Common Prayer* and the orthodox Anglican liturgy. There were exceptions to the rule, as in case of the Fifth of November, a special day that was set apart to give thanks for the deliverance of King James and his government. The Fifth of November, "Gunpowder Plot," or "Guy Fawkes Day" was an anomaly in that it became an annual Thanksgiving, and it was adopted by the Puritans as their faction's most significant national commemoration. Ironically, there was no biblical support for an annual thanksgiving of this sort, a fact that some Anglicans were pleased to point out. An essential quality of God's special providences was that they were unique and unpredictable. Having an annual thanksgiving flew in the face of Puritan theory by presuming to predict or take for granted God's unrevealed will.

As Horton Davies points out, the Puritan holiday pattern was strikingly different from the old ecclesiastical calendar and must have appeared shockingly radical, even blasphemous, to the unconverted.[2] The old calendar was unchanging, passive, and backward-looking, bound to a cyclical view of history wherein the annual roll of holidays appeared in a familiar and predictable manner. The stories of Christ and the saints were repeated within comfortable traditions of celebration and abstinence as season followed season. The Puritan version, in contrast, was dynamic and focused on the present and the future, on God's immediate intervention in daily life, and looked forward to God's kingdom, Christ's return, and the triumph of the saints. It was also far simpler—no Christmas, no Easter, no saints' days, nothing about what had happened over 1,600 hundred years of Christian history but only about how God's providence was manifest, here and now.

Among the Puritans, the recognition of instances of special providence was especially important. The Puritans considered the doctrine of providence as the foundation of their religious view of life. Momentous events were reckoned as the revelation of God's plan for his chosen people. God, they believed, was not just the great creator and ruler of the world but also its active executive, perpetually involved in the micromanagement of everything that happened on earth from the greatest of events to the most insignificant. Providence was the way in which the divine plan played out in history—scripted in every detail by the omniscient author but still flexible enough to allow humanity free will in its predetermined role in the great drama of creation. As with any script, the final outcome was determined at the outset, but the unfathomably complex scenario was beyond the understanding of any mortal man. God's will might be unknowable and often distressing to the faithful, but they believed that the unfolding of providence was concerned with their personal guidance and examined every event for indications of his intentions.

A key element in the working of providence was that, at or before the beginning of time, each individual had been cast in the role of a leading or supporting actor in the central plot of mankind's damnation and salvation. The "stars"—the "elect," who were predestined to be saved through the purely gratuitous mercy of God (as all mankind was sinful and unworthy)—had quite a different significance in universal history from their eternally damned fellow beings. Their parts were central to the drama; all others, whether emperors or beggars, were just spear-carriers and bit players of little importance. Those who hoped or believed that they were among the elect understandably had a keen interest in the unfolding of God's plan. They not only eagerly took part in national or public days of fast and thanksgiving but also declared such days for their individual Puritan congregations, and private Puritan families had household fasts and thanksgivings of their own.

These special days were tied to evident acts of providence, of which there was no lack. As the cosmic drama unfolded (to carry our metaphor further), there were a number of "plot complications" scripted in to challenge and test the major players—to put them through their paces, as it were. These took the form of "notable judgments and speciall mercies" in the shape of great calamities or special blessings that God visited upon the faithful. Judgments might take the form of great droughts, floods, fires, military disaster, or plagues, whereas mercies could include crops saved by providential showers, the safe arrival of a supply ship, the recovery of a sick ruler, or victory in battle. When the former took place, the proper response was to declare a special Fast day dedicated to prayer and humiliation during which the godly would gather together to search their consciences for sin so as to repent and appease God's righteous wrath. Also, days of humiliation were commonly declared to request God's furtherance and guidance for future undertakings, not just as a response to examples of divine displeasure. A fast might be held before starting a journey, beginning a project, or ordaining a minister. A thanksgiving on the other hand was appropriate only after some special mercy had been granted or, at the very least, a period of time had passed without notable disasters but rather a pattern of blessings such as successful harvests, economic prosperity, and good health. There was often a debate whether thanksgivings celebrating these "generals" were allowable, the outcome depending on the temper of the times and the degree of religiosity in each community.

Days of humiliation were observed by all-day church attendance and abstinence. No one who was between sixteen and sixty and in good health might work or eat until the end of the day. The members of the congregation were expected to dedicate this time to listening to exhortations, prayers, sermons and to meditating on their sinful nature. If on the other hand God had sent some special providence, the faithful would gather to sing his praise in a similar full day of thanksgiving with sermons, psalms (but not newfangled hymns), and thankful prayers, and then perhaps meet for a feast in God's honor. In contrast to earlier medieval religious festivals, Puritan providential holy days were distinctive in their solemnity and pious intensity—days filled with prophesying, psalms, and prayers with little time set aside for bodily needs. In addition to the days of thanksgiving declared by Puritan congregations or the nation at large, observations of God's especial providence by individual households were also encouraged as long as they did not conflict with the Sabbath or public holidays.[3]

The Puritan holidays served as a regulatory device whereby the nation, community, or family adjusted its behavior so as to stay in tune with God's will and remain in divine favor. Thanksgivings praised God for his goodness and made sure that his people's gratitude was made evident. Providential "mercies" were seen as signs that he was pleased with his people, while "judgments" with their attendant calamities were believed to be sent by God to mark his displeasure with the way things were going. Days of humiliation were used to identify the reasons for God's displeasure and to put the community back on track when it strayed from the path of righteousness. Such days also served the Puritan establishment as a means of controlling the behavior of the community in God's name, and maintaining the rule of the godly against its enemies and malcontents. If unregenerate individuals were guilty of grievous sins and flouting God's commandments, he would punish the whole community just as a teacher might keep an entire class after school for the actions of a few mischievous students. It became the responsibility of the godly therefore to see that these sinners were discovered and punished so that the community's relationship with God could be repaired. This allowed the Puritan leaders considerable discretion in rooting out and punishing wrongdoers, and ensuring that their neighbors conformed to a stringent system of laws and morality. It was this tradition of providential holidays—whereby fasts and thanksgivings were key elements in maintaining God's putative will on earth—that the Puritan migrations brought to New England.

The three religious holidays that the Puritans brought to America were the Sabbath, days of humiliation and fasting, and days of thanksgiving. The Sabbath set the basic pattern of how religious days were observed. The faithful were commanded to prepare for the Sabbath at three o'clock (the hour of Christ's death) on the "eve" or afternoon before Sabbath with family devotions and prayers. The families made sure that meals and other necessary labors such as feeding livestock were so arranged as to call for the least amount of effort on the day itself. On Sunday morning they went to church at around 8:30 and remained there the whole day, with a short break at midday, listening to sermons, singing psalms, listening to exhortations to live more godly lives, and participating in other uplifting spiritual exercises.

Fast and Thanksgiving days were two sides of the same providential coin. Both involved preparation on the previous evening and attendance at church for much of the day itself. Only those tasks which could not be postponed, such as feeding the family, watering the livestock, or rescuing people in danger, were allowed. Normal work or travel was forbidden, as were sports and other worldly pastimes. The fast was the more significant of the two, and as we have seen, fasting was widely utilized in preparation for prayer or indeed any important activity. The Plymouth colonists declared a Fast day in Leiden before the momentous departure from Holland to Southampton and America. Fast days naturally involved refraining from food and drink, although not complete abstinence, from the beginning of the eve to midafternoon on the day of the fast itself. At the official end of the fast at 3:00 or 4:00 pm (devotions might continue later), there was normally a modest meal. On thanksgivings, the religious preparations and attendance at morning services were the same, but there might be more culinary preparations on the day before, and the afternoon meeting was shortened or perhaps eliminated so that the people might celebrate with feasts and fellowship — but not with frivolity, sports, or such secular activities as characterized the 1621 Plymouth event. In time, as the original Puritan impulse declined and a more secular way of life evolved — that is, as Puritans metamorphosed into Yankees — the old New England holidays took on new associations, leading ultimately to the modern Thanksgiving tradition. It is this process that constitutes the true history of the American holiday.

The first *documented* providential holiday in New England was a Fast day declared during a serious drought in Plymouth Colony in the summer of 1623. When the colonists began planting their fields in April, the weather was favorable and seasonable. Six weeks after the final sowing, however, drought threatened both the crops and the very existence of the little settlement.

But it pleased God, for our further chastisement, to send a great drought; insomuch as in six weeks after the latter setting there scarce fell any rain; so that the stalk of that [which] was first set, began to send forth the ear before it came to half growth; and that which was later [set], not likely to yield us any [corn] at all, both the blade and the stalk hanging the head in such a manner as we judged it utterly dead. Our beans also ran not up, according to their wonted manner, but stood at a stay; many being parched away, as though they had been scorched before the fire. Now were our hopes overthrown; and we discouraged: our joy being turned into mourning.[4]

The previous year's harvest had not been good. If the approaching harvest failed as well, Plymouth Colony might not survive another year. The colonists met in hope that by humbling themselves before God, they would gain his mercy and be able to survive in New England for "his glory and our good." The day of fasting and humiliation — "appointed by public authority, and set apart from all other employments" — was held on a Wednesday, most probably July 16, 1623.

The skies were clear when the colonists gathered for public worship and spent eight or nine hours together in the meetinghouse, praying, singing psalms, and listening to sermons and exhortations. When they came out, they were gratified to see that it had clouded over. The next morning "soft, sweet and moderate showers" began, which continued off and on for the next two weeks. The wilted corn and the colonists' drooping spirits were revived, and the crops saved. The Indians noticed the providential rescue of the crops. Hobbomock, a Wampanoag *pinese* (superior warrior and counselor) who lived near the English settlement, noticed that the colonists were having a religious service in midweek, only three days after their previous service, and asked a boy why they were doing so. When the gentle and effective rains came the very next day, Hobbamock told the neighboring Indians about the impressive power of the white man's god, who had "wrought so great a change in so short a time."

The Plymouth colonists were no less impressed by this providential mercy. Having so dramatic an example of God's favor and acceptance, they felt that they should do something substantial to show their gratitude and not "smother up the same" or "content ourselves with private thanksgiving for that which by private prayer could not be obtained." They therefore declared that another solemn day be set apart and appointed for the glory, honor, and praise, with all thankfulness, to God. This first recorded Plymouth Thanksgiving probably occurred on Wednesday, July 30, the day before the *Anne* arrived in Plymouth with friends from England and Holland. The day was again spent in church, presumably in much the same manner as the Fast day but with quite a different tone. Possibly there was some sort of communal meal afterward.

In this single two-week period we have the first examples of the Puritan providential holidays in New England. Even Puritans needed some ritual in their lives. One question that might arise is, Why did they wait until 1623 to declare a Fast and a Thanksgiving when there had been plenty of earlier events that could have justified such observations? The simple answer is that we do not know that they did not have earlier Fasts or Thanksgivings. If they did, no reliable record of them has survived. However, the very early years are recorded in sufficient detail by Bradford and Winslow that it is quite unlikely any official proposal for a public Thanksgiving has been omitted. Even in Holland the Robinson Separatists appear to have been parsimonious with special days (or at least in the recording of them), as we know of only three Fast days observed before they left Holland. They declared a Fast in the autumn of 1617 to ask for divine guidance when the idea of emigration to America was first being considered, and another in late 1619 during the troubled negotiations with the Virginia Company and

King James. Their final day of humiliation and fasting, just before the voyage to America, began on July 21, 1620:

So being ready to depart, they had a day of solemn humiliation, their pastor taking his text from Ezra viii.21; "And there at the river, by Ahava, I proclaimed a fast, that we might humble ourselves before God, and seek of him a right way for us, and for our children, and all our substance." Upon which he spent a good part of the day very profitably and suitable to their present occasion; the rest of the time was spent in pouring out prayers to the Lord with great fervency, mixed with an abundance of tears.[5]

As we have seen, the Puritan holidays were modeled after the Sabbath and resembled a "second Sunday" during the week. There was the evening of pious preparation on the day before, a day spent in church with services lasting three hours or more on either side of a brief noontime break, and then a meal afterward (on both Fast and Thanksgiving days) as individual families went over the lessons of the day in their own households. Holiday lessons might be focused on the immediate nature of the events that had occasioned their declaration, but otherwise the same order of prayers, psalms, and sermons was followed. The difference between the two was in the mood of the day and, of course, in the style of the meal that followed.

The days of the week that were selected for the holidays remained irregular until the mid–seventeenth century, when Wednesdays and Thursdays became the most common days for Fasts and Thanksgivings, respectively. There was no real order or fixed practice, however, and other days, even Fridays (despite possible unwelcome associations with Anglican and Catholic fasting), were appointed from time to time. Providential holidays could never be held on Sunday, as that day was sacred to the Sabbath. The reformers were anxious to avoid the Catholic and Anglican practice of combining Sabbath devotions with special thanksgiving services, which they deemed as inadequate to either purpose. In the early years both Plymouth and Massachusetts Bay favored Wednesdays for Fasts and Thursdays for Thanksgivings. Thursday was market day in both Boston and Plymouth, and on occasion a special sermon or "lecture" was delivered for the edification of the gathered populace. In Connecticut, Wednesday was the preferred day for both holidays. By the end of the seventeenth century, Thanksgivings usually fell in October, November, and December, while Fasts might be appointed at any time of year. Later the Fasts began to cluster in the spring, in March, April, and May, but theology and public troubles such as war or other disasters prevented predictable regularity until after the American Revolution.

The best-known candidate for the first providential holiday in New

England is of course the famous Plymouth harvest festival of 1621. The problem with classifying this celebration as a Thanksgiving—or indeed as the "First Thanksgiving," as Rev. Alexander Young would do for the first time in 1841—is that it meets none of the qualifications for an orthodox Thanksgiving. It was only later that it began to resemble contemporary Thanksgivings, once the holiday itself had become as much a secular holiday as the harvest festival had been. As William DeLoss Love later observed, "It was not a thanksgiving at all, judged by their Puritan customs, which they kept in 1621; but as we look back upon it after nearly three centuries, it seems so wonderfully like the day we love that we claim it as the progenitor of our harvest feasts."[6] The successful harvest was indeed a matter for giving thanks, and we may be sure that the colonists did so in the context of their regular Sabbaths and in individual homes after the manner of the "private thanksgivings" found inadequate in 1623. There is no indication in the primary sources, however, that the participants thought of it as a formal day of official Thanksgiving. More importantly, the extended nature of the 1621 celebration over several days or a week, the recreations, and the non-Christian guests are the very things that pious Separatists protested had no place in any Christian holy day.

There is no mention of another providential day in Plymouth Colony until 1630, when Governor Bradford was asked to declare a day of humiliation for Friday, July 30, in sympathy with the newly arrived Massachusetts Bay colonists. The Winthrop fleet had arrived piecemeal at the Salem settlement between June 12 and July 6, 1630. Despite having better resources and arriving in warm weather, the new colonists landed weakened by malnutrition and disease just as the *Mayflower* passengers had in 1620. The loss of those who had come so far only to die, especially among the women, was the impetus for Governor Winthrop's call for a public Fast. Plymouth was having its own tribulations with Isaac Allerton's financial shenanigans and the Billington murder case,[7] and it is possible that Plymouth joined Massachusetts in this observation.

The Massachusetts Bay colonists brought the same tradition of providential holidays as their Plymouth compatriots. During the 1629 emigration led by Francis Higginson there were two Fast days declared at sea, a thing that the sailors said they had never heard of before. The first was near the beginning of the voyage on Thursday, May 21. After weeks of contrary winds the colonists had finally cleared the English Channel and were well at sea. Following the practice of having a Fast to ask God to look favorably on their momentous enterprise, they observed a day of humiliation:

Thursday, there being two ministers in the ship, Mr. Smith and myself [Rev. Higginson], we endeavored, together with others, to consecrate the day as a solemn fasting and humiliation to Almighty God, as a furtherance of our present work. And it pleased God the ship was becalmed all day, so we were freed from any encumbrance. And as soon as we had done prayers (see and behold the goodness of God?) about seven o'clock at night the wind turned to north-east, and we had a fair gale that night as manifest evidence of the Lord's hearing our prayers.[8]

They had a second Fast for favorable winds on Tuesday, June 2, which they believed met with immediate results. After they arrived, they had a third Fast on Thursday, August 6, preceding their choice and ordination of elders and deacons for the new church.

The pattern was repeated with the larger Winthrop fleet in 1630: Fasts were declared for Friday, April 2; Friday, April 23 (Saint George's Day); Friday, May 21 (in regard to the weather); Friday, June 4; and on Monday, June 7, when the voyagers caught some very welcome fresh fish. They had their first Thanksgiving on Thursday, July 8, 1630, following the arrival of the last straggling ship, the *Success*, two days earlier. It might be noted that Friday, the orthodox Anglican day for fasting, was chosen by the Winthrop company, whereas more Puritan Wednesday or Thursday dates were chosen by the Higginson and Plymouth groups.

When colonists from Dorchester settled Connecticut in 1635 (pushing out the Plymouth men who had gotten there first) and the New Haven Colony was established in 1637, the common tradition of providential holidays was introduced in those new colonies. The first occasion for a providential holiday in Connecticut was the successful conclusion (from a colonial point of view) of the Pequot War in 1637. The war, which included a terrible massacre of Pequots at their Mystic village, was the result of events stirred up by Massachusetts Bay and its Connecticut settlements, for which the unfortunate Pequots got the blame. The Puritan colonies were immensely heartened by the "victory" and declared a day of thanksgiving and praise for October 12, 1637, which was observed in Massachusetts and in Scituate in Plymouth Colony as well. This event has sometimes been misidentified as the "first New England Thanksgiving" by modern partisans for Native Americans and damned as the racist origin of all American Thanksgivings, which is rhetorical nonsense. It *was* the first Connecticut Thanksgiving, however, and was followed by Fast and Thanksgiving days in those colonies after the manner of the other Puritan colonies.

We know about the Plymouth Colony celebration of the October 12 Thanksgiving at Scituate through the historical accident of the survival of Rev. John Lothrop's church records for Scituate and Barnstable (where Lothrop and his congregation moved in 1639). These brief records shed valuable light on how Fasts and Thanksgivings could be declared by an individual congregation as opposed to "public" providential days commanded for the entire colony by the civil magistrates. They also demonstrate how the chance survival of records skews our impression of the past. If Lothrop's notes had disappeared, as the early records of the other Plymouth Colony churches have, we would never have known about these providential celebrations, as they do not appear in the formal records of the colony. There may well have been many such holidays in Plymouth and elsewhere, but as it is, the Lothrop records provide us a unique glimpse of what took place at the earliest New England Thanksgivings.

Lothrop's records begin in 1634 before the Scituate church was formally covenanted. The potential congregation met for a Fast on November 6, 1634, at James Cudworth's house, and had another Fast on Christmas day before they were joined in a covenant on January 8—during yet another Fast. Altogether, the church observed thirty-four days of humiliation and fasting but only nine Thanksgiving days between 1634 and 1653. The reasons for the Fasts ranged from such local concerns as asking for blessings for upcoming investings of deacons, relief from drought, from sickness, or from the rise of heretical opinions to broader concerns over the Pequot War, the Thirty Years' War in "Jermany," and the Civil War in "Old England." English troubles were the motivation for eleven Fast days between 1642 and 1649, although local concerns were often included as well. For example a fast was declared on November 15, 1649, "principally for old England & alsoe for our owne particulars, God's hand beeing upon us by Sicknesses & disease many Children in the Bay dyeing bye the Chin cough & the pockes & wee beeing alsoe many visitted to Sickenesses or diseases."[9]

More important for the purpose at hand are Lothrop's descriptions of what occurred at the Thanksgivings held by the Scituate/Barnstable church. The congregation's first Thanksgiving was on December 22, 1636,

in ye Meetinghouse, beginning some halfe an houre before nine & continued untill after twelve a clocke, ye day beeing very cold, beginning with a short prayer, then a psalme sang, then more large in prayer, after that an other Psalme, & then the Word taught, after that prayer—& the[n] a psalme,—Then makeing merry to the creatures, the poorer sort beeing invited of the richer.

The next Thanksgiving, on October 12, 1637, was

performed much in the same manner aforesaid, mainly for these two particulars. 1. For the victory over the pequouts, ye 2. For Reconciliation betwixt Mr. Cotton and the other ministers.

The third Thanksgiving was the congregation's first at Barnstable, on December 11, 1639,

att Mr. Hull's house, for Gods exceeding mercye in bringing us hither Safely keeping us healthy & well in o[u]r weake beginnings & in our church Estate. The day
beeing very cold o[u]r praises to God in publicke being ended, wee devided into 3
companies to feast togeather, some att Mr. Hulls, some att Mr [Mayo's], some att
Brother Lumberds senior.[10]

   These brief descriptions are the only surviving examples of how Plymouth Colony Thanksgiving feasts were conducted in the early seventeenth
century. From what Lothrop tells us, we can see that early colonial Thanksgiving days involved a day in church even if services might be shortened
for sufficient reasons such as the severe cold in drafty, unheated meeting-
houses. Thanksgivings could culminate in a feast, which in these examples
appears to have maintained the spirit of community of the church service
instead of breaking up into family units, as occurred later.

   There were additional days on which servile labor was suspended and
religious exercises were undertaken in colonial New England, including Harvard (and later Yale) Commencement, Election Day, and Militia
Training days—and public executions. These "days of civic religion," as
Horton Davies calls them, were proclaimed by the magistrates and included sermons and prayer just as the overtly religious Sabbath, Fasts (or
days of humiliation), and Thanksgivings. Religion was not just for special
occasions in colonial New England but a pervasive element of daily life.
The sermons of the civic days and the occasional midweekly "lecture day"
were popular social entertainments, providing the news and commentary we now expect from television news programs, and they were often
published.

   By 1640, the Puritan holidays were established in every New England
colony except Rhode Island. Providential holidays might be declared both
by the churches and by civic officials, and Plymouth, Massachusetts, Connecticut, New Haven, and New Hampshire passed laws determining the
responsibility of civic authorities to declare public Fasts and Thanksgivings.[11] For example, here are two of the Plymouth Colony statutes concerning providential days:

Holy Days: That it be in the power of the Govr & Assist^s to commans solemn
dies of humiliation by fasting &c. and also for thanksgiving as occasion shall be
offered. (1636)

Servile Work &c. on Day of Humil: &c.: It is enacted that none shall p^{r}sume to
attend servile worke of labour or attend any sports on such days as are or shalbe
appointed by the Court for humilliation by fasting and prayer or for publicke
Thanksgiving, on penalty of __ shillings. (1682)

There was apparently an aversion to *official* colonywide Fasts and Thanks-givings in Rhode Island, and the only examples on record are those that the colony was obliged to observe during the Dominion of New England, when Sir Edmund Andros, the royally appointed dominion governor, commanded Thanksgivings and Fasts for all the colonies, starting with a Thanksgiving on Thursday, December 1, 1687. Andros' subsequent two Thanksgivings were on Sundays in the Anglican tradition, which was yet another bitter pill for the New Englanders. After Andros was deposed in 1688, the colonies returned to their earlier practices, and Rhode Island lapsed back into avoiding colonywide providential days altogether.

Second- and third-generation New Englanders, who had no personal memories of the old holiday calendar of Christmas, Easter, and the saints' days, grew up with Fasts and Thanksgivings as a familiar part of their lives, and this familiarity eventually led to a modification of the old sys-tem. The original strong association between the church and the state that supported the strict providential view was weakened by the troubles of the 1680s, as Richard Gildrie has pointed out, opening the way to some lati-tude in the old patterns of pious behavior.[12] Fast days had always entailed an option of being held in anticipation of events as well as in response to them, and there had been a custom (begun by Charles I but enthusiasti-cally adopted by his Puritan foes) of regular monthly Fasts in Parliament during the English Civil War.[13] By the end of the seventeenth century a new tradition of regular springtime Fasts and autumnal Thanksgivings existed in parallel to the original practice of declaring special holidays in response to providential events. The New Englanders took the possibility of scheduled regularity that Fasts if not Thanksgivings had enjoyed and made it the basis for seasonal celebrations. Orthodox Puritans such as Samuel Sewall objected to the liberties being taken with the old providen-tial rules ("T'was not fit upon meer Generals as the Mercies of the year to com[m]and a thanksgiving"),[14] but the majority overruled them.

The Traditional New England Thanksgiving

The new yearly Thanksgivings and Fast days did not begin in one colony and spread to the others but rather evolved simultaneously throughout the region. There was no single "First Annual Thanksgiving" or "First Annual Fast Day" that began an unbroken tradition for succeeding generations. According to William DeLoss Love, the fall Thanksgiving became standard practice first in Connecticut by 1650 and in the other colonies by the end of the century, while spring Fasts were regularized about a decade later in the same fashion. Although the vernal Fast generally occurred between February and May and the autumnal Thanksgiving between October and December, these days were not legally established events like our modern holidays. People still waited for the exact dates to be announced each year. There might be no Thanksgiving at all in years when conditions were as grim as they were during King Philip's War, but otherwise the annual holidays might be confidently anticipated in their season each year.

Although the providential significance of contemporary events remained a primary factor, the natural agricultural rhythms of the year also helped determine a seasonal cycle for the holidays. While spring held the promise of a new year, the season itself was a time of want and privation in colonial New England. The end of winter and the old year (the new year began on March 25 in the Julian calendar, which remained in use in England and New England until 1752) was a time of dearth when the remnants of last year's harvest ran low, winter-weakened bodies were most vulnerable to disease, and no fresh food was available beyond a few salad greens. Spring flowers and songbirds were nice, but the colonists could not live on them. The planting of seeds might be likened to a burial that promised a glorious rebirth, just as Christ had died and was reborn, but the promise was contingent on God's mercy. All sorts of potential calamities might come between seedtime and harvest—drought, insect plagues, storms, excessive heat or cold. Everything hinged on the success of the crops, and as there was nothing much to eat anyhow, it made perfect sense to pause and observe a day of fasting to ask God for his favorable dispensation in the coming year.

The agricultural harvest ended in late September, and slaughtering began with cool weather in October. Long after the harvest was over in the fall, the results for the year that had begun with hope and anxiety were totted up. It was a time for summing up God's judgments and mercies toward his people. A yearlong retrospective was undertaken and thanks given for the harvest, and for the health of the community now that the hot months that could bring plague or sickness were past. The harvest brought both a bounty of fresh food and the wherewithal for getting through another winter and spring. The hay was in stacks, grain awaited threshing or shucking in the barns, and larders were full of fruits and herbs from orchards and gardens. Livestock were slaughtered and put to salt, and the great flocks of wild birds fattening for the winter were ready for the eager fowler to shoot or snare.

Autumn was more often than not a time of plenty, bringing a sense of a job well done and relative leisure following a hard season of agricultural work, once the rigors of the early years had passed and family farms were well established. There was no other time of the year when as much fresh food was available, so it was a perfect time to feast before winter brought the next cycle of retrenchment. The people of New England used their Thanksgiving to mark the closing of the books for the agricultural year: there was a church service in which God was praised for his mercies and the bounty of the land, followed by a feast (figure 5)—but not a traditional harvest feast such as occurred in England around Michaelmas (September 29). Instead, their feasts marked the arrival of winter, much as the now-disused Christmas holiday had.

Eighteenth-century practice combined the old occasional holidays with the new seasonal ones in such a manner as to make it seem that fasting and giving thanks had always been done that way. By the middle of the century, New Englanders were so used to annual Fast and Thanksgiving days that they tended to believe that such days had been customary throughout the history of the colonies. Colonial historian Thomas Hutchinson wrote of the ancestors of the New Englanders:

They constantly, every spring, appointed a day for fasting and prayer to implore the divine blessings upon their affairs in the ensuing year, and in the fall, a day of thanksgiving and public acknowledgement of the favors conferred upon them in the year past. . . . It has continued without interruption, I suppose, in any one instance, down to this day.[1]

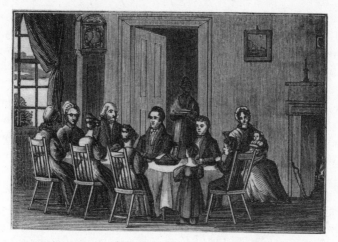

5. *Thanksgiving Dinner*, from Charles Goodrich, *The Universal Traveler*
(1837), opposite p. 36. An early New England family reunion and
Thanksgiving dinner.

Oral tradition smoothed over the doctrinal disputes and irregular observances that the holidays had undergone in becoming annual, and presented
an idealized past that contributed to later belief that there had always been
a late-fall Thanksgiving.

Providential holidays were not limited to the more puritanical colonies.
During the eighteenth century, Rhode Island began to appoint Fasts and
Thanksgivings, while New York, Pennsylvania, New Jersey, Delaware,
and even Virginia had their own occasional Fasts or Thanksgivings. The
American Revolution brought the observance of the providential holidays
to a national level when Fasts and Thanksgivings were declared for the entire thirteen colonies. The first was on June 12, 1775, when the president of
the Continental Congress, John Hancock, declared a Fast day in the United
Colonies for Thursday, July 20. Hancock declared another pancolonial Fast
for Friday, May 17, 1776. Henry Laurens, the president of the Continental
Congress, proclaimed the first national Thanksgiving for Thursday, December 18, 1777.[2] This Thanksgiving followed the New England model with
its Thursday date and an admonition in the proclamation:

And it is further recommended, That servile Labor, and such Recreation, as,
though at other Times innocent, may be unbecoming the Purpose of this Ap-
pointment, be omitted on so solemn an Occasion.

George Washington declared his first Thanksgiving as president on October 3 for Thursday, November 11, 1789, and a second national Thanksgiving for Thursday, February 19, 1795. John Adams declared no Thanksgivings

during his term, but he had two Fast days; Wednesday, May 9, 1798, and Thursday, April 25, 1799. James Madison proclaimed wartime Fast days for Thursday, August 20, 1812; Thursday, September 9, 1813; and Thursday, January 12, 1815. Madison also declared the last national providential holiday before the Civil War, a Thanksgiving for the conclusion of the War of 1812 on Thursday, April 13, 1815. In between the national holidays, the New England states continued holding their regular spring, fall, and occasional providential days. In the years that followed 1815, all the New England states including Rhode Island, Vermont (after 1777), and Maine (after 1820) maintained the spring Fast and fall Thanksgiving tradition.

The classic Thanksgiving holiday that eventually became a national ideal was an established fixture of New England life. After the ten national providential Thanksgivings between 1777 and 1815, the holiday tradition was maintained by annual Thanksgivings proclaimed by the individual states. No longer a holy day dependent on God's particular providence, the late-autumn holiday celebrated faith (if not orthodoxy), family, friends, and a successful year. There was still no fixed date for these annual events, a holdover from Puritan providentialism, but most were scheduled in late November or early December. Each year, the date was officially proclaimed by civil authority: the state governor would "advise" the churches that this was when they should observe the holiday.

The inhabitants of each state of course anticipated the announcement of their particular Thursday in November or December (dates sometimes varied from state to state), but the real action took place after the governor had set the day. Once the proclamation had been published and read in the churches, a flurry of preparations began. Housewives made pies days— even weeks—in advance, depending on cool seasonal temperatures for their safe preservation. On the evening before the holiday itself, all chores that could be done in advance were taken care of to clear the slate for a day of leisure. On the farms (and the vast majority of New Englanders were still farmers)[3] animals were foddered, houses cleaned, and fowls plucked for tomorrow's cooking. In town, householders visited the market to bargain for the necessary ingredients of the feast. Rev. William Bentley of Salem found the prices a bit steep in 1804:

[November] 28. Markets full, but poultry kept up its price from 12½ to 16 cents, Turkies, Geese, 10c., Ducks, pair 75 cents. Fowls, 12 cents. Sausages, 12½ cents lb. Pork low. Flour rising from 8 to 12, &c. Corn dear, & price not fixed. Beef 10 cents. Much of this price is to be put at the free Circulation of bank Bills & Checks.[4]

A brief supper ("a sort of 'picked-up' dinner")[5] was provided for the family and for guests who had already arrived before everyone went to bed in anticipation of the day itself. The holiday was a time of gathering together as family, friends, and neighbors met at church and in the homes of the community, just as they had in Scituate almost two centuries earlier. However, there was seldom any discouragement of secular entertainment, especially if it did not occur on the day itself. Thanksgiving balls were quite a popular addition to the holiday. Another custom found on the North Shore of Massachusetts was the Thanksgiving Eve visits by poor people (especially Revolutionary War veterans) to more well-off households to ask for charity, which were met with gifts of food supplies such as flour, rice, or the like. Children used the occasion to dress up in ragged clothes and pretend to be needy petitioners as a prank.[6]

Thanksgiving Day itself began with the household getting up at dawn, which at that time of year meant they arrived fully dressed for breakfast rather later than they would on a workday. After breakfast, the cooking of the dinner was begun, and family members prepared for meeting (one went to "meeting," not to "church," in New England). Not everyone went to meeting, however, as someone had to oversee the preparations for the feast, and the youngest children were not expected to attend the service. The sheer amount of labor involved in preparing the huge dinner for family and assorted guests was a burden to housewives and servants alike, as Mrs. Anne Lyman noted in a rare departure from the generally rosy reminiscences of the old-time holiday in a letter to her son in 1840:

We got through Thanksgiving as usual, — after a great struggle on my part — with fifteen at the table, who seemed to enjoy themselves highly — I did not. I am sure, however, that I have much to rejoice in. . . . But the reflections connected with the past most always make these annual festivals, to people who are as advanced as I am, to be days of sad retrospection.[7]

The meetinghouse bell began to ring at ten o'clock, and soon after the congregation arrived and sorted themselves into family pews. Attendance varied from year to year depending on the weather and the enthusiasm of the meeting goers. In 1800, although meeting attendance was still expected of any respectable citizen, only one in fifteen Americans was an actual member of a congregation.[8] Most churches had only a "forenoon" meeting, with the standard order of service. Thanksgiving sermons were often political or topical in nature, the sermon's length being determined by the aspirations of the minister and the expectations of his audience. Although organs were still a rarity, instrumental music was very popular at the beginning of the nineteenth century, and modern hymns were sung by the choir and congregation in addition to psalms. An important part of the Thanksgiving service was the collection for the poor — which might have been begun the week before—with the proceeds given to less-well-off families to ensure that they too would enjoy a proper dinner. The conventional charity of the season also included gifts of prepared food sent to poor relations and neighbors who were not included in the household gatherings.

When the morning service was over at noon or one o'clock, families and guests returned to their homes to await dinner, which was usually served at two or three o'clock. The turkey predictably was the foundation of the feast, but it also included chicken pie, roast beef, the various vegetables available to New Englanders in November or December, pies, and puddings, and ended with dried fruits and nuts. Cider (which was always alcoholic) and wine were commonly served before the temperance movement organized its challenge to this custom. Children in some families might eat separately from the adults—Thanksgiving was not a child's holiday, as much as they might enjoy it, but one in which adult activities such as games and dancing included the younger members of the family. After dinner, the company gathered for various pastimes such as games, conversation, songs, storytelling, or visits to other households. There was a supper later on, if desired. The more pious households kept up the older tradition of a discussion of the sermon followed by fireside prayers, and most families had some sort of prayer at the end of the short late-autumn evening. Schools were often closed for the entire week, and the Friday following a Thursday Thaksgiving was sometimes enjoyed as a day off work as well.

The most significant characteristic of Thanksgiving at the beginning of the nineteenth century, however, was that it was still an unselfconscious part of contemporary life. Holiday traditions were simple and unpretentious, focusing on the immediate basics of New England life: church, household, food, and domestic leisure. It was a time to review the current year, reminisce about one's personal past, and recall family members and friends who were not among the guests by reason of distance or death. Most importantly, it carried no suggestion of commemoration. There were no Pilgrim or historic associations connected with Thanksgiving. The holiday was not perceived symbolically as an evocation of olden times or invested with sentimental significance beyond its gathering of clans and its family reminiscences—when "conversations run backwards," as the nineteenth century Plymouth author Abby Morton Diaz observed. It was rather simply unquestioned tradition, the accepted thing to do at each year's end.

Thanksgiving took the place of Christmas in New England, acting as a seasonal break of meeting and feasting before the worst winter weather and gloomy days set in. Except for a few foreign immigrants and Episco-

6. George H. Durrie, *Home for Thanksgiving*, painted in 1861 and published by Currier and Ives in 1867. Connecticut artist Durrie specialized in New England snow scenes. His representation of a family reunion by sleigh captures the popular impression of Thanksgiving before the Pilgrims became associated with the holiday.

palians, practically no one celebrated Christmas in New England until the 1830s, and Thanksgiving was the major early winter holiday. Farm families would not think of late November as "harvest time," and the earlier harvest was just one of the various events of the year evoked in the proclamations during the summing up of the preceding year. There was a common association of Thanksgiving Day with snowy weather, when one might go to grandfather's house in a sleigh (figure 6) or go sledding and skating after dinner, rather than with the autumn colors and field crops we envision today. The harvest theme became prominent only when the people celebrating the event were divorced from the land, through moving to cities and suburbs, and started thinking about their agricultural heritage and the Pilgrim story.

After 1820, New England culture shifted from intellectual Calvinism to emotional evangelicalism, from living on farms to life in factory towns, and homespun virtue was replaced with commercial consumption. As John R. Gillis has said about the succeeding generations who made Thanksgiving their own, "The Victorians—or more specifically, the Protestant middle classes—were the first to experience the pastness of the past."[9] The example of the passing Revolutionary generation now became the touchstone for appropriate holiday behavior, and the historical element began to suffuse Thanksgiving sentiments. The rising generations would soon locate the archetypal Thanksgiving in an idyllic and unrecoverable past, nostalgically evoking the celebrations of the colonial and early national eras to give the holiday a sentimental antiquarian atmosphere quite unlike the immediacy it had enjoyed earlier. Before considering the Victorian contribution to the Thanksgiving holiday, we will take a closer look at the constituent parts of the traditional holiday.

Official proclamation of Thanksgiving by civil or church authorities initiated the holiday, as it had since New England was founded. Even today the president of the United States issues an official announcement each year, and the state governors issue their own proclamations, since each state still has jurisdiction over its holidays, just as the separate colonies did in the eighteenth century. This has become a perfunctory exercise today, however. Thanksgiving proclamations are issued annually by the governor of Massachusetts, for example, but in recent years they have not been printed and distributed to be read in public schools as they were a generation ago.

The earliest proclamations were simple handwritten announcements sent out by the governor to the many churches in the colony. The first surviving *printed* proclamation was for a Fast in 1670. Early eighteenth-century Massachusetts Bay proclamations were about twelve by sixteen inches in size, with the royal arms at the top and "God Save the King" at the bottom. An example from this period is the 1723 Dummer proclamation in the collection at Pilgrim Hall in Plymouth, Massachusetts.

By the HONOURABLE William Dummer Esq;
Lieutenant GOVERNOUR and Commander in Chief of His Majesty's
Province of the Massachusetts-Bay in New-England:
A Proclamation for a General
THANKSGIVING.

FORASMUCH as amidst the various & awful Rebukes of Heaven with which we are righteously aflicted, We are still under the highest and most indispensible Obligations of Gratitude for the many Instances of the divine Goodness in the course of the Year past, More especially, That it has pleased Almighty GOD to prolong the Life of our most gracious Sovereign Lord the KING, Their Royal Highnesses the Prince & Princess of Wales, and Their Illustrious Offspring, and to give an happy Increase to the Royal Family; To defeat the wicked and desperate Conspiracies against His Majesty's Sacred Person and rightful Government, and to Direct the Councils of the Nation to such Measures for the Suppressing & Punishing the same, as under GOD may prove the Means of their lasting Quiet & Security; So far to succeed the Administrations of His Majesty's Government in this Province, To continue our invaluable Privileges, To restore Health to us, To give us great Plenty of the Fruits of the Earth, to Defeat in some Measure the repeated Attempts of the Indian Enemy against us, and to defend so many of our frontier Plantations from their Rage & Fury, To guard our Sea-Coasts against the rapacious & bloody Pirates, and deliver many of them into the Hands of Justice; and above all that He continues to us the precious Benefits & Liberties of the Gospel: I have therefore thought fit, by and with the Advice of his Majesty's Council, to Order & Appoint that Thursday the Twenty-eighth of November Currant be solemnly Observed as a Day of Publick THANKSGIVING throughout this Province, exhorting both Ministers and People in their respective Assemblies to offer up their unfeigned THANKS to almighty GOD for these and all other his unmerited Favours; And all Service Labour is forbidden on the said Day.

Given at the Council Chamber in Boston the Sixth Day November 1723. In the tenth Year of the Reign of Our Sovereign Lord GEORGE, by the Grace of GOD of Great Britain, France and Ireland, KING, Defender of the Faith, &c.

By Order of the Honourable the Lieutenant Governour, W. DUMMER by and with the Advice of the Council, Josiah Willard, Sec.

GOD Save the King.

After the Revolution the proclamations increased in size to fifteen by twenty inches, and "God Save the King" was replaced with "God Save the Commonwealth of Massachusetts." By the early nineteenth century, Massachusetts proclamations were being distributed in a two-column format nineteen by twenty-four inches in size, which remained the standard until the end of the century. Some of the texts were quite long, but a moderate example from 1827 can be compared with the example from a century before:

Commonwealth of Massachusetts.

By His Excellency
Levi Lincoln,
Governor of the Commonwealth of Massachusetts,
A Proclamation
for a Day of Public Thanksgiving and Praise.

IN the rich enjoyment of the blessings of public tranquility, of health, and the abundance of the harvests, the People of this Commonwealth have passed through another revolution of the Seasons, and in devout contemplation of the goodness of a divine and merciful Benefactor, who has sustained, and nourished, and loaded them with benefits, their hearts will be elevated to acknowledgments of gratitude, and animated to fervent ascriptions of adoration and praise.

To afford opportunity, at the accustomed period of the year, for an united expression of these sentiments and feelings of pious joy, I have thought fit, with the advice and consent of the Council, to set apart THURSDAY, THE TWENTY NINTH DAY OF NOVEMBER NEXT, to be observed as a *Religious Festival* of

THANKSGIVING throughout the Commonwealth. And I do invite the People of every Christian denomination, to repair, on that day to the houses dedicated to the worship of Almighty God, there to commemorate the signal mercies of his providence, in the preservation of their lives, and in the multiplied circumstances of comfort and happiness with which they are enjoyed; — To recognize the divine superintendence in the peace and prosperity of the nation; in the security of the institutions of popular government; in the indulgence of the rights of conscience; in the diffusion of the means of instruction and knowledge; and in the cultivation and improvement of civil and social relations; — To rejoice that charity and philanthropy are engaged in the relief of the afflicted, intelligence and moral virtue in vindicating the rights of the oppressed, and that the spirit of Christianity is in exercise to communicate the influence of the Gospel to the ignorant and the vicious of the whole earth.

AND truly and deeply sensible of our dependence upon the grace and mercy of God, may we seek, by resolution of devoted obedience to his will, by penitence for sin, and by supplication and prayer, the continuance of his favor; — humbly commending ourselves in our individual interests and wants, and in all associations with Society, Government and Country, to his future protection and blessing.

THE People of the Commonwealth are requested to abstain from whatsoever is inconsistent with the appropriate observance of the occasion.

Given at the Council Chamber in Boston, this seventeenth day of October, in the year of our Lord one thousand eight hundred and twenty seven, and the fifty second of the Independence of the United States.

Levi Lincoln

By His Excellency the Governor, with the advice and consent of the Council.
God Save the Commonwealth of Massachusetts

The large broadsides were decorated with a woodcut of the commonwealth seal at the top, while God was enjoined to save the Commonwealth of Massachusetts at the bottom. Connecticut proclamations adopted a large-size sheet from 1783 to 1850 comparable to the Massachusetts examples, and the Rhode Island and Vermont sheets were similar. In New Hampshire, proclamations were usually smaller, especially after paper became scarce following the Revolution.[10]

Proclamations followed a customary format that enumerated the blessings and mercies of the current year and petitioned for their extension into the future. They differed in length from a couple paragraphs to pages of pious prose describing the benefits of the preceding season and beseeching "the Great Author" (or some other sobriquet of God) to keep up the good work in the coming year. The earlier proclamations put religious virtue, along with agricultural prosperity, domestic tranquillity, peace, and liberty, at the top of their lists of blessings experienced and desired:

And whereas it has been his divine pleasure to continue his manifestations of great goodness to the people of this State, in multiplying the fruits of the earth, promoting the diffusion of religion, advancing the interests of knowledge, prospering internal improvements, and vouchsafeing the enjoyment of liberty, peace and plenty.[11]

Which were followed by more mundane mercies:

He would bestow his benediction upon the interests of this State and Nation, prosper our Agriculture, Manufactures, Commerce and Fisheries, and bless the means of education and instruction in science and in moral and religious truth.[12]

The abstract blessings were gradually overtaken by the recognition of the year's tangible rewards in agriculture, public health, freedom (or relief) from disaster, educational advancement, industrial expansion, commercial prosperity, and, in New England in particular, the success of the fisheries. Lincoln's 1863 proclamation, which was actually written by Secretary of State William Seward,[13] is a classic example of the genre in which reasons for thankfulness are found even in times of hardship (the text can be found in chapter 4).

The emphasis in nineteenth-century Thanksgiving proclamations continued to be on contemporary circumstances rather than historical example. Although ancestors and history were alluded to from time to time, official Thanksgiving long remained a living tradition that did not require the authority of the past.

The Thanksgiving proclamation was issued from two to four weeks before the holiday itself, and the text published in newspapers and read out in the pulpits several times before the day arrived.[14] Once the proclamation was published, the preparations for the day began in earnest. These included gathering and processing provisions for the dinner, sending out invitations to family and friends, arranging for travel to the family homestead or getting the host's house in order (which might involve cleaning everything from the stables to the chimney), attending Thanksgiving balls, and, for the minister, outlining the sermon and order of service.

A sense of what the preparations entailed in an ordinary New England family can be found in Martha Ballard's diary between 1785 and 1811.[15] Beyond its interest as a unique chronicle of a female medical practitioner in post-Revolutionary Maine (then still part of Massachusetts), the diary contains a wealth of information on daily life in New England at the time. Mrs. Ballard was not always able to attend Thanksgiving services or even

7. Winslow Homer, *Thanksgiving Day—the Church Porch*, from *Frank Leslie's Illustrated Newspaper*, December 23, 1865, p. 217. A sober Thanksgiving service just after the Civil War.

observe the day at home owing to the exigencies of her work as midwife, but the annual event was obviously an important milestone in the social year. Mrs. Ballard regularly produced pies in profusion, including apple, pumpkin, and mince, with the help of her daughters and local girls who were hired as servants from time to time. The Ballards also bought what were then called "grocery stores," that is, staples and supplies that would not spoil quickly such as spices, sugar, coffee, and chocolate (for drinks). Fowl and meat predominate among fresh foods mentioned, as vegetables were largely taken for granted. Turkey is mentioned several times (they had it twice in the same week in 1792) but also (and most often) chicken, as well as beef and pork, sometimes all at the same meal.[16]

The first duty on Thanksgiving Day itself was to attend church (figure 7), a responsibility recalled by Charles Dudley Warner and others as tedious. "Thanksgiving itself was rather an awful festival—very much like Sunday, except for the enormous dinner."[17] Thanksgiving was most particularly the holiday of the Congregational heirs of Puritan tradition. While the

Congregational church was still "established" (that is, the official legal church) in Massachusetts and Connecticut, it was financially supported by the government and able to lord itself over competing denominations such as the Episcopalians, Baptists, Methodists, and the evangelical sects. This legal superiority was removed from the state constitutions in Connecticut in 1818 and in Massachusetts in 1833, making all Christian churches equal before the law. Congregationalism then had to compete with the other denominations for voluntary funding and membership. This and the secession of the liberal or Unitarian wing of the church in 1825 had an unsettling effect on the social position of the New England churches and began the gradual de-emphasis on the role of the church in what had been its most prominent holiday. The secularization of the holiday was a matter of concern for the more conservative members of the community, which is well described in Henry Bliss's 1815 poetical description of the day, *Thanksgiving, A Poem, In Two Parts*[18] (see appendix 1).

While the old "standing orders" of church establishment were still in force, the service was similar for each congregation, the main variation being whether it continued through both forenoon and afternoon sessions or was just a morning service. Typical examples are found in the diary entries of Anna Green Winslow (1771), Rev. William Bentley (1798), Julia Cowles (1803), and Martha Ballard (1808),[19] and in Mrs. Hale's early novel *Northwood* (1827):

The psalm was performing when they entered. The tune was "Old Hundred," with a bass viol for an accompaniment. They sung with energy, and made up in tone what they lacked in harmony; yet while there were some fine tenor voices, and the Englishman [a visitor and the narrator] allowed the performance to be tolerable, but he said there was wanting the full, swelling peal of the organ, to lift the soul to heaven; and nothing could in church music, he thought, supply the place of that instrument. Mr. Cranford had been reclining in the pulpit, so as not to be visible, but a moment after the singing ceased, he arose, and the whole congregation, by a simultaneous movement, arose with him, "and stood up." When, clasping his hands, he raised his eyes towards heaven, where the prayer he poured forth seemed ascending, Mr. Frankford admitted the possibility that his talents might merit the praises they had received. Not a foot was moved nor a loud breathing heard; all seemed to realize that they were in the presence of a holy God; and when the *amen* was pronounced, there was not a heart in the assembly that could not have responded, "so be it!" Again they sung, and then Mr. Cranfield, who had been industriously turning over the leaves of the Bible as if searching for his text, arose and looking around, a profound silence was maintained, while, with a slow and solemn pronunciation, he "invited their serious attention to what might be offered from that portion of the sacred scriptures recorded in the prophet Isaiah, twenty-sixth chapter and fifteenth verse: 'Thou hast increased the nation, O Lord, thou hast increased the nation: thou art glorified; thou hast removed it far unto all the ends of the earth.'"[20]

The service began with a hymn (or instrumental music), followed by an opening prayer, another hymn, the sermon, a third hymn, the contribution or offering, and the closing prayer and blessing. Instrumental music was an important part of contemporary New England services. Some congregations installed organs as early as the mid–eighteenth century, while others used chamber instruments such as bass viols. Sermons, usually topical or political, lasted over an hour, and many were later published, ostensibly "by demand" of the audience.[21] There was some socializing after the service was over, and then the congregation separated and went home to dinner.

Just as attending meeting was a primary social function on Thanksgiving, so was bringing people together to share dinner. What was important to a prosperous householder was the number of kin, friends, and charitable invitees that could be assembled to partake of his largesse. The emphasis on the *family* gathering, or reunion of kin, had not yet achieved the importance it came to have in later Victorian times. The father of the house was honored by the people he could extend hospitality to, and the mother by her ability to prepare a meal that would provide everyone with a generous superfluity of food. The paterfamilias was the founder of the feast, however, and it was to "grandfather's house"—not grandmother's—that the sleigh traveled over the river and through the woods in the original version of the famous Thanksgiving poem by Lydia Maria Child (1844).[22] Later, after the holiday had been taken over by the distaff side of the family, the verse was changed to "grandmother's house," but that would be in the future. Still later, once Thanksgiving became an autumn rather than early winter holiday, the poem was turned into a *Christmas* song by the Andrews Sisters—for as everyone now knows, sleighing is about Christmas, not Thanksgiving![23]

Family members made up the greater proportion of the guests when large family networks still lived in close proximity, but neighbors and visitors who were not kin were equally welcome. Following the dinner, the company might go out and visit other households, extending the social aspect of the day, or the minister and other guests might drop in for an hour or so. If there was snow on the ground (and the contemporary ideal was a "white Thanksgiving"), the popularity of nighttime sleigh rides enhanced the idea of travel. Community members might also use the after-dinner hours to regroup for weddings, which were a household rather than church affair at the time.[24] For the first third of the nineteenth century, at least, the

Thanksgiving holiday did not venture beyond its traditional components: the religious meeting, a remarkable turkey dinner, family entertainments and weddings, and community activities such visits and balls. Later in the century, the gastronomic pleasures of the day would overshadow the church service, and new activities such as football would supersede the turkey shoot—but the fundamental elements of church, family dinner, and community activities remained the day's common essentials until the end of the nineteenth century.

The Classic New England
Thanksgiving Dinner

We now come to the most renowned part of the New England Thanksgiving tradition, the dinner. In the early years of the nineteenth century, the church service and the dinner still shared top billing for the day, but the dinner would soon triumph and claim the primary role in the day's festivities. The focal point of the dinner was then as now the turkey, but other meats such as beef, mutton, ham, or pork could be substituted without a sense of incongruity. The chicken pie was almost as traditional as the turkey that it accompanied as an indicator of a true New England Thanksgiving. Although the constituent elements of the traditional Yankee dinner may seem familiar enough, our predecessors' tastes were sometimes rather different from those we are used to nowadays. (For examples of typical period recipes, please refer to appendix 2.)

The turkey had been a high-status food since it was first introduced into England in the 1530s. Game and fowl were always more prestigious than "butcher's meat," taking more expense and effort to acquire and prepare. The turkey assumed the place of honor that had previously been assigned to the goose in ordinary folks' feasts (the very wealthy having swans and peacocks). This preference traveled with the immigrants to New England, where they found numerous wild turkeys for their purposes. Governor Bradford notes that the Plymouth colonists found "a great store of wild turkeys, of which they took many" in the fall of 1621. To be safe, however, the Massachusetts Bay colonists listed turkeys (and rabbits) among the stock they intended to bring from England in 1630. These historic birds, while sometimes growing large (dressed turkeys weighing twenty pounds or more were not uncommon), looked nothing like the grotesque, bulbous birds of today, and as recently as the 1940s domestic turkeys still exhibited the sleek lines of their colonial ancestors.[1]

8. *Driving Turkeys to the Picking-House*, from *Harper's Weekly*, December 2, 1871, p. 1132. Collected from various farms, turkeys were driven in a flock to where they were killed, cleaned, plucked (or "picked"), and made ready for cooking.

The turkey was not only the showpiece of the dinner but also the primary icon of the holiday itself. Whether they came from the barnyard or from the wild, everyone expected to find turkeys at Thanksgiving time. The wild turkey was hunted and trapped in a number of ways. The most sporting was to stalk the birds along their trails and roosts, and shoot them as they ran (turkeys are fast and resolute runners) or flew off. The dedicated table hunter, on the other hand, might go out at night with torches to where the birds roosted in trees and take as many as he needed from their sleeping perches. While the big birds were often wary and hard to catch (when awake), they also acted with fatal stupidity at times. Audubon tells the story of sneaking up on a flock of turkeys and shooting three with one shotgun blast. "The rest, instead of flying off, fell a strutting round their dead companions, and had I not looked on shooting again as murder without necessity, I might have secured at least another. So I showed myself, and marching up to the place where the dead birds were, drove away the survivors." Audubon also relates how building a sort of covered pen out of logs and baiting it with corn easily trapped the birds. They entered a low slot at the bottom under a log, but after they had eaten, their only idea was to try to escape upward between the logs, never thinking to crawl out the way they had entered. These live captives were sometimes taken and raised in the farmyard (figure 8). Another contemporary turkey hunter was the French gastronome Brillat-Savarin, who visited Connecticut in

1794. He traveled deep into the woods to the Bulow family's farm and went out shooting on an October evening, bagging some partridges and gray squirrels. Coming by luck on a flock of turkeys, Brillat-Savarin was able to shoot one, much to his delight, while his companion was unable to find the one he was *sure* he had hit. Brillat-Savarin's turkey, whose memory has entered into culinary legend, was later served to an appreciative audience in Hartford.[2]

Wild turkeys became scarce after the American Revolution, and it was their tame farmyard counterparts (sometimes raised from wild turkey eggs found in the woods) that were more likely to become the offering on the Thanksgiving table. Turkey hunting was only a memory in New England by the mid-nineteenth century. "The very last wild turkey known to have been seen in [Massachusetts] was killed on Mount Tom, November 1, 1847. The specimen is still preserved in the museum of Yale College." Elisha Lewis in 1856 predicted the extinction of the species, saying, "Scarcely a bird is now to be encountered on the whole northern and eastern Atlantic seaboard. The destroying hand of the white man is stretched forth, and his victims are vainly seeking an asylum far beyond the confines of the 'Father of the Waters' [the Mississippi]." With too few remaining to be hunted in the wild, the sport of the turkey shoot was substituted.[3]

James Fenimore Cooper provides a good description of this practice—a Christmas custom in New York—in chapter 17 of his novel *The Pioneers* (1823).[4] The birds had been raised by a local black farmer and were offered up in the following manner: "The bird was fastened by a string of tow, to the base of the stump of a large pine, the side of which, towards the point where the marksmen were placed, had been flattened with an axe, in order that it might serve the purpose of a target, by which the merit of each individual might be ascertained. The distance between the stump and this point was one hundred measured yards; a foot more or a foot less being thought an invasion of the right of one of the parties." The assembled sportsmen then were able to take a shot at the bird (which in this case was hidden behind a snowbank with only its head showing) at a price agreed on with the owner. The man who killed—or bloodied—the bird got to take it home. As Thomas Low described the sport, "Turkeys are put up to be shot at so many rods' distance, at so much a shot, and the poor shots pay for the turkeys which the good ones carry home."[5] As in shooting galleries at modern carnivals, it took luck and skill to hit one's target, considering the distance, the movement of the bird, the firearms of the day, and the amount of alcohol consumed (figure 9).

Most families simply "harvested" one of their barnyard flock or bought a bird at market. "Turkeys are singled out for the block, and die 'without a sign.' Chickens follow in fateful order close after. There is an indiscrimi-

9. *Turkey-shooting*, from *Harper's Weekly*, January 17, 1874, p. 60. In this Thanksgiving contest, the prize for the best shot was a holiday turkey.

nate spirting [*sic*] of fresh blood all around the chop-log, a great flutter of feathers and headless hornpipes over the scattered chips, and the annual door-yard butchery is over. . . . Everyone is busy—is at work. The carcasses of fowls are getting plucked in a darkened back-room."[6] Once the deceased turkey was delivered by sport, purchase, or from the farmyard pen, it was turned over to the housewife for preparation. Fowl are easily plucked immediately after death, but preparing these birds was a tedious business of gutting, scalding, and plucking. Turkeys were usually roasted for the feast, but some might be boiled as well—a method of cooking that did not require close attendance. Contemporary recipes for roasting are, technically, not unlike those used today for oven-baked turkeys, but boiled turkey is probably unfamiliar to most modern cooks. Done well, it too is a dish suitable for a feast.

Fish, except perhaps for oysters, were seldom seen at a Thanksgiving feast. Fowl and meat were the most important constituents of the meal, followed next by the pies. Vegetables were the least valued—even the symbolic pumpkin—although they were regularly included in the bill of fare. Pickles and preserves were supplied to offset the rather bland nature of Yankee cold-weather cuisine.

The pumpkin had long had its own iconic status as the symbol of New England frugality and self-sufficiency. The large squash supplied a lot of food for the negligible effort of raising it. Its plainness suited the Puritans' aversion to luxury and ostentation, although even they found it too bland for unalloyed consumption. One of the very first published New England recipes is for the "Ancient New-England standing [i.e., of regular and habitual use] Dish" in Josselyn's *New-England Rarities* (1672), using vinegar and spices to make boiled pumpkin palatable.

But the Housewives manner is to slice them when ripe, and cut them into dice, and so fill a pot with them of two or three Gallons, and stew them upon a gentle fire a whole day, and as they sink, they fill again with fresh Pompions, not putting any liquor to them; and when it is stew'd enough, it will look lik bak'd Apples; this they Dish, putting Butter to it, and a little Vinegar, (with some Spice, as Ginger, &c.) which makes it tart like an Apple, and so serve it up to be eaten with Fish or Flesh: It provokes Urin extreamly and is very windy.[7]

The pumpkin was often credited with sustaining the colonists through the hardship of the early years, as in Benjamin Thompson's *New England's Crisis* (1676):

The times wherein old Pompion was a saint,
When men fared hardly yet without complaint
On vilest cates; the dainty Indian maize
Was eat with clamshells out of wooden trays
Under thatched huts without the cry of rent,
And the best sauce to every dish, content.

Similarly, the 1774 satirical ballad "New England's Annoyances" (which may have originated as early as the 1640s) makes pumpkins a necessity:

If flesh meat be wanting to fill up our dish,
We have carrets and pumpkins and turnips and fish;
And when we have a mind for a delicate dish,
We repair to the *clam-bank* and there we catch fish.
Instead of pottage and puddings and custards and pies,
Our pumkins and parsnips are common supplies;
We have pumkin at morning and pumkin at noon,
If it was not for pumkin we should be *undoon*."

However, the trope of frugality and hard fare is the very opposite of what is being represented at the Thanksgiving dinner, so while "Saint Pompion" was traditional to New England cookery, it was sweetened and whipped into a pie filling rather than appearing in its old role as a vegetable dish.[8]

The other vegetables served at the Thanksgiving table were the common sorts available in the Northeast at that time of the year (which meant no green peas or raw salads) such as winter squash, potatoes, carrots, onions, turnips, parsnips, and perhaps the newly introduced celery. The vegetables were taken for granted and often omitted from descriptions of early Thanksgivings. "Roots and pot-herbs," as vegetables were called in the seventeenth century, were slighted in earlier menus both in England and America. By themselves, they had always been primarily food for poor people, which did nothing for their popularity. Vegetables might be used as ingredients in pottages containing meat or fish, or in "simple and compound sallets," that is, vegetable dishes using one (simple) or several (compound) ingredients that could be boiled and buttered, as well as in raw salads. The rare vegetarian (or "Pythagorean") was looked on in England as an unheard-of eccentric until John Evelyn's *Acetaria* (1699) urged people to consider the healthful nature of vegetables and fruits in their diet. Even then, ordinary people considered them largely as starvation food, animal fodder, or inessential flavorings in a diet made up of meat, grain, and fish. At the end of the eighteenth century, vegetables in America acquired the name of "sauce"—usually rendered "sass" or "sarse"—the implication being that they were nice but superfluous additions to a meal. Carrots and parsnips were "long sass" (deriving perhaps from the boiled medieval "long worts") while potatoes, turnips, and onions were "short sass" in the terminology of the time.[9] Interest in Thanksgiving vegetable dishes eventually increased, following the enthusiasm for diet reform and vegetarianism in the 1830s and 1840s.[10]

The most famous sauce of the day was of course that of the cranberry. John Josselyn, who spent over nine years in New England, provided a good description of the cranberry in 1672:

Cran Berry, or *Bear Berry*, because Bears use much to feed upon them, is a small trayling plant that grows in Salt Marshes that are over-grown with Moss; the tender Branches (which are reddish) run out in great length, lying flat on the ground, where at distances, they take Root, over-spreading sometimes half a score Acres, sometimes in small patches of about a Rood or the like; the Leaves are like Box, but greener, thick and glistering; the Blossoms are very like the Flowers of our *English Night Shade*, after which succeed the Berries, hanging by long small foot stalks, no bigger than a hair; at first they are of a plane yellow Colour. Afterwards red and as big as a Chery; some perfectly round, others Oval, all of them hollow, of a sower astringent taste; they are ripe in August and September.

For the Scurvy
They are excellent against the Scurvy.

For the heat in Feavers.
They are also good to allay the fervour of hot Diseases.

The Indians and English use them much, boyling them with sugar for Sauce to eat with their Meat; and it is a delicate Sauce, especially for roasted Mutton; Some make tarts with them as with Goose Berries.[11]

The New England Indians introduced the cranberry to the colonists and also kept them supplied with the wild berries. The colonists' use of the cranberry, however, followed European precedents. It is often assumed that the colonists adopted many of the recipes of their Native neighbors, but there is little indication that this was the case. Most surviving colonial recipes follow English rather than Native tastes. Constance Crosby suggests that the cranberry may have recommended itself as a substitute for the English gooseberry or barberry in preserves and sauces.[12] Almost forgotten today as an ingredient in Anglo-American cookery, the "shoe peg" barberry was a common ingredient in sauces and preserves because of its acidic flavor and red color. The first cranberry recipes are quite similar to earlier barberry recipes, and they added the same touch of tart redness to a dull-colored as well as dull-flavored dinner.

Recipes for both barberries and cranberries are found in the first American cookbook, Amelia Simmons' *American Cookery* (1796). She also recommends serving roast turkey with "boiled onions, cramberry [sic] sauce, mangoes, pickles or celery."[13] Cranberry sauce and cranberry tarts or pies were standard Thanksgiving dishes by 1800, although the commercial cultivation of the berry did not occur until 1816, when Henry Hall, a Nobscusset (North Dennis) farmer on Cape Cod began the practice of transplanting cranberry vines into special "cranberry yards."

The pie was as much a New England institution as the turkey or Plymouth Rock. Even in the earliest years when wheat flour was scarce, pies and pasties were popular. The standing pie, which was made with a tough, solid rye crust that did not need a pan to support it, might contain almost anything, from fish and vegetables to an entire turkey. Most of the Thanksgiving pies and tarts were made with a short paste and required baking dishes or pans. Pies were a serious part of the regular diet of the region, eaten as often in the morning as at dinner or supper. Harriet Beecher Stowe evoked the expectations evoked what was expected of the housewife in the matter of the pies:

The pie is an English institution, which, transplanted on American soil, forthwith ran rampant and burst forth into an untold variety of genera and species. Not merely the old traditional mince pie, but a thousand strictly American seedlings from that main stock, evinced the power of the American housewives to adapt old institutions to new uses. Pumpkin pies, cranberry pies, huckleberry pies, cherry pies, green-currant pies, peach, pear, and plum pies, custard pies, apple pies, Marlborough-pudding pies, — pies with top crusts, and pies without, — pies adorned with all sort of fanciful flutings and architectural strips laid across and around, and otherwise varied, attested the boundless fertility of the feminine mind, when let loose in a given direction.[14]

The labor involved was so great that there was a reaction against the pie later in the nineteenth century, as Plymouth author (and early feminist) Abby Morton Diaz depicts:

> "And why must we have pies?" I demanded in tones of smothered indignation. "Why not bread and butter, with fruits or sauce, instead?"
>
> "Pie-crust does make a slave of a woman, though," said Mrs. Fennel. "There's nothin' harder than standin' on your feet all forenoon, rollin' of it out."
>
> "Denno' 'bout doin' without pie," drawled Mr. Fennel. "'Pears if bread'n sarse'd be a mighty poor show for somethin' to eat."
>
> "'Twould take off the heft of the cookin'," said Mrs. Fennel thoughtfully; "but (with a sigh) "you couldn't satisfy the men-folks."[15]

Pies reached their apogee of importance at Thanksgiving when households vied for the largest number—they were made in bulk not only for the day itself but also to last the winter—that could be brought to the table. The making of pies and the preparation of their ingredients such as mincemeat was the earliest of the Thanksgiving preparations (figure 10), sometimes weeks before the event itself. The pumpkin pie was usually made just before Thanksgiving Day because of its time-sensitive custardlike filling, but some made pumpkin pies with a filling that would dry rather than spoil. In 1904, Charles Dudley Warner reminisced about the pies of his youth: "They used to be made up by the oven-full and stored in the dry cellar, where they hardened and dried to a toughness you would hardly believe. This was a long time ago, and they make the pumpkin-pie in the country better now."[16] Mincemeat could be prepared weeks ahead of time, with children doing the laborious stoning (seeding) of the raisins, chopping the apples, lean beef, and suet, and mixing them with the spices. It was then put into a stoneware jar with some brandy to ripen, or made into pies that were warmed over before serving: "Weeks later, when you have occasion to use [the pies], carefully raise the top crust, and with a round edg'd spoon, collect the meat into a bason, which warm with additional wine and spices to the taste of your circle, while the crust is warmed like a hoe cake, put carefully together and serve up, by this means you can have hot pies through the winter."[17] Mincemeat was a throwback to medieval cookery, when dried fruits were regularly added to spiced and sweetened meat dishes. The use of fresh apples was modern, and in time the meat itself was omitted, as it usually is today. Commercially prepared mincemeat was

10. *Preparing for Thanksgiving*, from *Ballou's Pictorial Drawing-Room Companion*, November 11, 1855, p. 321. In a traditional New England kitchen, preparations for the Thanksgiving feast sometimes began weeks before the actual holiday.

one of the earliest products that was regularly bought rather than made by the Victorian homemaker.

Apples were New England's favorite fruit, and featured in their own pies as well as in the mincemeat. Apple pie may be an icon of America today, but as Mrs. Stowe observed, it was part of the heritage that the colonists brought to the New World, where both apples and pies were previously unknown. Apple trees, introduced in the seventeenth century, flourished in New England. They first bore fruit in the 1630s, and a generation later John Josselyn was told by Henry Wolcott of Connecticut that he had in one year gotten five hundred hogsheads of cider from his orchard.[18] By 1800, there were orchards all over New England with apples, pears, and other fruits that, if not as handsome as our modern large and unblemished fruit, were greatly esteemed by the population (and by the wild bears). The use of raw fruit was still suspect as a cause of illness, and the larger part of the apple crop was destined for the cider press or pies, dumplings, and other cooked dishes. There were a great many varieties of apples available in the nineteenth century before the need for commercial standardization and bulletproof, shippable fruit drove them out of existence. Andrew Jackson Downing lists 643 varieties in his *Fruits and Fruit Trees of America* (1845).[19] Cider was the primary way in which the product of the orchards was preserved, although some fruit was packed in straw-filled barrels or cut up and dried in garrets and sheds. Families usually had several types of apples for immediate fall consumption and in storage. William T. Davis remembered how his father had five different barrels of apples in their cool Plymouth cellar in the 1820s, "one each of Rhode Island Greenings, Baldwins, Russsets, Holmes apples and sweet apples."[20]

The apple pies of the early days of the Republic were not much different from the better apple pies today, except that they might include extra sweeteners such as rose water (as in Amelia Simmons) or molasses (as in Mrs. Howland's *New England Economical Housekeeper*). As Mrs. Child noted in the *American Frugal Housewife*, the acidity of different varieties of apples varied so greatly that no set amount of sweetener could be prescribed in a recipe. Another pie that employed apples was the "Marlborough" pie, which Edward Everett Hale associates with the holiday. "To this hour, in any old and well-regulated family in New England you will find there is a traditional method of making the Marlborough pie, which is a sort of lemon pie, and each good housekeeper thinks her grandmother left a better receipt for Marlborough pie than anybody else did. We had Marlborough pies at other times, but we were sure to have them on Thanksgiving Day."[21] The Marlborough pie was made with a lemon-flavored apple pudding filling.

The other pudding that regularly appeared on New England Thanksgiving tables was the suet-rich plum pudding. Although it is now associated far more with Christmas after the English tradition than with Thanksgiving, the big, round, boiled plum pudding is often mentioned in early accounts, and even survived to appear on Thanksgiving postcards at the beginning of the twentieth century.[22] The pudding might be served first in the old-fashioned manner, arrive with the main course, or follow with the pies, but it was yet another marker of the feast. As a child in 1847, Louisa Crowninshield Bacon found the pudding some recompense for the formal nature of the day:

All the grandchildren had their hair curled for the occasion and had suffered all the night before from having to lay their heads on hard, bumpy, brown curl-papers. The arrival of the plum-pudding, boiled in a round shape, stuck all over with blanched almonds and strips of citron and blazing with burning brandy or alcohol, repaid us a little for our suffering.[23]

A newer addition to the standard New England bill of fare was celery. Introduced into England at the end of the seventeenth century, celery was found to be actually improved by being kept in the ground until cold weather in the North, which made it milder in flavor. Celery was therefore grown in late summer or fall and harvested in the early winter, making it the only suitable "green" (i.e., fresh but not necessarily green in color) vegetable for the Thanksgiving table.[24] The sweet (or "Spanish") potato, on the other hand, did not flourish in New England (Amelia Simmons thought that new stock might improve the crops). Despite its modern popularity as a Thanksgiving standard, this southern favorite was not included in standard Thanksgiving bills of fare until later in the nineteenth century.

The menu might have local or family variations, but the basic outline of what was proper and fitting to serve on Thanksgiving was now established. Mrs. E. A. Howland gives us a basic bill of fare for Thanksgiving in the *New England Economical Housekeeper,* published in the 1840s:

ROAST TURKEY, stuffed.
A PAIR OF CHICKENS stuffed, and boiled with cabbage and a piece of
    lean pork.
A CHICKEN PIE.
Potatoes; turnip sauce; squash; onions, gravy and gravy sauce; apple
    and cranberry sauce; oyster sauce; brown and white bread.
PLUM AND PLAIN PUDDING, with sweet sauce.
MINCE, PUMPKIN, AND APPLE PIES.
Cheese.[25]

We have already introduced cider in the section about apples, but more deserves to be said about this standard New England drink. While wine, beer, and hard liquor (usually rum or brandy) was available in the region, cider was the primary indigenous tipple, and tipple it was, as the term always refers to what we now call "hard cider." (The stuff sold as "cider" today is simply unfiltered apple juice, not real cider.) It was made in large quantities and consumed throughout the year, although it was best in the cooler months. Cider was the most efficient way to preserve the apple crop, just as cheese was for milk. The apples were collected and pounded into a mash or "pomace" either by large mallets or by a horse-powered crushing mill. Once the juice had been squeezed out of the pomace with a hand-turned screw press, it was collected, barreled, and left to ferment, and the pulp was fed to the pigs.

The late eighteenth and early nineteenth century was a time of heavy alcohol consumption in America. "All the colonists drank cider, old and young, and in all places—funerals, weddings, ordainings, vestry-meetings, church-raisings, etc. Infants in arms drank mulled hard cider at night, a beverage which would kill a modern babe. . . . Old men began the day with a quart of hard cider before breakfast. Delicate women drank hard cider. All laborers in the field drank it in great draughts that were often liberally fortified with drams of New England rum. The apple crop was so wholly devoted to the manufacture of cider that in the days of temperance reform at the beginning of [the nineteenth] century, 'Washingtonian' zealots cut down great orchards of full-bearing trees, not conceiving any adequate use of the fruit for any purpose save cider-making."[26] Not only "small" drinks such as sherry, Madeira, beer, or cider but also a considerable amount of brandy, rum, and distilled "cider brandy" or "applejack" was consumed in punches, flips, and other mixtures. Distilleries, both small homegrown stills and large commercial enterprises, flourished as they turned molasses and cider into more potent drinks. The resulting rowdy behavior and labor problems led the Federalist elite and other reformers to institute the "temperance" movement, first on a local basis in New York in 1808 and in various New England towns, and then nationally with the establishment of the American Temperance Union. It was not long before "temperance" was being used to mean "abstinence," much as the idea of any smoking whatsoever is anathema in the antitobacco movement today. Apples survived, but both towns and entire states (Maine being the first) went dry under the social pressure of the reformers, and Thanksgiving tables were reduced to milk, lemonade, or water.

Before teetotalism became a New England obsession, Thanksgiving dinner ended with punch, cider, nuts, apples, and dried fruit. There were more wild nuts in the region then than now — American chestnuts (now pretty well extinct), shellbark hickory nuts, black walnuts, and hazelnuts being the most popular native species. As George B. Emerson noted, "Hazel-gathering is even now, in some parts of New England, a pleasant little festival for children; and the remembrances of the nooks among the woods, and the thickets among the river banks, to which the search for nuts leads, are not unwelcome, in graver and busier years."[27] The hazelnut was a smaller version of the filbert, and it was said that a sackful of nuts might yield a teacupful of meats. The hickory was more substantial but armor plated — it took quite a blow with a hammer to open one, and the black walnut was similar, except its thick covering stained the fingers a deep orange brown. Chestnuts were the best.[28]

The last components of the early national Thanksgiving were the holiday recreations. Thanksgiving was one of the few extended periods of leisure in the New England calendar. It lasted at least from Thursday to Saturday evening, longer than any other contemporary holiday, including Washington's Birthday, Election Day, Militia Muster, or the Fourth of July. Not everyone was a good homebody, and men used the time to go hunting, gambling, or gather in taverns while women bought new outfits and met the menfolk at the numerous balls and dance parties. However, most of the descriptions and memories concerning Thanksgiving pastimes were of a more innocent sort.

11. *Family Party Playing at Fox and Geese*, from *Ballou's Pictorial Drawing-Room Companion*, November 28, 1857, p. 345. Games such as fox and goose or blindman's buff were popular family entertainments at Thanksgiving.

Once the guests left the table, the rest of the afternoon (if any) and the evening were spent in the approved pastimes of the time (figure 11), which often continued the following day and Saturday as well, at least until the Sabbath began at nightfall. Edward Everett Hale remembers being allowed to enter the sacred front parlor and look at the picture books, such as *Hogarth's Engravings*, illustrated books of travel, and the "illustrated annuals" of the time.[29] Then, after dinner, children played a number of card games or even an early board game: "Before long we would be in the corner playing commerce, or old maid, or possibly 'slap everlasting'; or the Game of Human Life would be produced, with the teetotum, and one would find himself in the stocks, or in a gambling-room, or in prison perhaps, or happily, at the age of sixty-three years, on glory."[30] A teetotum was a sort of spinning die, like a Jewish dreidel, that had letters on it determining the moves around the board.

Jacob Abbott, like poet Henry Bliss, contrasted the pious observation of the holiday with the worldly one: "At the close of the dinner, the formal religionist, who thinks he has done his duty by attending church, goes out for amusement, by riding or walking. The Christian, mindful that it is a day for thanksgiving to God, assembles in the parlor the circle of domestics and of friends for devotion. The thanksgiving hymn is read, and the voices of the family are heard in the sweet cadences of the hymn, as they melt away in the consecrated dwelling. As the sun goes down the evening prayer is offered, and grateful hearts beat happily, in anticipation of an eternal meeting, and an eternal scene of thanksgiving, in the heavenly

world. The evening is passed by the older members of the family in conversation, and by the children in those animating sports which diffuse such
joy around the evening fireside. Such was a New England thanksgiving;
perverted by many, but a blessing and a comfort to not a few."[31] "Thomas
Lackland" (George Canning Hill) remembered, "The evening brings its
own pleasures again. Then the old-fashioned family games begin—blindman's-buff, puss-puss in the corner, snapup around the chimney, forfeits,
and their many ludistic congeners."[32]

One of the most comprehensive descriptions of the postdinner activities, and one that includes everything from dances to sleigh rides, is found
in "John Carver's" *Sketches of New England* (1842):

The dinner over, the preparation for the coming festivities commences. These
are of various kinds throughout the town, as the habits of different families may
dispose them. The more sober see the pastor and taste his sparkling cider; some
gather in a neighbor's dwelling, and find rich jokes over the cracking of hickory-
nuts and eating of the good dame's preserves; some patronize the ball in my
landlord's spacious chamber, and seek "no sleep till morn" in the excitement of
the dance; while others find, in the social chat of home but seldom visited, more
pleasure than abroad.

If there is snow on the ground, however, everything assumes a different aspect.
No sooner is dinner passed, than a project is on foot to drive over to some country
neighbor's, ten or fifteen miles off. The horses are all in requisition; the largest
sleighs are procured; the colts are attached to the cutters; and the whole family
starts off for a merry sleigh ride. Two hours, at most, are sufficient for the drive,
and cheerful faces and warm fires are waiting your arrival. Then comes the merri-
ment of the evening. The young folks hastily arrange the dance, and while partners
are procured, and places selected, old Peter Peterson, who has played for fifty years
to sires and children, tunes up the violin. Contra dances, cotillions and jigs, come
each in turn, and while the old people crack of their marriages and courtships,
births and burials, in the corner, or go with the housekeeper to cheese-press and
pantry, the others merrily foot it till called to supper. Then comes the clattering of
knives and forks, the cracking of the lively cider, the merry laugh, the broad jest, the
quick repartee; then the games which country folk only know how to enjoy—some
to the rattling gammon, some to the sober whist; others play hunt-the-slipper, or
magic music, or blind-man's-buff; and sports, rough and boisterous perhaps,

"Where romping miss is hauled about.

By gallantry robust,"
But, nevertheless, undisturbed by a single care, close up the evening.[33]

The most organized of the Thanksgiving entertainments was the community ball, a form of entertainment that was very common from well

12. New England Thanksgiving ball invitations (1840–1888).

before the Revolution and continued through the nineteenth century. Many of these were by invitation (figure 12), and represented the social climax of the year in an atmosphere of elegance and refinement. Other dances were more informal, although just as significant to the participants, and appeared very modest to later generations. One of these was remembered from Abby Morton Diaz's father's time in the early years of the nineteenth century in Plymouth, Massachusetts:

Cornish's tavern, eight miles or so on the old stage road that goes from Boston through Plymouth down to the Cape. Nabby Cornish! She was simple, sort of unfacultied; never knew when to put her potatoes in the pot. . . . Thanksgiving and Forefathers' we youngsters took the girls up there, sleighing. . . . Up at Cornish's we just took that tavern and all that was in it, and rummaged and helped ourselves and turned things upside down. And we had a great supper, and we danced four-handed reels, and some did the old double-shuffle, and we played plays. I presume you never played "Oh, come, my Loving Partner," nor "All the way to Boston," nor "Snip up." And the singers used to sit round the great fireplace and sing: —

"Madam, you shall have a coach and six,
Six black horses black as pitch,
if you'll be my true lover — "

all the verses of it, and of —

"There was a Man lived in the West,
He loved his eldest daughter best,
Bow ye down, bow ye down."[34]

These elements collectively made up the classic New England Thanksgiving. In the years following 1820, they would be spread far beyond their point of origin as Yankees poured out of New England into the western states, bringing their customs and their self-assured righteousness to whatever new places of residence they might choose. Also, the sentimental culture of the mid–nineteenth century would look back at the homey and less complicated rural lifestyle of the early Republic and glorify Thanksgiving as a holiday epitomizing the virtues many citizens felt had been lost in the industrialization and modernization of American culture.

The Nation Embraces
Thanksgiving, 1780–1880

The adoption of the Thanksgiving holiday outside New England was in part a result of the great Yankee exodus that occurred after the American Revolution. The war had brought debilitating debt and inflation to the small New England farmers and shopkeepers, a burden compounded by high state taxes by which local governments tried to recover from the same problems. This precipitated the desperate protest of Shays' Rebellion (1786–1787), in which economically threatened farmers rose up against the tax demands of the government and foreclosures on their properties. The Revolution had also decimated New England's merchant and fishing fleets. The administrative closure of the British colonial ports in the Caribbean to American vessels following the war cut off many profitable trade connections (for both regions), while the French and Spanish closed their colonies to their erstwhile ally in orthodox mercantilist fashion. Although John Adams was able to get an advantageous clause in the treaty of 1783 that allowed Americans to fish in Canadian waters and even cure their catches on that coast,[1] many investors now sought more promising opportunities than trade in the developing industries of cloth and iron manufacturing. Peace removed the threat of frontier raids by the British and their Indian and Tory allies, clearing the way for the release of pent-up desire for better farmland. A steady flow of Yankee emigrants passed into northern New York, the Northwest Territory, and beyond, bringing with them all the particular attitudes and traditions of their old home.

Changes in Yankee life accelerated with the hardships during the War of 1812, when a beleaguered New England went so far as to consider secession at the Hartford Convention in reaction to the ruinous national embargo. The flow of expatriate New Englanders increased to a flood with the opening of easier pathways west such as the National Road in 1818 and the Erie Canal in 1825. Steam power in boats and later in railroads not only facilitated immigration into the new territories but also made it possible for the West to return the favor by becoming the new food source for New England. Soon frontier settlements were full of industrious former New Englanders who retained an exceptional fondness for their old home and applied themselves to re-creating Yankee culture on the new frontier. Among the customs that were introduced into an expanding America were the two New England holidays that embodied the expatriates' dream of home, Forefathers' Day and Thanksgiving.

Forefathers' Day (December 22) was the commemoration of the landing of the Pilgrim Fathers in Plymouth in 1620. It had been introduced in Plymouth, Massachusetts, in 1769 by the members of the Old Colony Club as a celebration of Plymouth Colony's independent origins and in response to oppression by the English Crown that the club members, like their forefathers, found objectionable. Conservative Federalists in Boston subsequently adopted Forefathers' Day in the 1790s as a celebration of the traditions of old New England in reaction to the unsettling social changes and democratization of the time. Forefathers' Day was also adopted by the members of the "New England Society of New York" in 1805 as their annual celebration. Like other immigrants in the city such as the Irish, Germans, and Scots, Yankees found themselves at a disadvantage away from their home turf. Much as the Ancient Order of Hibernians did for the Irish, New England societies reassured their members of their identity and facilitated cooperation and mutual support. The first New England society was organized in New York by prosperous expatriate New Englander merchants and professionals to celebrate their common heritage and to advance their commercial interests, rather to the annoyance of the New Yorkers who found Yankee self-absorption irritating. By 1816, the Boston *Columbian Centinel* could report, "Patriotic institutions of this denomination have been formed or are forming in most of the Southern and Western States."[2] New England societies were founded in Charleston in 1819, in Augusta in 1825, and in New Orleans, Louisville, Detroit, Cincinnati, Springfield, Illinois, and San Francisco by 1850. They brought first-generation Yankee emigrants and their heirs together for social conviviality, reverence of their ancestral origins, and charitable work among the poorer members of their community. Each of the societies adopted December 22—Forefathers' Day—as an annual celebration of their New England roots. Yearly reiterations of the Pilgrim story by oration, sermon, or discourse, symbolic of the entire New England enterprise, played an important part in embedding the image of the Plymouth Forefathers and their famous rock in the national consciousness.

Forefathers' Day was the original holiday honoring the Pilgrims—long before the Plymouth colonists had any association with Thanksgiving.

Instead of harvest symbols and autumnal feasts, the Plymouth Pilgrims were initially associated with the *Mayflower* voyage, the landing on "Forefathers' Rock," and the terrible First Winter in which half the company died. It was only after the full text for the chronicle of that first year in *Mourt's Relation* (1622) and Governor Bradford's manuscript "Of Plymouth Plantation" were recovered (in 1822 and 1853, respectively) that the full story was revealed. Until the 1850s, therefore, the Pilgrims were known primarily as the stalwart and persevering first founders of New England. Their role as hosts to Massasoit and his men at the harvest festival of 1621, or in the famous Standish courtship triangle, did not become widely known until later. Before the 1850s, Forefathers' Day in bleak December was their only ceremonial commemoration.

Outside Plymouth (where the *Columbian Centinel* said Forefathers' Day was a "woman's holiday" because of balls and other events involving women),[3] December 22 belonged to the men of the community. Forefathers' Day was an example of what has been characterized as the "masculine" form of historical celebration, focusing on parades, orations, formal dinners, and the erection of monuments to the great men and events of the past. This sort of festive activity was standard in the early nineteenth century, as on the Fourth of July, when public celebrations included not only elite dinners but also fireworks, parades, and rowdy behavior among the less genteel members of the community. Such historical commemoration can be contrasted with an alternate "feminine" approach to history that focuses on the quotidian rather than the heroic, the domestic rather than the public, and social over political culture. This new pattern of historical observation first appeared in the mid–nineteenth century. Here the focus was on the daily life of the household and the importance of home and family to society—not battles and heroic ventures. In the place of bronze and granite monuments, there were historic houses, replicas of colonial kitchens, and displays of household antiques such as teapots, spinning wheels, and warming pans—all employed to tell the story of how both heroes and common folk lived when there were no battles to be won and the epic adventures were over. If Forefathers' Day was an example of the masculine style, by the 1850s Thanksgiving was beginning to exemplify the feminine. The New England societies and their rhetoric helped popularize the Plymouth Pilgrims and provide them with cultural significance, but Forefathers' Day men-only celebrations could never capture the hearts or the minds of Americans as Thanksgiving did.

The Thanksgiving themes of feasting, family reunion, and tradition were sympathetic with the cultural temper of antebellum times. The second quarter of the nineteenth century was a time of economic recovery but also one of uncertainty and factional disputes. The growth of antago-

13. *Thanksgiving Dinner—Ephraim's Speech*," from *New York Illustrated News*, November 26, 1859, p. 25. One of many depictions of a contemporary Thanksgiving dinner down on the ancestral farm.

nistic regionalism after the Missouri Compromise in 1820 brought new challenges to the young nation revolving around the issue of slavery. During this antebellum era, the activists and reformers of New England did everything they could to restrain the spread of slavery (and alcohol) and to badger the slaveholders. The growing pains of the Republic and the divisive issues of the era made people long for the (imagined) stability of the "good old days."[4] People looked back on the troubled Revolutionary era not only as a time of patriotic resolve and heroic action but also as the end of an era of rural virtue stretching back unchanging to the time of Pilgrims. Thanksgiving became an embodiment of this ideal, now less focused on present or future "mercies" and more on the past, mirroring a longing for a childlike security in home, family, and tradition. Accounts of traditional Thanksgivings were now often presented as memories of childhood or as seen through the eyes of a child, in homes where old customs would never be the same again (figure 13).

By the antebellum years, the home had become the moral center of America, the domain of motherhood, nurture, and propriety. American culture had come a long way from the masculine virtues of the Revolutionary era, and while fatherhood, like the Revolution itself, was still revered and honored in theory, it was now the distaff side of the family that commanded the most deference and respect. The period was dominated by feminine sentiment and what we now think of as "Victorian family values," with their stress on the sacredness of the home, family, and children and the importance of the women's sphere. Marriage expectations had changed as well. The husband was still the "head of the household," but the partnership was more egalitarian than had once been the case, and the housewife "enjoyed an increasing degree of influence or autonomy within the family."[5] The domestic partnership also embodied what would be labeled "the feminine mystique" and the hypocrisy, repression, and hypersensitivity that went along with this.

Similarly, Thanksgiving, which earlier honored the family patriarch as he gathered his kin and dependents about him at the close of the year, became at midcentury the province of the mother of the household, a celebration of family and of domestic virtue. The center of production had moved from the separate yet cooperative male and female spheres of the colonial farmstead to the income-producing factory, shop, or office job only for the father of the family. He now "brought home the bacon" rather than raising it himself. However much the old agrarian way of life might still color cultural perceptions and sentiment, it no longer dominated New England's economy. Seeing no future in the hilly, stony farms of southern New England, workers looked for new opportunities elsewhere, on the frontier or in the new workshops and factories. The urban housewife, whose mother had helped her husband slaughter the pigs and preserve the bacon, found herself reduced to simply buying and cooking it—or hiring someone else to do so. She oversaw a household dependent entirely on her husband's income, her previous contribution to the economic status of the family replaced by a responsibility for commercial consumption. Children, no longer valuable as contributors of household labor, became the pampered focus of their mother's nurturing until they too could leave home for their own careers or households.[6]

The housewife's role had changed considerably as well. There was less physical work expected of the middle-class homemaker than there had been of her mother in the "age of homespun," when so much of what the family wore and ate was the direct result of household labor. The new American housewife bought her food and clothing, hired other women to cook and clean, and thus had more time available for fussing over children or "ornamental and ceremonial behavior" involving complicated rituals of etiquette and the practice of genteel crafts such as embroidery or home decorating.[7] She became an active participant in the growing consumer culture, making decisions about the purchase of many new products from packaged mincemeat, canned foods, and cookstoves to the vast array of ornamental articles and gewgaws that so delighted our Victorian ancestors. The increased availability of commercial products included reading materials specifically aimed at a leisured woman's edification and entertainment, ranging from cookbooks, didactic children's stories, and etiquette manuals to ephemeral fiction and essays.

Thanksgiving had two strong factors in its favor in the antebellum period. As a "feminine" holiday focused on home and family, it was in harmony with the values and goals of the contemporary "domestic movement," and it was an established holiday at a time when American (and English) society was realizing a need for such cultural amenities. There were fewer holidays in English-speaking countries in the early nineteenth century than at any time before or since. The legacy of the cramped Puritan calendar, the industrialist's rationalized dismissal of anything that interfered with labor and commerce, and, in America, the Revolutionary break with English custom left very little scope for celebratory leisure, in New England in particular.[8] The problem had not been as pressing when most people worked for themselves on farms or in small workshops where work was more like housework than modern office or factory labor. One could take time away from the job when necessary and vary tasks to suit one's mood of the moment, except during haying or harvest. When the clock and the supervisor owned one's time, the lack of flexibility and variety became painfully evident. There was only one truly national holiday—the Fourth of July—in the early nineteenth century. Individual states had been celebrating Washington's Birthday since the 1780s, but in Massachusetts, for example, it only became a legal holiday in 1856, and it did not become a national holiday until 1885. Other special days such as the Militia Muster or Election Day were local in character and involved duties quite as much as they did leisure. Otherwise every day except the Sabbath was nominally a workday.

The demand for holidays, which grew even stronger toward the end of the century, is demonstrated by the progress of both Christmas and Thanksgiving across the new nation. Christmas had been generally celebrated in New York and in the South in colonial times, but the unruly nature of its observance had led to a decline in its public acceptance both in England (where it was the only surviving annual public holiday by 1838) and in the colonies.[9] However, it made a dramatic comeback in the nineteenth century, when the new sentimental literary culture, represented in the works of Washington Irving and Charles Dickens, promoted its revival. Stephen Nissenbaum observes: "The [Christmas] movement swept the nation during the two decades that began in the mid-1840s. By 1865, twenty-seven out of thirty-six states (along with four territories) had set December 25 apart as a day when certain kinds of ordinary business could not be legally transacted."[10] In a reversal of Thanksgiving's spread beyond New England, a "reformed" Christmas made headway into the region after the mid–eighteenth century, first among urban Episcopalians

14. *A Thanksgiving Dream of Home*, from *Frank Leslie's Illustrated Newspaper*, December 5, 1868, p. 184. A lonely traveler (or exile) far from the comfort of family and a Thanksgiving dinner at home.

and liberal Congregationalists (and rowdy "Anticks"—poor men and boys who confronted respectable householders for handouts), and then more generally in the next century, eventually reaching out into the conservative countryside. By the 1850s Christmas had even been accepted in backwaters such as Plymouth, Massachusetts, although "more through its appeal to the aesthetic rather than religious sense of the people."[11] Some of the southern states—North and South Carolina, Mississippi, Missouri, Florida, and Texas—were the last to legalize the holiday, well after the old Puritan strongholds had succumbed by 1861, presumably because many communities in the more rural, traditional South had not previously felt the need to.

Thanksgiving achieved national popularity somewhat in advance of Christmas. The demand for holidays, along with Thanksgiving's respectable character (in contrast to the undisciplined revelry associated with both Christmas and the Fourth), may have supported this progress, but the Yankee diaspora across America was an equally important factor. For most former New Englanders, Thanksgiving became a sentimental window to an idyllic past that, at least once in the year, evoked dreams of childhood on the old homestead (figure 14). The old custom of gathering at the patriarchal table became a tradition of annual reunion that drew crowds of displaced Yankees back to their ancestral haunts from as far away as the West Coast or Florida. Those exiles who could not make a pilgrimage back to New England set about to re-create traditional Thanksgivings in the southern and western states and territories. Instituted by people with shared memories of what the holiday should be like, Thanksgiving retained its Yankee characteristics wherever it was adopted: the governor's proclamation, the late November date, the "secular" sermon, the gathering of family and friends, seasonal recreations, and the turkey dinner.

Thanksgiving became an annual event in neighboring New York in 1817 and in Yankee-dominated Michigan by 1824, but it was not until the 1840s that the New England holiday was generally adopted by other states. Once the Thanksgiving movement gained momentum, events moved quickly. Within the 1850s, the holiday became an annual event in New Jersey, Pennsylvania, Ohio, Wisconsin, Illinois, and Iowa.[12] By 1858 Franklin Hough could confidently claim that "this custom is now observed in nearly every State and organized Territory in the Union," although he was unable to secure examples of proclamations from six states and most of the territories for his compilation of official declarations for that year. "Wherever the practice prevails," Hough observed, "schools, public offices, banks and places of business generally are closed, at least for part of the day, and religious services are held among most if not all regularly organized denominations."[13]

The new media of popular magazines and novels proved to be another powerful vehicle for the promulgation of the American Thanksgiving. Sarah Josepha Hale, editor of *Godey's Lady's Book*, began her advocacy of Thanksgiving in 1837. Ten years later she started a campaign to have the last Thursday in November declared Thanksgiving in every state and territory. She directed a stream of editorials and letters to the governors of the states to achieve this result, and by 1860 was gratified to report:

We may now consider *Thanksgiving a National Holiday*. It will no longer be a partial and vacillating commemoration of gratitude to our Heavenly Father, observed in one section or State, while other portions of our common country do not sympathize in the gratitude and gladness. It is to be a regularly recurring Festival, appointed by the concert of the State Governments *to be observed on the last Thursday in November* thus made, for all future time, THE AMERICAN THANKSGIVING DAY.... We do earnestly hope and pray that *the last Thursday in November* may be established as the American Thanksgiving Day. Then, on *that Day*, our citizens, whether in their own pleasant homes, or in the distant regions of Oriental despotism, would observe it on board every ship where our flag floats there would be a day of gladness wherever our missionaries preach the Gospel of "goodwill to men," the *day* would exemplify the joy of Christians; and in our Great Republic, from the St. John's to the Rio Grande, from the Atlantic to the Pacific, all our people, as one Brotherhood, will rejoice together, and give thanks to God for our National, State, and Family blessings.

Thanksgiving observance had spread to thirty states and two territories by this time.[14] The Civil War interrupted this progress, but wartime conditions would provide an even greater boost to Thanksgiving's national status.

It was during the war that the first national Thanksgivings since 1815 were declared. Ironically, the first was not a Yankee occasion. President Davis and the Confederate Congress proclaimed a national Thanksgiving service for the South, at least, on Sunday, July 28, 1861, following the victory at Bull Run. The northern states had little to celebrate in 1861, although Thanksgivings were still declared by individual northern states that November in the customary fashion. The Union had its turn when President Lincoln declared Sunday, April 13, 1862 (on the forty-seventh anniversary of the 1815 event) a national Thanksgiving for the victories at Forts Henry and Donelson, and Shiloh. The Confederacy had a second and final Thanksgiving on Thursday, September 28, 1862, following the second battle of Bull Run. In 1863, the Union celebrated *two* national Thanksgivings, one on Thursday, August 6, following the victory at Gettysburg, and then a second holiday that Lincoln declared for the last Thursday in November. It is this second Thanksgiving that began our modern sequence of national Thanksgivings.[15] While the others were all providential wartime observances after the old style, the last was different—it was a "for the generals" (general mercies, not military generals), New England–style, end-of-November celebration of the sort Mrs. Hale had been lobbying for all along:

Thanksgiving Day 1863

By the President of the United States of America—a Proclamation

The year that is drawing toward its close has been filled with the blessings of fruitful fields and healthful skies. To these bounties, which are so constantly enjoyed that we are prone to forget the source from which they come, others have been added which are of so extraordinary a nature that they can not fail to penetrate and soften even the heart which is habitually insensible to the ever-watchful providence of Almighty God.

In the midst of a civil war of unequaled magnitude and severity, which has sometimes seemed to foreign states to invite and to provoke their aggression, peace has been preserved with all nations, order has been maintained, the laws have been respected and obeyed, and harmony has prevailed everywhere, except in the theater of military conflict, while that theater has been greatly contracted by the advancing armies and navies of the Union. Needful diversions of wealth and of strength from the fields of peaceful industry to the national defense have not arrested the plow, the shuttle, or the ship; the ax has enlarged the borders of our settlements, and the mines, as well of iron and coal as of the precious metals, have yielded even more abundantly than heretofore. Population has steadily increased notwithstanding the waste that has been made in the camp, the siege, and the battlefield, and the country, rejoicing in the consciousness of augmented strength and vigor, is permitted to expect continuance of years with large increase of freedom.

No human counsel hath devised nor hath any mortal hand worked out these great things. They are the gracious gifts of the Most High God, who, while dealing with us in anger for our sins, hath nevertheless remembered mercy.

It has seemed to me fit and proper that they should be solemnly, reverently, and gratefully acknowledged, as with one heart and one voice, by the whole American people. I do therefore invite my fellow-citizens in every part of the United States, and also those who are at sea and those who are sojourning in foreign lands, to set apart and observe the last Thursday of November next as a day of thanksgiving and praise to our beneficent Father who dwelleth in the heavens. And I recommend to them that while offering up the ascriptions justly due to Him for such singular deliverances and blessings they do also, with humble penitence for our national perverseness and disobedience, commend to His tender care all those who have become widows, orphans, mourners, or sufferers in the lamentable civil strife in which we are unavoidably engaged, and fervently implore the interposition of the Almighty hand to heal the wounds of the nation and to restore it, as soon as may be consistent with the divine purpose, to the full enjoyment of peace, harmony, tranquility, and union.

In testimony whereof I have hereunto set my hand and caused the seal of the United States to be affixed.

Done at the city of Washington, this 3d day of October A.D. 1863, and of the Independence of the United States the eighty-eighth.

ABRAHAM LINCOLN[16]

Although there is no direct evidence that President Lincoln was responding to Mrs. Hale's campaign (he did receive letters from her concerning the holiday), it seems reasonable to assume that her success in gaining national recognition for the holiday figured in his decision to appoint a Thanksgiving for the last Thursday in November 1863 (figure 15). Yet even though the second Thanksgiving of 1863 is an important milestone in the history of the holiday, its significance should not be exaggerated. The previous adoption of Thanksgiving by nearly all the states and territories had already achieved national recognition for the holiday. We know from hindsight that Lincoln's second 1863 proclamation initiated an unbroken tradition, but this could not be foreseen. As Mrs. Hale was fully aware, Lincoln's November Thanksgiving might never have been repeated. She continued with unabated effort to secure not only national status but the legal standing of a federal holiday for Thanksgiving to ensure its continuity. This is exemplified in her *Godey's* editorial for 1871:

We have long endeavored to secure the celebration of this great festival upon the same day in every American State and Territory, so that it might be a National Holiday. In 1863 the Southern States could not be reached. Application was made to President Lincoln, who issued a proclamation, the first since that of Washington from the representative of the nation, and appointing the same day, the last Thursday of November. His example has been yearly followed by his successors.

But one thing is wanting. It is eminently fit that this National Holiday shall rest upon the same legal basis as its companions, the Twenty-second of February and the Fourth of July. As things now stand, our Thanksgiving is exposed to the chances of the time. Unless the President or the Governor of the State in office happens to see fit, no day is appointed for its observance. Is not this a state of things which calls for instant remedy? Should not our festival be assured to us by law?

In this she was unsuccessful, and the holiday was sustained by custom alone until 1941.

15. Sarah Josepha Hale, editor of *Godey's Lady's Book*, from *Harper's Bazar*, June 28, 1879, p. 416; and Abraham Lincoln, from *Harper's Pictorial History of the Civil War* (Chicago: Star Publishing Co., 1896), p. 47. Lincoln's second proclaimed Thanksgiving in 1863 became the first of our modern series of holidays, and may have been inspired by Mrs. Hale's campaign.

Lincoln also proclaimed a Thanksgiving for the last Thursday of November in 1864. In addition to reinforcing the continuity of the holiday, the 1864 Thanksgiving involved a massive effort on the part of the Union League Club of New York to provide the Union troops with a proper Thanksgiving dinner. The Union League resolved as follows: "We desire that on the twenty-fourth day of November there shall be no soldier in the Army of the Potomac, the James, the Shenandoah, and no sailor in the North Atlantic Squadron who does not receive tangible evidence that those for whom he is periling his life, remember him. It is hoped that the armies in the west will be in a like manner cared for by those nearer to them than we. It is deemed impractical to send to our more Southern posts. . . . We ask primarily for donations of cooked poultry and other proper meats, as well as mince pies, sausages and fruit."[17] This attested to how central the traditional dinner had become for celebrating a true Thanksgiving.

Organized by George W. Blunt with dedicated humanitarian Theodore Roosevelt, Sr., as treasurer, the Union League enlisted the express companies to transport the donations of food for free to the central depot on Trinity Place in New York. Delmonico's and other restaurants volunteered to prepare and cook the fowl. From the Getty's Building depot, Thanksgiving provender was dispatched to the various army camps as well as to local military hospitals and posts. Public response to the call was impressive. People from across the New York and New England region sent not only money or turkeys but also every imaginable kind of foodstuff. The contributions are carefully listed in the Union League report in thirty-seven pages of small print. An example of the variety can be seen in an invoice from Nichols, New York:

> 1 Barrel Apples, given by C.V.S. Bliven.
> Box No. 1 — 1 package dried apples, 3 packages chestnuts, 1 package black-
> berries, 2 packages fried cakes, 2 packages cookies, 6 mountain cakes,
> 13 mince pies, 2 gallons pickled cabbage, 1 can catchup, 1 bottle catchup,
> 1 can tomato pickles, 4 pieces 20 lb cheese, 2 rolls plus 4 lb butter [a roll of
> butter being a standard bulk unit that might weigh from 5 to 10 pounds].
> Box No. 2 — 6 turkeys, 1 goose, 2 ducks, 33 chickens, 3 mince pies, 1 keg
> tomato pickles, ½ bushel apples.
> Box No. 3 — 1 turkey received too late for shipment in No. 2.[18]

There were also plenty of cranberries, cranberry sauce, and all the vegetables associated with the traditional dinner. In all, the campaign received $56,565.83 in cash donations (of which over $51,000 was spent on poultry) and 225,000 pounds of fowl, all of which was forwarded to the military.

The soldiers were reported to have been quite pleased and grateful for both the food and the effort, even if the result sometimes fell short of the ideal. "The want of proper appliances compelled most of the men to broil or stew their turkeys, but everyone seemed fully satisfied, and appreciated the significance of this sympathetic thank-offering from the loyal North. One soldier said to me, 'It isn't the turkey, but the idea that we care for,' and he struck the key-note for the whole festival."[19] The logistics of such an enterprise were unprecedented, and some of the food did not arrive on time or was lost through damage and spoilage, but by and large the effort proved a great success. More significantly, it demonstrated the commitment of the American people to the Thanksgiving holiday, and introduced it to every serviceman.

In 1865 Andrew Johnson proclaimed the first Thursday in December as Thanksgiving, but after this single aberration each subsequent American Thanksgiving has been in late November. President Johnson acknowledged the new tradition when he began his 1867 proclamation as follows: "In conformity with a recent custom that may now be regarded as established on national consent and approval. . . ." By 1869, a writer for *Frank Leslie's Illustrated Newspaper* seconded the idea, observing: "A quarter of a century ago, and even later, Thanksgiving Day was appointed by the Governors of States, and was not particularly observed except by New England people, outside the land of the Pilgrims. It has grown rapidly within a decade, and the Proclamation of the President of the United States has tacitly superceded the invitations of the governors. As a national day, therefore, let us accept it." Following the Civil War an annual national Thanksgiving was proclaimed each year by the president, and the holiday became a standard milestone in the American civic year.

While the firm hand of tradition kept the basic essentials of the holiday true to their nostalgic roots, new elements were introduced as well, the most important being the annual college football game. The "annual Thanksgiving Day game between the previous year's two leading college football teams [was] an idea hatched in 1876 by the student-run Intercollegiate Football Association," which was founded in that year.[20] Football had its roots in the anarchic and violent English games played between villages, often resulted in maiming or even death, where the goal might be to get the ball to the opposing parish's church porch by any means possible. North American Indians played similar games over long distances on beaches and open land. Colleges had played casual soccer-style football from the 1860s until Harvard adopted rugby football rules in games against McGill in 1876, which was the beginning of the modern American game. College was a defining experience for the American middle class by the end of the nineteenth century, and all of its accoutrements and rituals, in particular the sport of football, became highly fashionable. In 1891 *Harper's Weekly* could report: "There may be some who like family

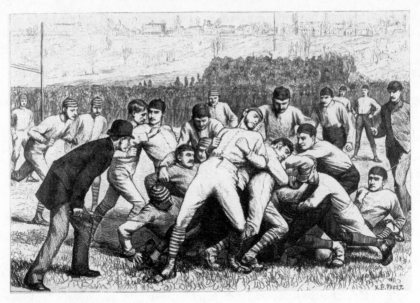

16. A. B. Frost, *Football Match between Yale and Princeton, November 27*, from *Harper's Weekly*, December 20, 1879, p. 985.

dinners; and there are other wicked ones who sympathize with the young woman who assented to having a family dinner by saying, 'Yes, and let us have any other family but our own.' It may not be so everywhere, but around New York city, . . . a great and powerful and fascinating rival has come to take the place of the Thanksgiving day dinner, . . . the Thanksgiving Day Game. And now everyone goes out to see Princeton and Yale decide the football championship instead of boring each other around the dinner table" (figure 16).[21]

Entertainment had always been an important part of the holiday tradition, either as family activities or with community-wide participation. Even before the war, the firemen of New York had held "public reviews," and militia companies conducted parades and turkey shoots, followed by the very popular Thanksgiving balls.[22] Articles and illustrations of football games now joined stories about family dinners in the popular press each November as Thanksgiving embraced its new sporting tradition. Just as the earlier winter associations were being replaced with idyllic harvest scenes, the spectator sport of college football supplanted hunting or the turkey shoot.

Proclamations, sermons, reminiscences, contemporary reports, and other primary source documents provide a historic understanding of the nineteenth-century Thanksgiving, but for an impression of how the holiday was perceived by those who celebrated it, we might turn to contemporary literary and artistic representations. In the next chapter we will survey the manner in which the holiday was dealt with in popular literature, and the ways in which Thanksgiving appeared in art, illustration, and other graphic media.

Nineteenth-Century Holiday Imagery in Literature and Art

The national adoption of Thanksgiving would not have occurred without the efforts of expatriate New England advocates such as *Godey's* editor Mrs. Sarah Josepha Hale and all the anonymous Yankees who worked to introduce the holiday in their respective towns and states. Their efforts to "sell the holiday" to the American people were greatly enhanced by the explosion in popular periodicals after 1830. Earlier, the public's impression of Thanksgiving—what it signified and what was appropriate to its celebration—derived largely from personal experience, hearsay, or a few references in texts or newspapers. The "serious" Thanksgiving publication was still the sermon, and its prominence continued unabated through the Civil War. In the 1830s and 1840s, however, a technological revolution in the publishing industry took place, powered by the rapid improvement in printing technology through steam presses, pulp paper, cloth binding, steel engraving, and cheap lithography. Spurred by cheap printing, writing became a profitable enterprise, whereas once only the independently wealthy or artistically determined could afford to toy with authorship. In very short order, the era of mass production opened up vast new markets, such as "domestic fiction," for aspiring writers, many of them women: "The leading producers of domestic fiction (castigated as 'a damned mob of scribbling women' by an envious Hawthorne) were all making tidy profits. The *Atlantic* was paying poets fifty dollars a page, as opposed to the two dollars offered by the *New England Magazine* in 1835; compensation for literary journalism would triple between 1860 and 1880."[1] It was these "scribbling women" and their male counterparts who carried out the literary exposition of Thanksgiving, ensuring that even those unfortunates who had not grown up with the holiday in New England would understand the significance of the day and how it should be observed.

The social shift toward separate male and female domains (outside the home versus domestic), and the cultural shift toward the perspective of women and children (i.e., toward the domestic "feminine" sentiments described in the previous chapter), were reflected in popular literature of the time, which was dominated by women's magazines and illustrated weeklies such as *Frank Leslie's Illustrated* or *Harper's Weekly*. *Godey's Lady's Book*, followed by its imitators *Graham's* and *Peterson's*, far outdistanced all masculine rivals. When *Godey's* was in decline in the 1860s, it could still claim 150,000 subscribers as opposed to *Harper's* 110,000."[2] The feminine influence also produced a flood of best-selling "domestic novels" depicting the tribulations of pure-hearted but oppressed women struggling to defend home life against the cold, treacherous external world. The moral fortification of the home — under the aegis of the enlightened homemaker — against the rough-and-ready masculine world of business and politics became a dominant middle-class fixation in the antebellum period. As Ann Douglas has demonstrated, the middle-class women involved in this "domestic revolution" found ready allies among the liberal clergymen of the era, who had been deprived of the political and social clout of their established Puritan predecessors. Laying claim to the social conscience of their generation, they instituted a regime of "sentimental" values in place of the old Enlightenment no-nonsense rationality and the tough-minded, aggressive Calvinist theology of the previous era. Obliged to rely on diffused "influence" in place of political or economic power, this intelligent and dedicated alliance effectively manipulated the popular press to promulgate its agenda. Feeling and sensitivity were presented as morally superior replacements for worldly and economic seriousness.

As often where women were concerned, sentiment was wanted, not facts. Literally hundreds of nostalgic memoirs were penned in the Civil War period about vanished rural ways, old New England farmsteads, a once-abundant country Thanksgivings presided over by all-capable and generically hospitable housekeepers; such reminiscences, while valuable as a response to cultural change, hardly give a trustworthy account of it.[3]

It was through such efforts that women and clerical authors constructed the popular impression of the Victorian Thanksgiving holiday, with all its sentimental associations with domestic virtue.

The shift to sentimental values from "rational" or scientific ones had a tremendous influence on how Americans viewed and valued holidays. Holidays in general lost much of their earlier theological and political emphasis and were reworked under the influence of Victorian culture, in which emotionality was encouraged and individual sensibilities were played on to heighten domestic, patriotic, and pleasurably pathetic responses to the symbolic significance of each particular occasion. Evocation of emotional states and the manipulation of feelings by sentimental literature transformed Thanksgiving from a sober religious occasion followed by a decorous family dinner into an indulgent domestic-centered spectacle imbued with nostalgia, social sympathies, and narratives of melodramatic family predicaments. This emotive turn was enthusiastically endorsed by most Americans and indeed flourishes even today among the less sophisticated—despite the reaction against Victorian sentiment by intellectuals in the twentieth century—as can be seen in the mawkish holiday decorations and simplistic moral narratives that thrive in popular culture alongside the "social realism," political concerns, and postmodern ironic detachment favored by the elite.

Public discussion about the behavior and significance appropriate to the holiday was presented in the popular literature of the day. It was through the flood of ephemeral stories and now-forgotten nineteenth-century novels that the contemporary construction of Thanksgiving took place. Most of these were published first in the popular journals of the time, and in early children's books. There were no exceptional texts comparable in influence to Washington Irving's Christmas scenes at *Bracebridge Hall* (1822) or Clement Moore's *'twas the Night Before Christmas* (1823), but the Thanksgiving theme did attract a few well-known authors. Harriet Beecher Stowe's descriptions of the day in *Oldtown Folks* (1869) and Louisa May Alcott's "An Old Fashioned Thanksgiving" (1881) are still read today (and found on the Internet), although their survival is due more to the celebrity of the authors than to long-term literary excellence. The pieces that had any staying power were excerpted for inclusion in the collections for schoolroom use that became popular at the end of the century, but most disappeared unnoticed. Interestingly, very few treatments of the holiday appear in the works of the major New England "local color" authors, despite the centrality in their work of maudlin Yankee themes such as poverty, enervated bloodlines, old maids, and the tyranny of custom. Perhaps the Thanksgiving story was already considered too much a regional stereotype by the time these stories appeared at the end of the century.

The predominant literary treatment of Thanksgiving before the colonial and Pilgrim themes became fashionable involved the holiday dinner, acts of charity, the gathering of the family in the ancestral mansion, and the return of distant or missing family members to the security and order of the home. These tropes might be presented as exemplary depictions of the holiday and the ethics that made it possible, or as cautionary tales that warned against the social forces outside the home that threatened this domestic idyll. The traditional meal itself remained a constant, and accounts differed only in the degree of descriptive detail and whether it was the feast of a prosperous farmer or city merchant, or a more modest meal enjoyed by representatives of the virtuous poor. Far more important in Thanksgiving domestic fiction was the interplay of character and motives among the guests assembled around the table, not unlike similar themes played out today in films and television shows dealing with the holiday.

Fictional use of Thanksgiving could be nothing more than an incidental inclusion of the holiday in a story of contemporary (and especially New England) life. Or it could exploit the domestic symbolism of holiday themes such as the family homestead and reunion to frame conflicts between the familial ideal and the perceived dangers of worldly temptation. In George Hill's *Dovecote* (1854), for example, the melodramatic story of little Milly, who found a safe haven on the old New England farm of Dovecote, is interrupted by an affectionate description of a classic Thanksgiving that has no relevance to the story other than to reinforce the sunny picture of agrarian life. A good example of the full development of domestic subject matter is the 1850 novelette by Cornelius Mathews, *Chanticleer: A Thanksgiving Story of the Peabody Family*. The plot of the story is that Elbridge, grandson of old Sylvester Peabody, has been missing for a year, under suspicion of having murdered a Rev. Barbery before he fled. As the story begins, Peabody's other grandson Sam hears the rooster Chanticleer crow for the first time since his brother Elbridge left, and predicts his return. Sam's grandfather, old Sylvester, who has the role of the wise and charitable rural patriarch, had declared Elbridge dead to their affections. As the Thanksgiving guests arrive, we see how each of them, having left the sanctuary of the family farm, has been seduced by the ways of the world. The eldest, William, is a successful merchant and landowner who has become obsessed with property, symbolized by an obscurely worded ancient deed hidden in the family house that might or might not give title to some local estate. Oliver has become a prosperous farmer in Ohio and married Jane, a Quaker (who may be guilty of a sort of reverse pride in her simplicity). His only interest is in crops, prices, and agrarian improvements. A very wealthy married daughter, Mrs. Carrack, has condescended to come this year after having avoided her humble parents for five years. She arrives in a grand coach with her two footmen and her supercilious dandy son, Tiffany. The widowed mother of Elbridge and a son-in-law, Captain Charley Saltonstall, who has retained a rough simplicity of manner and generosity, are contrasted to the Peabody siblings.

Amid the usual subplots—involving, in this narrative, good-hearted black servant Mopsy and her pumpkin, young grandson Sam, and the humorous misadventures of the unfortunate Tiffany—the holiday proceeds in classic fashion through the Thanksgiving meeting and the dinner until two strangers appear. They of course turn out to be Rev. Barbery (who had dropped everything to join the gold rush) and Elbridge. The latter, realizing that he was under suspicion, had gone after the luckless Barbery and brought him back to prove his innocence. On his lonely travels he pointedly avoided his uncharitable siblings, passing by Oliver's home in Ohio and avoiding Tiffany in New Orleans. Sylvester is reconciled to his errant son but requires that he immediately marry his abandoned sweetheart, Miriam. She of course agrees, and this happy resolution redeems the others (barring Tiffany). William burns his old deeds, and Mrs. Carrack and Jane take part in a wool-spinning contest to show that neither has lost that fundamental domestic faculty.

In *Chanticleer* we have a full panoply of contemporary Thanksgiving symbols: the ancestral farmstead with its generous patriarchal master, the menace of worldly success and luxury in contrast to the homey virtue of old-fashioned rusticity, the embarrassment of the overrefined dandy out of his urban element, reunion with the prodigal child, true love and constancy rewarded, the classic Thanksgiving wedding, and even the symbolic virtue of the spinning wheel.

Another Thanksgiving story in which the virtue of the family home is didactically contrasted with the evil of the world is "Thanksgiving: A Home Scene," which appeared in the *Ladies' Repository* in December 1874. The story opens in the happy farm household of Kate and Edward Roberts and their four young children as they await the return of their eldest son from college for Thanksgiving. The themes of simplicity, self-sufficiency, and contentment are stressed: "[they were] just about to seat themselves at the tea-table, which was covered with the many delicacies that farm could supply,—golden butter from their own dairy, honey from their well-kept hives, baked apples, delicate biscuits, and dainty cake: all home comforts, which Mrs. Roberts took pride in seeing on the table."[4] Many years before, Fanny, one of Mrs. Roberts' friends, who thought that bringing together a wealthy socialite and a shy, awkward countryman would be amusing, had introduced the Robertses to each other. However, the two unexpectedly hit it off, and Kate, much to the consternation of her fashionable circle, married Edward and went to live an old-fashioned life on the farm. Looking forward to Thanksgiving, Kate tells her husband that the elegant Fanny, who had married a wellborn, stylish young man, has not prospered: "the once beautiful, light-hearted Fanny Ludlow is but a faded wreck of her former self," with an improvident husband who frequents gambling halls while she tries to support them with paid needlework—that Victorian woman's curse. The Robertses therefore send a large hamper of Thanksgiving food to Fanny and her family, graphically demonstrating the superiority of rural simplicity to urban luxury and dissipation.

Thanksgiving fiction almost always involved middle-class families of English descent, although virtuous representatives of other groups such as poor or "decayed" Yankee families, honest Irish workers, or black servants were occasionally introduced as exemplary foils to unprincipled villains or ruined relations. Most stories were set in the present, or a generation or two earlier, and concerned with the usual tribulations of sentimental fiction such as saintly sisters or orphan children who die young, poverty brought about by deserting husbands or intemperance, or star-crossed lovers and hard-hearted fathers. The classic New England Thanksgiving described in *Oldtown Folks* (1869) by Harriet Beecher Stowe is set just after the Revolution. *Oldtown Folks* uses the Thanksgiving theme to show the contentment of the Badger clan in their rural homestead, but also as an occasion that introduces the cosmopolitan villain, Ellery Davenport, to his future wife, the innocent orphan Tina. Similarly, in Mary J. Holmes' "The Thanksgiving Party" (1865), Thanksgiving is the setting in which wealthy and snobbish Lucy Dayton's pursuit of Hugh St. Leon is thwarted when he marries the penniless Ada Harcourt—who turns out to be the well-bred daughter of a wealthy man who was ruined several years earlier. Also, Lucy's beloved delicate sister, Lizzie, dies—which sends Lizzie's lover out to be a missionary and starts Lucy on the path to moral recovery.

There are other sentimental tales involving reunions and Thanksgiving Day marriages, tales of soldiers returning after rumors of death to the folks back home, of acts of seasonable charity rewarded and brittle selfishness defeated, of prodigals welcomed back to the genuine family life of the countryside or bemoaning their fate in urban poverty and degradation. The unexpected return of a soldier or western émigré who saves the farm for the old folks at home was a perennial favorite, as in the *Harper's Weekly* story "Zenas Carey's Reward" (1863). Old Zenas and Melinda Carey take in a homeless veteran on Thanksgiving, in memory of their son who died at Gettysburg, only to find that their guest is a missing heir of a local magnate. The guest then forgives their mortgage and becomes like another son to them. An alternative "return" in which no redemption takes place is in Hawthorne's "John Inglefield's Thanksgiving" (1840), which he published under the pseudonym "Rev. A. A. Royce." Here the errant child is sixteen-year-old daughter Prudence, who briefly returns to her father's fireside where her twin sister, her brother, and the former apprentice Robert sit following the day's dinner. For a moment she becomes again a part of the family she left months before for some unnamed enormities, becoming an actress or something worse, but she does not repent, and flees the fireside unshriven.

It was now the hour for domestic worship. But while the family was making preparations for this duty, they suddenly perceived that Prudence had put on her cloak and hood, and was lifting the latch of the door.

"Prudence, Prudence! where are you going?" cried they all, with one voice.

As Prudence passed out of the door, she turned towards them, and flung back her hand with a gesture of farewell. But her face was so changed that they hardly recognized it. Sin and evil passions glowed through its comeliness, and wrought a horrible deformity; a smile gleamed in her eyes, as of triumphant mockery, at their surprise and grief.

"Daughter," cried John Inglefield, between wrath and sorrow, "stay and be your father's blessing, or take his curse with you!"

For an instant Prudence lingered and looked back into the fire-lighted room, while her countenance wore almost the expression as if she were struggling with a fiend, who had power to seize his victim even within the hallowed precincts of her father's hearth. The fiend prevailed; and Prudence vanished into the outer darkness.[5]

Similar themes are worked with typical coincidental twists in the plot of J. G. Holland's Yankee epic in free verse, *Bittersweet* (1858). Set in the requisite old red New England farmhouse on a stormy Thanksgiving Eve, the poem begins with the gathering of the clan: two sons with their wives and families who have little to do with the story, and the individuals who are central to the plot—old Israel, the patriarch, his daughters Ruth and Grace, Grace's husband David, and their adopted sister Mary. They become involved in a discussion of theological problems of sin, temptation, and faith that were still of great interest to the New England reader (*Bittersweet* was a much-reprinted best seller in its day), prefiguring the troubles related in the rest of the book. The party then breaks up. David and Ruth go on a tour of the cellar stores of cider, apples, salt meat, and other staples, while Grace and Mary go off to talk. They exchange stories of the faithlessness and adultery that married life has dealt them. Grace begins by telling Mary that she discovered David had been unfaithful to her, and how she angrily responded to his transgression. Mary, however, tops this with the confession that not only did her lazy husband Edward cheat on her but when he sank into drink and debauchery, she began to sink with him until he went off with his frowsy mistress in a balloon on July 4. Once Mary had recovered from all this, she vengefully tried to seduce a married man who had hired her to make an embroidered purse for his wife. Fortunately he resisted and even helped her to repent, which was how she was able to return to the sanctity of her old home.

Later that evening, when the family has regathered, a boy's telling of the Bluebeard tale moves Ruth to denounce the innate bloodthirsty nature of men and boys, while David makes the very sentimental observation that

The girl is nearest God, in fact;
    The boy gives crime its due;
She blames the author of the act,
      And pities too.

The denouement occurs when a ragged stranger rescued from the storm turns out to be the wretched Edward, who asks Mary to forgive him. Mary, in so doing, reveals that the man whom she tried to seduce but who ended up helping her was none other than her sister's husband, David. Grace realizes that the "affair" she had so bitterly resented was in fact David's effort to redeem Mary, not actual adultery. All are reconciled, and irredeemable Edward, having accomplished his purpose, appropriately dies.

Children played an important role in adult Thanksgiving fiction, both as characters and as narrators reflecting the voice of the author in recalling the wonderful holidays of yesteryear. Mrs. Stowe used the boy Horace to narrate *Oldtown Folks*, which was based in part on her husband Samuel's memories of South Natick, Massachusetts, and her/Horace's portrayal of Thanksgiving is very similar to recollected accounts of the old-time holiday in contemporary nonfiction. In Julia Mathews' *Uncle Joe's Thanksgiving* (1876), a group of children work together to raise funds to return a small cottage to its onetime owner, the superannuated Uncle Joe, and his granddaughter "Delight." The story also involves a returned reprobate, who dies after reconciliation with his family, and a good-hearted Irish couple. The presentation of the deed to the house takes place following a Thanksgiving sleigh ride, and this scene takes full advantage of the charitable associations with the day, while leaving the church service and dinner as understood.

The Thanksgiving theme was also a popular vehicle for the didactic purposes of children's literature. A children's story illustrating familiar ideals is *Mary and Ellen; or, The Best Thanksgiving* (1854), which contrasts the temperaments and holiday experiences of two classmates: selfish Mary, who plans to visit her grandparents along with prosperous relatives from Boston and California, and humble Ellen, who expects no celebration at home with her poor, sickly mother. As might be expected, Mary has the worst of the two Thanksgivings. Her uncooperativeness almost prevents her from going to her grandparents' house. She then overeats, spending part of the day quite uncomfortably but still enjoying the stories and popcorn. Ellen's holiday on the other hand is redeemed first by the effort of her mother's genial black caretaker, Aunt Ceely, who arranges for a basket of food to be sent to the Fisher household, and then by Ellen's missing seaman father, who turns up having made a fortune in the California goldfields.

The American Sunday School Union found Thanksgiving a suitable subject for their tiny tracts to catechize children, such as thoughtless young Annie in *Thanksgiving-Day* (ca. 1866), in the proper Christian attitude of thankfulness:

> M[other]: What is the reason we keep thanksgiving-day?
> A[nnie]: O, I suppose for a holiday, like Christmas, and new-year's day,
> 　　or like my birth-day. Is it not, mother?
> M[other]: It is for a better purpose than this, Annie. . . .

A standard depiction of the classic holiday, with patriarchal widower, gathered grown children, and two vacant chairs (for departed mother and daughter) can be found in *The Family Gathering; or, Thanksgiving-Day* (n.d.). Another family inquisition from *Dotty Dimple at Play* (1868), in Sophie May's popular children's series, provides a glimpse of the popular appreciation of Thanksgiving:

> After the silent blessing, Mr. Parlin turned to the youngest daughter, and said, "Alice, do you know what Thanksgiving Day is for?"
>
> "Yes, sir; for turkey."
>
> "Is that all?"
>
> "No, sir; for plum pudding."
>
> "What do you think about it, Prudy?"
>
> "I think the same as Dotty does, sir." Replied Prudy, with a wistful glance at her father's right hand, which held the carving knife.
>
> "What do you say, Susy?"
>
> "It comes in the almanac, just like Christmas, sir; and it's something about the Pilgrim Fathers and the Mayflower."
>
> "No, Susy; it does not come in the almanac; the Governor appoints it. We have so many blessings that he sets apart one day in the year in which we are to think them over, and be thankful for them."
>
> "Yes, sir; yes, indeed," said Susy. "I *always* knew that."[6]

Many people did feel that Thanksgiving was primarily "for" turkey and plum pudding, or perhaps pumpkin pie and cranberry sauce, and that like the modern Christmas it was primarily a time of indulgence, not piety. Educated adults appreciated its religious nature, although the religious element was far weaker by the mid- to late nineteenth century than it had been. In all the children's books examined for this study, only the two Sunday School Union titles assume attendance at church on Thanksgiving Day. In the others, the only individual who is described as having attended church is Aunt Ceely in *Mary and Ellen*.

Few of these stories, whether written for children or for adults, had accompanying illustrations. They relied almost completely on literary means to describe (and prescribe) the holiday's characteristics, echoing perhaps

New England's aniconic culture of sermons, essays, and verse. However, texts were only one of the ways in which the Victorians constructed the meaning of their evolving Thanksgiving holiday. From the 1830s on, an ever-increasing torrent of mass-produced graphics brought about a revolution in popular perception. Inexpensive prints and woodcut illustrations had long been popular in chapbooks and on broadsides, providing a rough visual complement to the text or captioning. Such images may or may not be considered as "art," but their central importance in this instance is as an alternative "language" that created and provided meaning sometimes quite independent of any verbal expression. As W.J.T. Mitchell observes,

[L]anguage and imagery are no longer what they promised to be for critics and philosophers of the Enlightenment—perfect, transparent media through which reality may be represented to the understanding. For modern criticism, language and imagery have become enigmas, problems to be explained, prison-houses which lock the understanding away from the world. The commonplace of modern studies of images, in fact, is that they must be understood as a kind of language; instead of providing a transparent window on the world, images are now regarded as the sort of sign that presents a deceptive appearance of naturalness and transparence concealing an opaque, distorting, arbitrary mechanism of representation, a process of ideological mystification.[7]

Popular mid-nineteenth-century illustrated serials such as *Gleason's* (later *Ballou's*) *Pictorial*, *Harper's Weekly* (and *Harper's Monthly* and *Harper's Bazar*, to a lesser extent), *Frank Leslie's Illustrated*, or, for the family market, *Every Saturday*, the *Youth's Companion*, the *Child at Home*, and *Hearth and Home* published both Thanksgiving stories and impressive holiday-themed engravings each year, but seldom in conjunction. The stories were usually unrelated to the pictures, which had their own short textual explanations. The often elaborate engravings, however, are a valuable source in themselves as a medium through which to view the Victorian Thanksgiving. Until the technological revolution in print took place, there had been few visual representations of Thanksgiving. Popular perceptions of the holiday were shaped entirely through personal experience or by hearing and reading about it. Texts would continue to be the most important means by which the American Thanksgiving was defined and bounded, but images grew to become another essential method through which popular culture determined what Thanksgiving was all about.

The first pictorial representations of Thanksgiving, such as those by John W. Barber (1828) or Charles Goodrich (1836), depict simple families assembled around a Thanksgiving table (see figure 5). These quaint, rather primitive images would soon be superseded by much more dynamic and realistic representations.[8] Popular prints proved to be an effective vehicle for increasing public appreciation of Thanksgiving and for communicating its association with the themes that remain recognizably "Thanksgiving" today, such as New England, turkey dinner, and family reunions. The most famous such image is Connecticut artist George H. Durrie's painting *Home for Thanksgiving*, which was published by Currier and Ives in 1869. Durrie specialized in winter scenes in New England, and *Home for Thanksgiving* shows a young man who has arrived at a Yankee farmhouse with his wife and child in a sleigh being welcomed by the old father and mother (see figure 6). No other nineteenth-century picture achieved the dissemination of Durrie's image in later years, but scenes of reunions in family homesteads and crowded dinner tables presided over by the aged head of the family were repeated again and again in the illustrated papers.

Most popular Thanksgiving illustrations in the 1850s were images of contemporary celebrations. Each November or early December, journals such as *Gleason's, Harper's,* and *Frank Leslie's* offered seasonal cover and story illustrations of the Thanksgiving holiday. These include the return to the old homestead, preparations for the feast (including pictures of turkeys being hunted, bought, slaughtered, and served), family and friends assembled at the dinner table, and after-dinner entertainments. A typical example that appeared in *Gleason's Pictorial* for December 6, 1851, has a festive Thanksgiving dinner attended by men, women, and children with their aged hosts; the grandfather cutting a turkey; and a servant bearing a huge plum pudding. For November 11, 1854, *Gleason's* depicted a turkey hunt. *Ballou's Pictorial Drawing-Room Companion* for November 28, 1857, features a selection of images, including a family at dinner and the same people playing fox and goose and blindman's buff with some abandon after the meal (see figure 11). There is also a wintry "coasting" or sledding picture and a "husking party" in the issue. The *Harper's Weekly* issue of December 5 for the same year has an analogous picture of a large New England family at table (with the youngest children at a separate table) and two servants, and a lively image of blindman's buff played in the kitchen. The *Harper's Weekly* Thanksgiving issue for the following year has the standard dinner and a Thanksgiving ball. An American turkey shoot was published in the *London Illustrated News* in 1859, while the *New York Illustrated News* offered yet another New England homestead dinner—with a strong emphasis on the cider barrel—in *Thanksgiving Dinner—Ephraim's Speech* (November 26, 1859). Off to the right are two lovers hidden in an adjoining room (see figure 13).

During the Civil War, Winslow Homer and other illustrators contributed scenes of Thanksgiving in the field where soldiers were doing their best to observe the holiday. In 1862, Homer published *Thanksgiving in*

17. Winslow Homer, *Thanksgiving in Camp*, from *Harper's Weekly*, November 29, 1862, p. 764. Soldiers are celebrating the holiday in a sutler's bower. Civilian sutlers, or provisions retailers, provided supplies not available from military stores.

Camp in *Harper's Weekly*, which depicts a sutler's tent and brush arbor in which men are receiving pies and drink for the holiday (figure 17). In 1864, the organization of the Union Club collection of food for the troops at Delmonico's and the Trinity Place depot was reported in *Frank Leslie's Illustrated Weekly*, while Thomas Nast chronicled the results of those same efforts among the soldiers and sailors. In *Thanksgiving-day in the Army*, Homer presents a sentimental print in *Harper's* (December 3, 1864) in which two battle-hardened veterans are seen pulling a wishbone. When conditions allowed, the military encouraged Thanksgiving activities as a temporary anodyne to the rigors of the battlefield, as shown in Lossing's *Civil War in America* (1866, vol. 1, p. 168). A full folio page by artist W. T. Crane is devoted to the "Thanksgiving festivities at Fort Pulaski, Georgia," on November 27, 1862, including blindfolded wheelbarrow races, greased pigs and poles, a sack race, the dress parade, a Thanksgiving ball, and other activities.[9] Illustrators also depicted Thanksgiving on the home front. The war's close was duly celebrated in 1865 by Winslow Homer in a pair of prints in *Frank Leslie's Illustrated*: *Thanksgiving Day — the Church Porch*, showing veterans, some with missing limbs, attending Thanksgiving Day services with their families (see figure 7), and *Thanksgiving Day — Hanging Up the Musket*, where the returning soldier hangs a musket marked "1861" beneath the remains of an old gun labeled "1776."

After the war, Thanksgiving prints appeared regularly in *Harper's*

Weekly, Frank Leslie's Illustrated, and other periodicals. These images varied over a limited range, from Thomas Nast's humorous cartoons of turkey-haunted nightmares suffered by overindulgent small boys to allegorical harvest compositions. Predictably, turkeys in the various stages of their role as principal entrée appeared regularly, as in the prewar *Thanksgiving—Way and Means* published in the November 27, 1858, issue of *Harper's Weekly*, but pictures of New England farms and dinners declined in frequency as the other regions of the country developed their own traditions. Images of the classic New England family gathering so popular in the 1850s and 1860s were replaced by representations of colonial Thanksgivings. These as a rule retained the wintry character of the earlier contemporary Yankee images until the Pilgrims and their autumnal harvest festival shifted the seasonal focus to the milder days of early fall or November's hazy, warm "Indian summer."[10] The decorations surrounding the text of President Andrew Johnson's 1869 November proclamation in *Harper's Illustrated* (November 30, 1869, p. 744) emphasize the peaceful harvest theme—including blacks picking cotton!—but include manufacturing and shipping as well.

When topics such as the return to the old homestead were revisited, they might be handled frivolously, as in the *Frank Leslie's Illustrated* 1883 drawing *Thanksgiving in New England—Returning Home from School*, in which a fashionable urban matron and her three idle daughters (and their cats) await the coach bringing their son and brother from college, or in *The Small-Breeds Thanksgiving—Return of the First-born from College* (*Harper's*, 1877), which depicts with the typical cynical condescension of the time an impoverished black family and the arrival of their son for the holiday dinner. As Franklin Hough observed in 1858, the Thanksgiving reunion was less often observed outside New England, and that theme may have seemed a bit threadbare to many Americans by this time.[11] A new perennial favorite, the depiction of women in the kitchen preparing the feast, is represented by Etyinge's *Mixing the Thanksgiving Pudding* (*Harper's Weekly*, December 6, 1879).

The use of blacks as representatives of Thanksgiving is interesting, as they are the only minority—except for Indians in historical images—to so appear on a regular basis. Except for Thomas Nast's impressively "multicultural" prints (see below), Thanksgiving drawings and cartoons are almost entirely populated with old-generation Americans. Almost no Irish, Germans, Jews, or other ethnic groups regularly depicted in the popular press turn up in Thanksgiving pictures, yet blacks do so on a regular basis. Many of the images are of black cooks and servants whose role is to serve the holiday dinner, but the African Americans' own Thanksgivings are common as well. Some examples are *Thanksgiving Day—the Dinner*

18. S. B. McCutcheon, *Preparing the Thanksgiving Dinner,* from *Harper's Weekly,* December 4, 1880. A respectful, sentimental image of a black family preparing their modest Thanksgiving dinner.

(*Harper's Weekly,* November 27, 1858); W.S.L. Jewett's *Thanksgiving—a Thanksgiving among Their Descendants"* (*Harper's Weekly,* November 30, 1867); E. A. Abbey's *Thanksgiving Turkey* (*Harper's Weekly,* December 9, 1879); J. W. Alexander's *Done Brown, Sho's Yo' Bo'n* (*Harper's Weekly,* November 26, 1881). There is a predictable seasonal variant on the stereotypical black chicken thief (an attribution shared by the white tramp), as can be seen in a cartoon in the *Harper's Weekly* "Thanksgiving Number" for 1887. As Jan Pieterse notes, blacks were often caricatured as poseurs in the process of middle-class assimilation, and after 1890 also gradually assumed the burden of stereotypical poverty, replacing the dim-witted Irish, indolent Germans, and wily Jews.[12] However, there are also dignified representations of black ministers, as in *What the Colored Race Has to Be Thankful For"* (*Harper's Weekly,* November 27, 1886) or *American Sketches: A Negro Congregation in Washington* (*Illustrated London News,* November 18, 1876). *Preparing the Thanksgiving Dinner* by S. B. McCutcheon (*Harper's Weekly,* December 4, 1880) depicts a black family getting ready for their dinner in the same respectable and sentimental fashion as is found in the many Yankee images over the years (figure 18). Even P. S. Newell's *After the Thanksgiving Service—Taking the New Minister Home to*

Dinner (*Harper's Weekly*, November 27, 1897), while uncomfortably racist to modern eyes, exhibits what passed for well-intentioned humor in contemporary ethnic illustration. There appears to have been a strong impulse to associate blacks with the holiday in illustration, although I have been unable to find any text explaining why this was so. Perhaps it assumed a reciprocal sympathy with New England and the abolitionist tradition, or reflects some association with the alliances that marked the Reconstruction period. The African American Thanksgiving was so well established by the end of the century that it could be parodied in *Judge* in 1896 to show a table of Republican politicians in blackface, hosted by a black President McKinley, gathered to eat a scrawny turkey labeled "offices" (referring to partisan patronage). This connection persisted into the early twentieth century, especially on Thanksgiving postcards.

Thomas Nast, to whom we are indebted for so much of our national iconography including the Republican elephant, Democratic donkey, and jolly Santa Claus, deserves credit for attempting to recast Thanksgiving as America's inclusionary holiday. As an immigrant himself, Nast apparently found in the Thanksgiving holiday a promise of national assimilation and/or ethnic equality. For example, in *Uncle Sam's Thanksgiving Dinner*, his November 20, 1869, drawing for *Harper's Weekly*, Nast presents a dinner table presided over by Uncle Sam and Columbia around which are seated representatives of all the nationalities of the world waiting to break bread, or rather turkey, together (figure 19). On the wall behind are pictures of Washington, Lincoln, and Grant (the current president), and the lumpy centerpiece is labeled "Self Governance Universal Suffrage." In *The Annual Sacrifice That Gladdens Many Hearts* (*Harper's Weekly*, November 28, 1885), Nast offers a similar image, as representatives of various nationalities — American Indians, Africans, Irish, Germans, Scots, and others — line up for a piece of turkey carved on the "Union Altar" by Uncle Sam in colonial costume. Partisans of the Progressive movement would eagerly adopt this conceptualization of Thanksgiving as a celebration of national unity and toleration rather than nativist tradition in their efforts to stir the immigrant melting pot. Nast never developed an icon for the holiday as he did with Santa Claus for Christmas or the Republican elephant and Democratic donkey; there was not much that could be added to the reigning turkey in that line. By the time the Pilgrims arrived on the iconographic scene, he had left *Harper's* and was no longer involved in crafting cultural caricatures.

Traditional Thanksgiving charity was another popular topic for illustration. The charitable impulse might be presented in a sentimental manner as in the delivery of a basket of food to a widow and her children (figure 20) in a dreary city garret (Sol Etyinge's *Widow's Thanksgiving* in *Harper's Weekly*, December 5, 1874) or in W.S.L. Jewett's *First Thanksgiving*

UNCLE SAM'S THANKSGIVING DINNER.

19. Thomas Nast, *Uncle Sam's Thanksgiving Dinner*, from *Harper's Weekly*, November 20, 1869, p. 745. Nast's irenic vision of immigrants seated in harmony around America's Thanksgiving table.

20. Sol Etyinge, *The Widow's Thanksgiving*, from *Harper's Weekly*, December 5, 1874, p. 1005. Charity was an important part of Thanksgiving's virtues, although in this case it seems unclear whether the widow has the wherewithal to deal with a large, uncooked turkey.

(*Harper's Weekly*, November 28, 1868), where a small street-girl is given a meal of leftovers and, incidentally, a glimpse of bourgeois holiday spirit. Alternately, it might be presented by straightforward reporting, as in *Thanksgiving Dinner at the Five Points' Ladies Home Mission* (*Harper's Weekly*, December 23, 1865), or as a critical contrast between the excesses of the Gilded Age and grinding urban poverty. An evocation of the failure of the tradition of Thanksgiving charity in the anonymity of the city is provided by Winslow Homer in *Thanksgiving Day—1860: The Two Great Classes* (*Harper's Weekly*, December 4, 1860), which contrasts the luxurious leisure of the wealthy with the desperate plight of the poor in scenes of someone stealing chickens or a lonely seamstress trying to earn a crust. The absence of charity is also evident in the humorous *Frank Leslie's Illustrated* 1864 cartoon "*So Near and Yet So Far.*" Here a small boy is overcome just by imagining what the dinner might be like in a saloon to which enormous supplies of game and food are being delivered, reinforcing the certainty of deprivation amid holiday indulgence.

Thanksgiving illustrations sometimes showed people attempting to honor the holiday under conditions quite unlike the cozy scenes of domestic harmony. The loneliness of a failure's shabby room (see figure 14) in *A Thanksgiving Dream of Home* (*Frank Leslie's Illustrated*, December 5, 1868) or the plight of men without family to turn to in *Thanksgiving among the Homeless—in a City Restaurant* (*Harper's Weekly*, November 30, 1872) were especially poignant to period sensibilities. Similarly, the Wild West, like the battlefield, was a place where a little Thanksgiving spirit was a heartfelt need. Even during the rigors of the gold rush, treasure-seeking Yankees felt the need to recognize their traditional holiday, as shown in *Thanksgiving in a Miner's Cabin* in *Gleason's* (May 3, 1851). Pioneer life had its risks, as a pictorial sequence titled *Thanksgiving in Michigan* on the cover of *Hearth and Home* (November 30, 1871) makes clear: a family's log house burns down, and they are forced to find refuge in a rough hut, but even if their Thanksgiving dinner is nothing more than bread and potatoes, they are still grateful for their lives and for supplies sent by the "Relief Association," which will allow them to start anew. In Frederick Remington's *Thanksgiving Dinner for the Ranch* (*Harper's*, November 24, 1888) two rough cowboys are seen riding home with some rabbits and an antelope for the boys back at the ranch, while his *White Man's Big Sunday* (*Harper's*, November 26, 1896), perhaps a reference to the "First Thanksgiving," shows a frontier housewife offering holiday food to several Indians who benefit from the charitable nature of the day.

The most significant new illustrative theme was the representation of Thanksgiving in colonial times. Historical paintings and drawings were exceedingly popular in late-Victorian America, even if such nineteenth-century historical art usually seems melodramatic and inauthentic to us today. It should be remembered that it was only recently that people had begun to be concerned with what the past actually looked like. For centuries, representations of the past had mirrored the fashions and styles of the time in which the illustrations were made rather than those of the period being depicted. The discovery of classical artifacts and the dissemination of their images in engravings had made it possible to approximate a generalized style of costume to represent biblical or ancient events even while the faces, landscapes, and furnishings depicted in the same images remained recognizably those of early modern Europe. As Roy Strong observes, it was the "wildly inaccurate" illustrated histories that appeared after 1770 that accustomed the public to the idea of "seeing" the past.[13] It was not until the end of the eighteenth century that a conscious attempt to represent history accurately emerged, and it was at least another century before artists became familiar enough with historic costumes and artifacts to approach historical exactness.

The late-Victorian fascination with America's colonial past was immeasurably advanced by the excitement surrounding the national Centennial and the Philadelphia Centennial Exposition of 1876. Interest in the relics and customs of the colonial era had been increasing for some time, resulting in the restoration of Mount Vernon—America's first "historic house"—and the "olde tyme" kitchens created and exhibited during the Civil War for the U.S. Sanitary Commission Fair (a forerunner of the Red Cross that assisted in the medical care of Union soldiers). There were at least six of these colonial kitchen fairs held in 1864 as charitable fund-raisers, in Brooklyn, New York City, Saint Louis, Indianapolis, and Philadelphia—all cities with New England societies. Although New York focused on the Dutch and Philadelphia on the German colonists, the other three were "New England Kitchens," and it was the New England model that became the standard. Organized by local women, the kitchen exhibits were pioneering attempts to represent the spirit of the colonial past to the general public, which led to the institution of the historic house museum. Each exhibit was equipped with a large fireplace where antique cooking utensils were used to serve homey New England fare to visitors at long tables under festoons of dried apples. Costumed matrons operated spinning wheels and made quilts to demonstrate outmoded homemaking skills, surrounded by antiques such as "grandfather" clocks, candlesticks, teapots, Bibles, and pewter ware. All this domestic activity was fascinating to a generation that had grown up with iron stoves, chinaware, canned goods, and oil lamps. Like the classic Thanksgiving dinner, the New England Kitchen was a tangible evocation of the simple domestic virtues of the Revolutionary era.[14]

A direct descendant of the Sanitary Commission's New England Kitchens was the New England Log-House and Kitchen exhibit at the Philadelphia Exposition in 1876. Like the earlier exhibits, the Log-House and
Kitchen evoked the virtues of the Era of Homespun and the industry of
the colonial housewife, even while it celebrated the very masculine War for
Independence. Marling notes that "the relentless domesticity with which
Washington and his era were presented at the Centennial Exposition suggests that conventional political and military history were matters of in-
difference to fairgoers and exhibitors alike."[15] The furnishings in the 1876
Log-House and Kitchen were not limited to Revolutionary-era antiques,
however, but included a wooden cradle alleged to be Peregrine White's
and "John Alden's" writing desk. A reproduction of "Elder Brewster's tea
service" (not that the elder ever served tea) was offered for sale. None of
these were actual *Mayflower* relics, but like the spinning wheels and other
objects they satisfied the avid curiosity about the antique that animated
the visiting public. Illustrations of the Sanitary Fair "kitchens" and the
relics on display were widely distributed by *Harper's Weekly, Frank Leslie's
Illustrated*, and Centennial guidebooks, inspiring Americans to begin collecting indigenous antiques and making everyone familiar with a selective
imagery of "old colonial days."

The Log-House itself was perhaps the most blatant anachronism of
them all. There had never been log cabins of this sort in colonial New
England, but the log cabin's symbolic role in contemporary American
culture dictated the necessity of its representation. The pioneer/patriot/
Pilgrim archetype celebrated at the exposition was therefore not only culturally compelling but also enthusiastically muddled. "Most of those who
recorded in print their reactions to the Log-House displayed a remarkably
elastic sense of history; the Revolutionary epoch stretched backward at
will, for instance, to take in John Alden and Peregrine White and oozed
forward again to accommodate a frontiersman's log cabin of nineteenth-
century design."[16] It is not surprising then that the attempt to represent
Puritan Thanksgivings resulted in scenes full of inconsistencies apparent
to the educated modern observer if not to her predecessors. The popularity
of the colonial past and the Pilgrims led to a whole new way of looking at
Thanksgiving history.

Like the sentimentality found in the literature of the time, this nostalgic
evocation of the "good old days" in tangible form followed the contemporary preference for an emotional rather than a cognitive appreciation of
the past, and paved the way for the eventual association of Thanksgiving
with its ultimate historic association, the Plymouth "First Thanksgiving"
of 1621. All these relics of the country's preindustrial past would in time

become icons and symbols endlessly reproduced in illustration and decoration to allow Americans to indulgently contemplate their emotive ties to Pilgrims and pioneers, and the ostensible significance of their autumnal holiday inheritance.

Enter the Pilgrims

The Revolutionary War had been a signal break with the past, not least in the broken continuity of old customs. The years that followed brought more changes that further disrupted America's social continuity.[1] The rise of industrialism and dislocation of long-established communities in the era of railroads and steamships made many people yearn for the security of tradition and the apparently stable social landscape of the past. The Civil War then made its own rupture with the past, and the "good old days" seemed to drift even further away. The postwar emphasis on family and nostalgia for an agrarian paradise lost fed the American people's continuing interest in the first colonists, whose culture exemplified those things and their ultimate origin in American history. It was in this way that attention was turned to the earliest New England immigrants, the Pilgrims of Plymouth.

For a century and a half following the 1620 landing, the Plymouth colonists were not recognized as anything more than the first small wave of the great New England Puritan emigration. They were honored by New England historians such as Nathaniel Morton (1669), Cotton Mather (1701), and Thomas Prince (1736) for their role in establishing the Puritan commonwealth, but the one-hundredth anniversary of their arrival passed unobserved in 1720. The first effort at commemoration did not occur until 1769, when the Old Colony Club of Plymouth instituted Old Colony Day—subsequently Forefathers' Day—the anniversary of the date when the exploratory expedition from the *Mayflower* first set foot on the shore of Plymouth Harbor. By a tradition dating to 1741, the mainland landing had taken place on or near a singular boulder on the Plymouth waterfront on December 11, 1620 (Old Style calendar). The Plymouth clubmen were not interested in the landing at the tip of Cape Cod on November 11, or the landing on Clark's Island in Plymouth Harbor on December 8. As the old Julian calendar had been discarded in favor of the Gregorian model only seventeen years earlier, the clubmen "adjusted" the anniversary by the eleven extra days that had been added to the calendar in 1752. This made the anniversary December 22, which became the established date for "Forefathers' Day."[2]

In 1774, the rock identified with the Forefathers' landing was levered from its bed, and its upper half, which had split off, was dragged up to the town square and placed at the foot of a liberty pole. Thus began the process by which the humble Plymouth colonists became the symbolic founders of New England and, by extension, the future United States as well. Their voluntary separation from the Old World to establish a new Christian commonwealth in America, independent of any royal assistance, was seized on as historical sanction for the American separation from England, and their high ideals and simple way of life were extolled as a model for all Americans. In contrast to the sordid history of early Virginia or the authoritarian nature of Massachusetts Bay, the Plymouth story was refreshingly virtuous and unexceptionable. The Pilgrim Fathers were rather anachronistically credited with Enlightenment values such as tolerance, a love of liberty, belief in public education, and a reverence for law, in addition to their deep religious faith. The Plymouth Forefathers were the ideal candidates for the the Revolutionary Founding Fathers' own "founding fathers." Also, it did not hurt that New England had a virtual monopoly on interpreting American history at the time, and had little competition in promoting its own forebears as the true founders of the nation.

The memory of the Plymouth Forefathers grew in public stature following the new nation's independence until they became, in Rev. Peter Gomes' felicitous phrase, little more than an example of "aggregate virtue." Massachusetts Federalists in Boston, who had enthusiastically adopted the December 22 "Old Colony" holiday, assigned the name "Pilgrim Fathers" to them in 1798, perhaps because the Plymouth colonists could only be the symbolic rather than the literal progenitors of the larger colony. Their most important mythic act, the climactic 1620 landing, became the moment of conception for the nation born in 1776. It was the landing, therefore, together with related elements such as the flight from England, the *Mayflower* voyage, and the terrible first winter, that dominated the literary and artistic representations of the Pilgrim Fathers in the early years of the Republic.

The Pilgrims' legend blossomed despite (or perhaps because of) a relative lack of original accounts. Governor Bradford's manuscript history of the colony had disappeared during the British occupation of Boston, leaving historians dependent on Nathaniel Morton's *New Englands Memoriall* (1669), a simplified version of his uncle William Bradford's chronicle. The detailed account of Plymouth's first year, familiarly known as *"Mourt's Relation"* (1622), was available only in the abridged version published by Samuel Purchase in 1625. No one then even knew that the Leiden Separatists had come from the Scrooby area in England before they fled to Holland. Interest in the Pilgrim Fathers spurred researchers to retrieve further information. The missing portions of *Mourt's Relation* were found and published in 1822, revealing the 1621 harvest celebration that was subsequently christened the "First Thanksgiving." Rev. Joseph Hunter's work in English archives resulted in the identification of Scrooby as the origin of the Pilgrim congregation in 1849. Hunter also oversaw the transcription of Bradford's *Of Plymouth Plantation* for publication in 1856 after the manuscript was rediscovered in the Fulham Palace library. However, the basic outline of the Plymouth Pilgrims' history had been quite sufficient to support the central narrative of courage, suffering, and perseverance. Rufus Choate insisted in 1843 that the Pilgrims were heroes in a heroic age, something more than ordinarily human, and unique in American history.

In 1807, an anonymous correspondent to the Boston *Columbian Centinel* proposed that a "Pilgrim Society" be formed and a "proper edifice be erected for the festive occasion. In one of its apartments may be deposited such appropriate portraitures and antiquities, as can be procured. . . . A monument, erected contiguous to the edifice, and inscribed to the memory of the Pilgrims, would be a valuable acquisition."[3] Commemorative impulses of this sort, which resulted in massive monuments, parades, orations, and civic dinners, we identified earlier as part of the heroic or masculine vision of history. Great men and glorious events are presented with broad sweeps of rhetoric and abstraction, making plaster (or bronze and granite) saints out of historical figures to emphasize the unsullied virtues and awesome accomplishments of the past. This process put the Pilgrim Fathers on a pedestal—quite literally—with the 1853 proposal for a massive granite monument supporting emblematic statuary celebrating the virtues of these heroic people. The cornerstone for a National Monument to the Forefathers was consecrated amid lavish speeches, a massive parade, and a banquet in Plymouth, Massachusetts, on August 1, 1859.

However, by the 1850s another view of colonial history was starting to receive attention—the history of real, ordinary people in everyday life. This domestic or feminine perspective on history did not dispute the classic narrative, but it did descend from the heights and take an intelligent interest in who the Pilgrims actually were, what they were like as individuals, and how they lived their lives. The new antiquarian or social history focused of the people themselves, their daily lives, their humble dwellings and belongings, and all the quotidian things that went on when there were no stirring voyages or battles to talk about. Instead of heroic canvases or granite effigies, the new historical perspective was expressed in smaller, more intimate paintings, engraved illustrations, and Rogers Groups.[4] Poetry, plays, novels, and pageants gave the Pilgrims more human appeal than their sainthood had allowed. The result was often sentimental and idealized, but it was a corrective to the previous austere, one-dimensional representation.

An early instance of this trend was the story of Mary Chilton. A tradition arose that Chilton was the first person to set foot on the sacred rock. She was actually in competition with John Alden for this honor, but as John Davis said in 1826, "As there is a great degree of uncertainty on this subject . . . we may expect from the friends of John Alden that they should give place to the lady."[5] Even though neither she nor John was anywhere near Plymouth Rock on December 11, 1620, Mary Chilton became the first Pilgrim woman to be individually celebrated through her association with the landing.

The most striking example of personal memorialization was the publication of Longfellow's *Courtship of Miles Standish* in 1858. The earlier trope associated with the landing of 1620 evoked separation from the Old World at a time when the American Revolution could benefit from such an image. The *Courtship* in turn brought a much-desired domestic quality to the Pilgrim story at a time when the fear of national division mitigated against the older themes of separation and rebellion. Longfellow's poem, published by Tichnor and Fields in Boston, achieved instant success. The publisher, through continual reprintings, sold twenty-five thousand copies in two months (at a time when twenty-five hundred was more than respectable), and more reprintings followed. Twenty-four English publishing houses brought out the *Courtship* simultaneously, and ten thousand copies were sold in London in a single day![6] The poem's importance is perceptively described by Rev. Gomes: "Had Henry Wadsworth Longfellow devoted himself to the Romance languages, of which he was Smith Professor at Harvard, rather than to mediocre but memorable verse, the perception of American history may well have quite different. Paul Revere would have remained an unknown Boston artisan, and the Pilgrims of Plymouth would be little more than aggregate virtue. It was Longfellow's disciplined meters and undisciplined history that launched them both into immortality."[7]

Although the legendary courtship found its most famous and influential expression in Longfellow's 1858 poem, the story of the Pilgrim lovers had appeared in print before. In 1814, Rev. Timothy Alden published the family tradition in the third volume of his *Collection of American Epitaphs*, which was later quoted in James Thacher's *History of the Town of*

Plymouth (1832) and Justin Winsor's *History of the Town of Duxbury* (1849). In 1843 the *Rover*, a small weekly New York magazine, published a version of the courtship story in verse attributed to "Moses Mullins, 1672." It was Longfellow's poem, however, that made Myles, Priscilla, and John household names. Two illustrated editions were published the following year, giving readers their first visual impressions of the Pilgrims as individuals, as opposed to the heroic gatherings shown in portrayals of the "embarkation from Holland," "signing of the Mayflower Compact," or "landing on Plymouth Rock." Illustrations by John Ehninger in the United States and John Gilbert in England in 1859 provided the basis for later artistic representations of the famous romantic triangle by artists such as George H. Boughton, Howard Chandler Christie, and N. C. Weyth.

The courtship was the first important Pilgrim story unassociated with the landing epic to achieve popularity. Representations of the Pilgrim lovers (especially in the work of the Anglo-American artist George H. Boughton) soon surpassed views of the landing (in number if not in size) as the most popular images of the Pilgrims. The story of John, Priscilla, and Myles gave a new humanity to the Pilgrims, and Longfellow's evocative poetry introduced a number of humble images—from Priscilla's spinning wheel to the apocryphal white riding bull—to American popular culture. The courtship did not supersede the older stories but rather expanded the Pilgrim corpus by introducing a new romantic theme quite different in tone from the dour tale of the landing and the first winter. With this for competition, it is no surprise therefore that Rev. Young's little footnote about a first thanksgiving in 1621, as we discussed in the preface, failed to make an immediate splash.

That footnote, however, had far-reaching effects. It brought the Pilgrim saga to a satisfactory conclusion, wherein the heroic sufferings of the fatal first winter—which saw the death of half the 102 *Mayflower* passengers as well as half the ship's crew—was redeemed by a triumphant "thanksgiving" or harvest festival involving the colonists and their Indian guests. It shifted the Pilgrims' symbolic significance, from fortitude in the face of adversity to the achievement of a successful first harvest and genial relations with their Wampanoag neighbors, so that the "First Thanksgiving" came to overshadow the *Mayflower* voyage and the landing on Plymouth Rock in art, literature, and patriotic rhetoric.

This is a particularly striking example of what Eric Hobsbawm and Terence Ranger have famously identified as the "invention of tradition." "The peculiarity of 'invented' traditions," they note, "is that the continuity with [the significant historical event] is largely factitious."[8] Invented traditions are a response to the breakdown of older social and cultural forms, which occurred with unnerving frequency during the Victorian-era shift from agrarian to industrial economies in Europe as well as America. Such traditions have helped establish social cohesion for real (or imagined) communities, legitimized new relations of authority as old mores and religious ties crumbled, and, most of all, promoted the socialization of fragmented populations by "the inculcation of beliefs, value systems and conventions of behaviour."[9] Original Plymouth traditions concerning the community's forefathers had already been revised to create a more inclusive "Pilgrim" narrative for a broader audience, but now that story, which had been crafted to the needs of the Revolutionary generation, was modified yet again to meet the requirements of nineteenth-century America.

This same process was mirrored in the crafting of a romantic new vision of Scottish Highland life with the invention of kilts (instead of the old belted plaids) and all sorts of newly defined "clan tartans" and badges, the construction of an ostensibly historic bardic system in Wales involving a fictionalized imagery of Druidism, and the revival of the Welsh language; in the creation of a pan-Germanic unified past by the erection of massive monuments such as the Hermannsdenkmal (1841–1875) or the Kyffhäuser (1890–1896) to bring the fragmented German states into a unified nation; and in the Pan-Indian movement in North America that established a politicized as well as romanticized view of Native American identity and culture in the early twentieth century that has significant echoes today.[10]

Invented traditions such as that of the Pilgrims evolve or are introduced to replace the lost traditions and customs that provided social cohesion and cultural continuity in preindustrial societies, but as Hobsbawm observes, they are only partial and inadequate substitutions for earlier verities. They do not occupy as much of the private lives of ordinary people as the true traditions of olden times, and they are far more easily contested or doubted by both critics and believers in modern cultures. They do, however, form the basis for national patriotism, especially in rituals involving their public performance—and as the substance of an ill-defined "Americanism," the Pilgrims and their Thanksgiving holiday were gratefully adopted by the middle class as a defense against the insecurities that threatened the lives of good citizens in modern times.

Thanksgiving is above all a middle-class holiday, and its popular observance among the mass of Americans remained firm even when its symbolic patrons, the Pilgrims, eventually came under attack by the liberal intelligentsia and the forces of modernism. The progressive struggle against what was identified as "Puritanism" cast a shadow over the Pilgrims and the middle-class mores embodied in their holiday. Michael Kammen notes that the conservative bent of American tradition was increasingly challenged by an emerging liberal ideology at the end of the nineteenth century and after:

. . . our two regions richest in a sense of tradition, New England and Dixie, each underwent a protracted phase (between about 1885 and 1925) in which leading spokesmen repudiated the past and cried out for liberation from the oppressive weight of tradition. Charles Francis Adams and Brooks Adams excoriated Puritanism, while William Grady appealed for the New South to rise, like that fabled Phoenix, from the ashes of the old. The repudiation of Puritanism was not confined to New England, moreover, and as that repudiation swept the nation during the 1920s, it verged upon a rejection of New England's hegemony over the exposition of American history.[11]

One response to the attack on Puritanism was to distance the Plymouth Pilgrims as far as possible from those witch-burning spoilsports in Massachusetts Bay. The impulse to differentiate the Plymouth colonists (gentle, colorful "Separatists") from their brethren in Massachusetts Bay (grim, repressive "Puritans") had begun as early as 1780 when George Chalmers, an immigrant Scots lawyer in Philadelphia, declared the Plymouth colonists to be a more worthy standard for American society than the bigoted Bostonians. A hypothetical dichotomy between the two New England Calvinist communities was strongly asserted by liberal historians and theologians in the nineteenth century. This division was given its most influential expression by English Congregationalist Benjamin Scott in *The Pilgrim Fathers Neither Puritans Nor Persecutors* (1866). Scott established the familiar formula of "Pilgrims good—Puritans bad" that was gratefully adopted by New Englanders as a way to maintain the precedence of their region by shifting the virtues previously accorded to the Puritans to the "more acceptable Pilgrims."[12] This effort did not escape criticism by partisans for other colonies, notably New York and Virginia. Kammen notes that concerted efforts to denigrate the role of the Pilgrims and Puritans in American culture were pursued by both modernists and southern sectionalists such as Lyon G. Tyler and Mrs. Mildred Lewis Rutherford.[13] Neither had any lasting success outside their narrow constituencies.

The Pilgrims did not escape disparagement altogether. Their role as model ancestors and harbingers of Enlightenment values came under particular attack by Maryland author William Macon Coleman, who challenged their moral and historical primacy in *The History of the Primitive Yankees; or, The Pilgrim Fathers in England and Holland* (1881). Coleman turned Scott's position on its head. He found the Pilgrims to be indeed a class apart, but a worse rather than better community than the Puritans, in contradiction to the understanding of their defenders.[14] He denounced the Plymouth Separatists in great detail as a particularly mean and despicable breed, taking satisfaction in denying all the claims for their beneficial influence on American culture. For example, he dismissed such examples of tolerance as Edward Winslow's account of John Robinson's generous "farewell sermon" as outright invention, and their descendants' filial pride as a ruthless deception:

The descendants of the Pilgrims of Plymouth Rock claim to derive from the English Puritans. They allege that these English Puritans laid the foundations of civil and religious liberty for mankind at large. And they hold it their proper mission on earth to carry forward and to complete the work that, as they say, their ancestors began.

They have notified the world of this claim with sufficient frequency and directness. It has been the ground-tone of the countless thousands of their sermons, speeches, and orations. It has inspired their more than ten thousand poets. For two hundred years the changes rung upon it from the annual commencements at Harvard down to the children's exhibitions in the country schoolhouses. Their churches have founded upon it and attempted to justify their intermeddling in the name of God and humanity. Their literature finds no theme so rich in pecuniary rewards. Their historians revel in giving it expression. And their politicians — how they have availed themselves of it to cover their robberies, let the history of this country tell.

This claim of descent from the English Puritans is fraudulent. It is utterly destitute of any basis of facts to support it. On the contrary, the truth is, that the Pilgrim Fathers were repudiated, bastardized, cast out, by these self-same Puritan worthies who are now boasted as progenitors.

If it should be asked why this claim has been allowed to pass so long unchallenged the answer is, that it is because nobody has been particularly interested in denying it. Then, after all, the Puritan is not savory, and a pedigree traced to this source has not been universally regarded as a legitimate cause of envy to those who posses no title to such a lineage."[15]

Progressives and reformers who conflated Puritanism with conservatism took up the anti-Puritan crusade in the early twentieth century. "Puritanism" to cultural pundits of the era such as H. L. Mencken, William Carlos Williams, and Randolph Bourne often meant Victorian and evangelical narrow-mindedness rather than seventeenth-century Calvinist social authoritarianism, but they felt that contemporary repression had its roots deep in colonial culture:

The result of that brave setting out of the Pilgrims has been an atavism that thwarts and destroys. The agonized spirit, that has been followed like an idiot with undeveloped brain, governs with its great muscles, babbling in a text of the dead years. . . .[16]

The land! don't you feel it? Doesn't it make you want to go out and lift dead

Indians tenderly from their graves, to steal from them—as it must be clinging even to their corpses—some authenticity?"[17]

This denigration of the popular pieties of American history of course roused conservative ire, and the defenders of tradition roundly criticized the "debunkers." This rearguard action was derided by the wits and intellectuals of the time, who continued to criticize and mock the Puritan straw man and his earnest sentimental defenders alike. However assured the debunkers may have been about their progressive ideals, they did not necessarily reflect the common opinions of their day. "It would not be difficult to find documentation for the proposition that the super patriot and the filio-pietist were more representative of the prevailing attitudes during the postwar era than was the debunker. But any such attempt could end in nothing conclusive, and would draw attention away from the many indications, including the very shrillness of the 'patriot's' protest, that the debunker spoke, however extremely, for the dominant mood of his time."[18] There was still a strong market for the old sentimental pieties and emotional responses to history, despite the best efforts of the earnest debunkers. The mood of the nation, however, was soon to be subjected to two sharp shocks—the Great Depression and World War II—which would turn the cultural tide strongly in favor of the indignant traditionalists.

That the Thanksgiving holiday had originated among the New England Puritans was universally acknowledged, but it had usually been referred to in a generic and diffused way as one of the many legacies from that era along with blue laws, excessive sobriety, and humorlessness, and it carried no particular association with the Plymouth Pilgrims. There was for many years no agreement as to when or where the first New England Thanksgiving had occurred. Some authorities, such as Franklin Hough (1858), considered the Massachusetts Bay Thanksgiving of February 1632 upon the arrival of the supply ship *Lyon* with supplies that saved the colony to be the first. This event that was the subject of an engraving titled "The First Thanksgiving at Boston, February 5, 1632," in *Every Saturday* (1871), and of a story in *Our Young Folks* (November 1866).[19] Others found the First Thanksgiving in Plymouth Colony, as Alexander Young did in 1841 when he identified the harvest celebration of 1621 as the first. Charles W. Elliott complicated matters by confusing 1621 and 1623 in his influential *New England History* (1857) by declaring that Massasoit had attended the first recorded Plymouth Thanksgiving in 1623, which led to inaccurate references in *Harper's Weekly*[20] and elsewhere. Each of these events was cited from time to time, until the 1621 Plymouth event eventually triumphed.

Among the earliest visual representations of the 1621 Plymouth occurrence were the presentation of three deer to the colonists on the cover of

21. *Thanksgiving Day among the Puritan Fathers in New England*, from *Harper's Weekly*, December 3, 1870, p. 781. One of the few representations of the 1621 "First Thanksgiving" before the outdoor dinner became the standard motif.

The Child at Home (November 1867); Edwin D. White's circa 1860 painting *The First Thanksgiving*; an illustration titled "*Thanksgiving Day among the Puritan Fathers in New England*" (figure 21) in the December 3, 1870, issue of *Harper's Weekly*; and *The First Thanksgiving, New Plymouth, 1621*, an illustration by W. L. Sheppard in *Harper's Bazar*, December 15, 1883, p. 792. Both White's painting and the anonymous *Harper's Weekly* print are of interiors, which was true of all representations of colonial Thanksgiving dinners until the publication of *Standish of Standish* (1889). White presents what looks like a single extended family at prayer, very much in the manner of the standard New England Thanksgiving dinner. The link to the Plymouth event is provided only by the presence of a single Indian man standing in observation behind the table (who may possibly have been intended to represent Hobbamock in his role of witness in 1623). The *Harper's Weekly* print has a number of colonists assembling around a table with six standing Indian men as potential guests. Sheppard's illustration is an interesting rendering of the "men returning from fowling," in which four men (and two boys) bring ducks, turkeys, and a rabbit to another man, presumably the governor. The text credits Rev. Increase N. Tarbox's 1879 article as the source for the image. What is more important than the historical veracity of these images is their capacity to inform the public about the Thanksgiving holiday's colonial origin. However, as we have seen, it was not the irenic "First Thanksgiving" with its peaceful meeting of the two races that dominated the Victorian impression of the colonial holiday. Instead, the dominant theme for colonial Thanksgivings was one of violence, where the Native presence was interpreted as a source of hostility and hidden danger, as represented in *Thanksgiving Day in New England Two Hundred Years Ago* (1869) (see figure 2). The idea that the threat of attack from "an implacable enemy," the Native Americans, was central to the colonial experience was firmly embedded in the popular consciousness.

There were isolated references to the Pilgrims' First Thanksgiving between 1841 and the publication of *Standish of Standish* in 1889, but none of any significance such as an influential editorial, book, or presidential proclamation. Diana Appelbaum discovered an early reference to the Pilgrims in a Thanksgiving proclamation from Iowa in 1844 and another in the 1851 Utah proclamation.[21] There are scarcely any references to the Pilgrims in Mrs. Hale's *Godey's* editorials, even after 1865, when she expressly credited the Pilgrim event as initiating the holiday. As we have seen, annual Thanksgiving illustrations and articles in the popular *Harper's Weekly* and *Frank Leslie's Illustrated* newspapers include only a few isolated representations of the 1621 — or 1632 — event. Two illustrations, J. W. Ehninger's *Thanksgiving — a Thanksgiving Dinner among the Puritans* and S. L. Jewett's *Thanksgiving — a Thanksgiving Dinner among their Descendants*, in the November 30, 1867, issue of *Harper's Weekly* compare a Puritan-era family Thanksgiving with a contemporary family's holiday dinner. The former shows a prosperous household (which by the solid architecture and antique furnishings would appear to represent an English setting) arranged around a table as the patriarch offers grace over a large roast of beef. Two servants stand in the shadows to his right, but there are no Indian guests or other attempts to evoke the colonial past. The latter depicts a brighter and more cheerful contemporary scene, where a New England family awaits the grandfather's carving of the turkey and a black manservant stands at the right foreground.

C. S. Reinhart's *Thanksgiving Week — 1621*, which appeared in the December 1, 1894, issue of *Harper's Weekly*, shows the "exercising our arms" mentioned in *Mourt's Relation*, in a contest between an Indian man with a bow and a colonist with a musket before a number of casual spectators (figure 22). This image presents an uneasier message than the now-familiar outdoor feast, where relations between the two cultures were closer to an armed standoff than a friendly dinner party. The Reinhart image reflects a far more popular Victorian conceptualization of early New England Thanksgivings, characterized by a climate of violence and tension between the New England colonists and the Native Americans. The popular press regularly presented images of combat and death when it dealt with colo-

22. C. S. Reinhart, *Thanksgiving Week — 1621*, from *Harper's Weekly*, December 1, 1894, pp. 1137–38. An alternative scene from the 1621 "First Thanksgiving" when, as *Mourt's Relation* states, "among other Recreations, we exercised our Armes." This peaceful contest between musket and bow perhaps reflects the decline in the theme of Thanksgiving violence.

nial Thanksgivings, in the manner of *Thanksgiving Day in New England Two Hundred Years Ago*. Another example, by Winfield S. Lukens in the November 22, 1897, issue of *Harper's Illustrated*, is titled *A Thanksgiving Tragedy*. The illustration depicts a dead New England colonist sprawled in a snowy field, his holiday turkey, hat, and musket beside him, as a group of armed Indian figures emerge from the trees at the upper right (figure 23). A sort of companion print (figure 23) depicts a sturdy young colonial man comforting his young wife (John and Priscilla?) outside their snowy log cabin, from which the door has been torn off, as a dead Indian lies at their feet. This was published by Charles Howard Johnson in 1895 (and later used on a Thanksgiving menu!).

However, interracial colonial violence was only one motif associated with Thanksgiving in the mid–nineteenth century. In 1869, Thomas Nast envisioned a quite different connotation for the holiday in a *Harper's Weekly* cartoon in which representatives of all the peoples of the world who had contributed to the population of the Untied States (including American Indians) are gathered in harmony around Uncle Sam's Thanksgiving table (see figure 19). He is joined by Columbia (his feminine equivalent before the Statue of Liberty took this role) and is carving a turkey beneath a picture of Castle Gardens (the predecessor of Ellis Island, now Battery Park), further emphasizing the idea of immigration. Nast's inclusionary

23. Winfield S. Lukens, *A Thanksgiving Tragedy*, from *Harper's Illustrated*, November 22, 1897, p. 1176; Charles Howard Johnson, untitled print, 1895. Interracial holiday violence—a colonial hunter lies dead in the snow beside his holiday turkey in Lukens' image, while Johnson's analogous print presents the Indian as both aggressor and victim.

ideal would have to wait for half a century to pass before it would supplant the older theme of violence.

The pathos of racial violence continued as a perennial theme in representations of colonial Thanksgivings in the illustrated newspapers, periodical cover art, and cartoons, such as those in the old *Life Magazine* (1883 — 1936). Like most stereotypes, the theme survived longest in humorous contexts, remaining a popular subject well into the twentieth century. For example, Norman Rockwell produced a humorous cover for the *Life* Thanksgiving issue of November 17, 1921, titled *A Pilgrim's Progress*, which shows a Pilgrim boy carrying the Thanksgiving turkey fleeing amid a hail of arrows, one of which has pierced his tall buckled hat.

Such negative images might have suited the humor of the day, but it was the sentimental and heartening Pilgrim First Thanksgiving that struck a resonant chord with the American public. It fulfilled the cultural desire for a romantic origin for the holiday and also provided the Pilgrims with a new role as tolerant American peacemakers, now that friction with England had a less compelling significance given the increasing Anglophilia of the time. Even serious scholars succumbed to its appeal. The exhaustive scholarly history of the New England holiday written by William DeLoss Love in 1895 has it both ways, historical as well as sentimental. His analysis of the event he calls the "Harvest Festival at Plymouth — 1621," which is so thorough and judicious that it has never been superseded, carefully points out the impossibility of the 1621 harvest celebration being considered as a true Thanksgiving. Nevertheless, he is willing to accept the popular reverence accorded the event:

It was not a thanksgiving at all, judged by their Puritan customs, which they kept in 1621; but as we look back upon it after nearly three centuries, it seems so wonderfully like the day we love that we claim it as the progenitor of our harvest feasts.[22]

It was this resemblance, along with the sentiments associated with it, that was the foundation for the belief that the holiday did indeed have its origin in Plymouth in the autumn of 1621, and that New England was the source of much that was good and generous in American history, not the prudery and bigotry that was often cited as its legacy.

The image of the Pilgrims and their Native neighbors dining in irenic harmony was an apposite symbol of the peaceful assimilation and Americanization the reformers sought. Jane G. Austin's description of such a gathering in her 1889 novel and W. L. Taylor's illustration *The First Thanksgiving Dinner, with Portraits of the Pilgrim Fathers* (1897) gave the story the boost it needed (see figure 4). The following year Kate Douglas Wiggin included a juvenilized account of the Pilgrim story with its Thanksgiving culmination ("All this happened nearly three hundred years ago, and ever since that time Thanksgiving has been kept in our country")[23] in *The Story Hour*, an anthology of stories intended for kindergarten pupils. Jennie A. Brownscombe's *First Thanksgiving at Plymouth* (1914), J.L.G. Ferris' "*First Thanksgiving* (ca. 1915), and Percy Moran's *First Thanksgiving in Plymouth* (1920) firmly established the dominant tone for future visual depictions of the event (see figure 1). Each shows an open-air feast derived from the Austin description and Taylor illustration in which Pilgrim hosts and Native guests dine together in a dignified manner on the autumnal bounty. Despite various minor physical inaccuracies such as log cabins and western Native costumes, these images faithfully reflected the brief moment in 1621 when the two cultures met in harmony as described by Edward Winslow.

One other possible factor influencing the favorable reception of Austin's First Thanksgiving was the cessation of the Indian wars in the West. Victories over the Native peoples, which strengthened the trope of the "Vanishing Redman" and stimulated widespread sentimental interest in Native culture, made it possible to reassess the representation of Thanksgiving's colonial roots. It was now not only feasible but also fashionable to think of welcoming the Native Americans to the table. Another possible factor was the progressive mind-set that flourished at the turn of the twentieth century, which sought to bring reform and a rational order to American society. The old, defensive construct of the new American nation as solely the legacy of a Protestant Anglo-Saxon past (which the Pilgrims embodied) was fading even as the earlier fear and resentment toward other immigrant communities was temporarily mellowing. It was now time to create unity out of diversity and invite others to join together at the national table, as Thomas Nast's beneficent cartoon had presciently suggested in 1869.

However, it took time for the 1621 First Thanksgiving to achieve hegemonic status. Until the 1940s, the Thanksgiving holiday was as often represented in popular culture by accounts of "old time Thanksgivings" of the late eighteenth and early nineteenth centuries or stories about contemporary holiday events as it was by the 1621 story; and the cartoon stereotype of colonial strife still flourished in *Life* and similar publications. The postcard fad that flourished between 1905 and 1912 produced a large number of Thanksgiving Day images, many of which employed colonists, Indians, and turkeys in various ways, but illustrations of the 1621 dinner are noticeably absent.[24] The Pilgrim story was still dominated by the themes of the 1620 landing and the "first triangle" of Myles, John, and Priscilla. A survey of standard primary school textbooks from 1894 to 1940 shows that references to the Pilgrims might omit any mention of the 1621 event.[25] The "First Thanksgiving" was not even represented in either of Plymouth's two major historical pageants, Margaret M. Eager's Old Plymouth Days and Ways (1896–1897) or George P. Baker's The Pilgrim Spirit (1921).[26] Baker had even originally contemplated including a Thanksgiving segment and then decided against it, even as he incorporated Norse explorers and peripheral scenes involving French ambassadresses.

Nevertheless, there was sufficient awareness of the 1621 myth among the American public to prepare the nation for a widespread acceptance of the "First Thanksgiving" by World War II. The hearty patriotism of the period celebrated the Pilgrims along with other national icons. Samuel Eliot Morison captured the prevailing consensus in 1937 when he observed, "the Pilgrims in a sense have become the spiritual ancestors of all Americans, whatever their stock, race or creed."[27] The First Thanksgiving soon replaced the *Mayflower*, Plymouth Rock, and the "courtship" as the Pilgrims' most significant contribution to the American way of life. The Pilgrim story now had a romantic happy ending, with all parties gathered together on an eternal golden autumn afternoon around a table laden with the fruits of the first New England harvest. The 1621 feast found its way onto calendars and into magazine advertising and cover art while the old violent images were buried in library vaults. From the 1930s on, an increasing number of children's books brought the story to younger generations, each adding its own fictional gloss to the picture. Greeting cards and schoolroom decorations left no uncertainty that the Pilgrims were at the core of the Thanksgiving tradition. In addition to the classroom decorations, ephemeral tales, and exercises found in school holiday anthologies, the Pilgrims were packaged as craft projects in which paper dolls and cardboard cutouts illustrated their supposed log cabins and colonial possessions. Earlier examples featured wintry landscapes and rough conditions, but soon these teaching aids shifted their focus to autumn and Thanksgiving themes. Teachers' workbooks provided master copies of cute Pilgrims, Indians, turkeys, and pumpkins to color.

By 1950, Thanksgiving was the primary focus of the Pilgrim story in popular culture. Critics were quick to debunk these stereotypical images as inauthentic—the belief that the Pilgrims lived in log cabins or sported the somber dress of the Quakers and Victorian evangelicals has been "exposed" on a regular basis for over fifty years—but the mythic significance attached to the holiday passed unnoticed. A filmed re-creation of the event in 1960 at the young Plimoth Plantation (founded 1947), which modernized the images and provided assurances of reliable accuracy, received extensive national press coverage and was shown in many schools. The association of the popular holiday with its supposed Pilgrim origin had become a self-evident historical truth—the world had been sold on the "Pilgrim" brand of Thanksgiving.

The Plymouth First Thanksgiving is an "etiologic tale," a story that has been told to explain and define the holiday through an account of its putative origins. As Thanksgiving is now believed to have originated with the Pilgrims, the modern holiday has as its symbolic patrons the hospitable Pilgrims and their Native American guests. Whenever we see a be-buckled Pilgrim and his natural prey, the turkey, or a generic American Indian amid the fruits of the harvest season, we are immediately put in mind of Thanksgiving. Jack Santino perceptively sums up their modern holiday meaning:

The images of the Pilgrims we see today may refer to those people specifically, at least in some people's minds, but most of the Thanksgiving Pilgrims are generic. So are the Indians. We have no "Chief Massasoit" candles on sale at the department stores. Rather we have cute Indians and nameless Pilgrims, usually a man and a woman. The first Thanksgiving, the Pilgrims, the fellowship with the Indians, all these have become mythic events in the American consciousness. Historically there has been a bias toward England as the cultural parent of the United States, and toward New England as the geographical place of origin, despite the fact that it is not the oldest or first area settled, nor were Englishmen the first or only settlers, Nevertheless, the Thanksgiving story has become a kind of origin myth for the United States. It is felt to be the first truly *American* event, and we call the Pilgrims our forefathers. It is not surprising, then, that we portray them as a male and female pair. They are our distant parents.[28]

Actually, that "male and female pair" are recognizable as avatars of the popular images of John and Priscilla Alden, but no matter. They have become an indelible part of the traditional iconic procession that cycles from babies with numerical banners to pink hearts and cupids, leprechauns and shamrocks, Easter lilies and fancy hats, Uncle Sam and fireworks, black cats and Frankenstein monsters, Pilgrims and Indians, to Santa Claus and presents beneath the tree.

Pilgrims Are for Kids

Thanksgiving in the Progressive Classroom

What Americans actually did on Thanksgiving changed very little after the mid–nineteenth century, except for a decline in church attendance and the introduction of football and, later, parades. Even today, the established sequence of family reunion, dinner, and leisure-time activities (including watching football games) repeats the pattern set in place a century and a half ago. The important developments in the history of the Thanksgiving holiday from the end of the nineteenth century until World War II were more in the way the holiday was presented and perceived rather than any changes in its observation. The adoption of the Pilgrims and harvest symbolism was the primary modification in the way the holiday was understood, but almost as influential was the innovative effort to instruct children in the significance of American history through a cycle of holiday observations, including Thanksgiving.

We are now so accustomed to the ubiquity of Thanksgiving stories, plays, and images in classrooms, not to mention mass-produced holiday decorations, greeting cards, and "holiday specials," that it is hard to imagine a time when Thanksgiving was observed without any of these props. Classroom utilization of holiday iconography, which started about 1890, was so effective that by 1907 Robert Haven Schauffler could preface an anthology of Thanksgiving selections in mock amazement that it had not been done before: "For years the imperative ungratified demand for such a book has almost suggested a dark conspiracy among literary folk, — a conspiracy which the present volume is intended to thwart."[1] Although there actually *were* earlier Thanksgiving collections, Schauffler's comment points up how quickly holiday exercises had become essential to grade school education.

It was in the classroom that Thanksgiving had its greatest impact at the turn of the twentieth century. Anyone who grew up in the United

24. Thanksgiving school pageant, Obenaus Studios, Albany, N.Y., ca. 1930.

States after 1890 was exposed to an annual sequence of classroom holiday activities through which civic education and American patriotism were inculcated. As each holiday approached, pupils were taught appropriate stories and songs; set to work to cut, paste, and color decorations; and involved in class exercises that pointed up the particular significance of the occasion (figure 24). Holiday observances introduced youngsters to the central themes of American history and, in theory, strengthened their character and prepared them to become loyal citizens. Thanksgiving, with its colonial harvest themes and idyllic images of Pilgrims and Indians feasting together on turkey, was one of the more significant of these cheerful pedagogic events. Also, the inculcation of those Thanksgiving images in generations of schoolchildren was probably a major factor behind the ultimate success of the Pilgrim Thanksgiving iconography.

This familiar cycle was not an important part of American education before the end of the nineteenth century. There had been earlier holiday activities for kids and children's books such as Hamilton's *Red-Letter Days in Applethorpe* (1866)[2] that explained the basis for holiday observances, but the complete subsumption of the civic calendar into the school curriculum was the result of a new progressive approach to education that paralleled the contemporary impulse to create new holidays for everything from labor and flags to birds and trees. This grammar school adaptation of civic ritual not only exposed students to the lessons of "Americanism" but also turned traditional holiday stories such as that of the Pilgrims into children's fare. When the turn-of-the-century schoolchildren grew up and began telling their own children about the Pilgrims, they naturally associated the story with their own childhood and consigned it to the category of nursery tale. Soon the Pilgrims, like Santa Claus, the young George Washington, and the Easter Rabbit, were generally thought of as "kids' stuff" and not accorded quite the serious adult attention that they had enjoyed earlier.

The First Thanksgiving trope institutionalized the significance American society found in the traditional holiday. The emotions that arose from the interplay of ideas communicated in the anthologies, classroom activities, and visual decorations coalesced into a standardized holiday myth for student internalization. However, schoolchildren were only one of the audiences for which the holiday lessons were intended. Children of immigrants or uneducated parents could explain the holiday to their families, for whom Thanksgiving's nondenominational character, subdued patriotism, and middle-class respectability were attractive selling points. "Not coincidentally, the visually oriented progressive celebrations were tailor-made to appeal to not only children and non-English-speaking immigrants but also to Americans enamored of popular commercial culture. . . . Holidays and festivals thus played a vital role in the progressive conception of community."[3]

The final decades of the nineteenth century were a time of unsettling social change. The comfortable complacency of mid-Victorian America was shaken by labor unrest, industrial monopoly, economic depression, and cultural tension. The latter was occasioned not only by the burgeoning political power of ethnic Americans but also by the great tide of new immigrants from southern and eastern Europe. The old elite was alarmed that these new cultural currents might overwhelm its traditional political and moral prominence. "Old Americans" felt beleaguered by both internal weaknesses and external dangers. They believed that their beloved Anglo-Saxon Protestant heritage was threatened not only by crime, vice, and intemperance but also by the raw economic power of the new railroad, oil, and banking combinations and the strange and frightening immigrant communities. "By 1900, Yankee stereotypes of the old immigrant groups [Irish, German, and French-Canadian] had become more sympathetic; but those of the new immigrant groups, whom the restrictionists wished to exclude, steadily deteriorated."[4] Whereas earlier the leaders of society had felt secure in the assumption that all Americans (or all who mattered) shared a common ancestry, body of religious principles, and cultural inheritance, they now realized that this was no longer the case.

The United States was no longer a young nation in which living memory could encompass most of its significant past. The development of an American public memory based on a new middle-class consensus (of which the annual holiday cycle in schools was a component) became the well-intentioned mission of patriotically minded reformers and pro-

25. *We Americans*, from *Life*, July 14, 1887, p. 22–23. This pointed comparison between the revered Pilgrims of 1620 and the inferior immigrants of 1887 clearly reveals the anxiety "Old Americans" felt about the rising tide of immigration in the late nineteenth century.

gressive spokespeople.[5] Also, technological progress and urbanization had undermined the agrarian values and traditions that had once unified a largely rural nation. The dominant middle class found their loyalties divided between the provincial ideals of the local community such as "modesty in women, rectitude in men, and thrift, sobriety, and hard work in both" and the opposing qualities that were valued in the new social terrain of cities, railroads, immigrants, gigantic industries, and mass marketing. The key to the future was still believed to lie in the traditions of the Anglo-Saxon mainstream, but their inculcation needed to be updated for modern audiences. A new social adhesive was needed to weld these disparate elements together so that the best of the old was not lost, conflicting interests could be mediated without violence, corruption prevented, and private gain subordinated to social order.

The Old Americans were determined to meet this challenge. They threw up social barriers to exclude interlopers, founded the Immigration Restriction League in 1894, denounced any and all perceived threats against their way of life (figure 25), and retreated behind a defensive orthodoxy that fostered a restrictive, more cohesive class structure. At the same time, they were determined to "Americanize" their new fellow citizens by aggressively educating them in the values and traditions of indigenous Americans.[6] The need to "Americanize" not only new immigrants but also the rising generations became a major concern for progressive educators and community leaders at the turn of the twentieth century. First, however, they had to define just what being an American entailed. Older nations had well-established national identities, but the United States had long been insecure about defining itself, and its citizens worried whether they were, in fact, truly "American" enough.[7]

Efforts at establishing what it meant to be a "true American" called for not only moral and political reform but also a reexamination of the nation's shared cultural heritage. An important part of this reexamination involved the study of American history and its customs, artifacts, and narratives. "Small-town America," in which the majority of Old Americans lived, had taken its Protestant heritage as a given, applicable to all. Its history was everyone's history, but the details were rather vague. When the WASP interpretation of the past was the only "game in town" and the Revolution part of living memory, there had been no inclination to scrutinize the past too closely. As Michael Kammen observed, "For a very long time, members of traditional societies had relied upon custom and comfortably assumed that genuine customs were inscribed 'in the memory of man.'"[8] Now that competing histories might have to be taken into consideration, there was a concerted effort to ensure that what had once been taken for granted remained the dominant interpretation of the past. The nostalgic fascination with things colonial (which might be extended to include anything preindustrial), which had been growing since before the 1876 Centennial, led to the enthusiastic collection of colonial relics and antiques, and the anecdotes and legends that went with them. Among these were the relics and stories of the famous Pilgrims of Plymouth, whose memory was soon inextricably linked with the Thanksgiving holiday.

Although they had no lasting impact, there were dissenters among the immigrants and the American poor who did not willingly accept the standardized view of history. One interesting example involving holiday observance was the "anti-Thanksgiving" declared by Chicago anarchists in 1885:

The day set apart by the well-fed, well-clothed, well-housed, and well-to-do classes to return thanks for the success that crowned their efforts to exploit the working class during the past year was Thursday, November 26. . . . The Internationalists therefore arranged for an indignation meeting of the working people, to who was addressed the following announcement:

Grand Thanksgiving services of the Chicago workingmen, tramps, and all others who are despoiled and disenfranchised, on Market square (Randolph and Market streets) Thanksgiving Day, November 26, 1885, at 2:30 o'clock p.m. Good "preachers" of the gospel of humanity will officiate. Everyone is invited.

Learn how turkeys and other nice things may be procured. *The Committee of the Grateful.*

According to the account in the *Alarm*, an anarchist publication, two thousand people showed up in the mud, slush, and cold to hear the radicals denounce the rich and powerful on the occasion of Thanksgiving, at which Albert Parsons thundered forth atop a salt barrel and William Holmes (both of whom might have come from "Old American stock") read resolutions mocking the middle-class sentiments of the day.[9] Such things frightened the leaders of society and strengthened their resolve that the young people of America be indoctrinated in the accepted values of their country to offset the influence of anger and despair among the poor.

The introduction of holiday observances in schools, Ellen Litwicki found, began with the observation of Washington's Birthday following the Washington Inauguration Centennial in 1889.[10] There was concern that students, especially those who came from immigrant families, were not being properly prepared for citizenship. The goal of fostering patriotism in a time when American society was undergoing alarming changes led to the swift adoption of the holiday cycle in primary education. "In the 1890s school holidays grew rapidly as venues of patriotic education. In Chicago and across the nation, schools introduced exercises for Lincoln's Birthday, Memorial Day, and the new holiday of Flag Day, and the public schools emerged as one of the most important arenas for the celebration of patriotic holidays."[11] By 1900 educational publishers were providing compilations of supplementary materials in the form of plays, verse, pictures, and stories for the major holidays — and a number of new or minor ones as well. "In the early twentieth century, holiday celebrations became a schoolhouse institution, as a veritable industry emerged to produce holiday exercises and supplies."[12]

The small, inexpensive booklets these publishers produced followed the example of cheap anthologies of dialogues, songs, orations, and verse for adults that were published in great numbers following the Civil War.[13] The earliest school holiday collections, such as Hood's *Special Days in the Primary Grades* (1897),[14] contained poems and songs categorized by patriotic school holiday (Columbus Day, Lincoln's Birthday, Memorial Day, Washington's Birthday, and "Miscellaneous"). Soon other holidays such as Thanksgiving, Christmas, Valentine's Day, and Easter were added to the list. New holidays such as Arbor Day, Flag Day, and Labor Day were included following their introduction. Irish's *Days We Celebrate* (1904) has entries for Arbor Day, Christmas, Easter, Flag Day, the Fourth of July, Halloween, Labor Day, Lincoln's Birthday, Memorial Day, New Year's, Saint Valentine's, Thanksgiving, and Washington's Birthday, while Kellogg's

Special Day Exercises (1911) even includes daily exercises for Shakespeare, Emerson, Longfellow, and "Michael Angelo"![15]

Individual holidays had their own booklets as well (figure 26). One of the first anthologies dedicated solely to Thanksgiving, Schell's *Thanksgiving Celebrations* (1901),[16] contained a variety of materials including President McKinley's 1900 Thanksgiving proclamation, Mrs. Hemans' "The Landing of the Pilgrims," songs with musical notation, scriptural readings, recitations, and "exercises" or dramatizations, and closed with a suite of songs celebrating rural themes from spring through harvest. The exercises were characteristic of the time, involving fairy-tale elements such as brownies, or personifications on the order of "Spice Boys," "Milk Maids," and "the Goddess of Pumpkin Pies." In addition, there were the standard Pilgrims and modern children. A monologue on the "First Thanksgiving" by Pauline Bristow conflates Jane G. Austin with Longfellow to arrive at a Thanksgiving description that ends with the acceptance of Alden's famous proposal. There are even echoes of the old-fashioned holiday storytelling with versions of "Bluebeard" and "The Legend of Sleepy Hollow." This wide range of activities, intended to meet the needs of all ages and grades, was repeated in teachers' magazines and other supplementary collections of Thanksgiving materials published and reprinted during the next few decades. Variety also helped ensure that teachers who were destined to repeat the seasonal round year after year would not become bored.[17] Elizabeth Pleck found that "[b]y the 1920s, Thanksgiving was the most celebrated holiday in the schools, edging out Christmas by a single percentage point, according to one survey of elementary school principals."[18]

Some collections, such as the one by Schauffler or Dickinson's *Children's Book of Thanksgiving Stories* (1916),[19] contained stories and poems drawn from previously published books and magazines, while others were made up of original if pedestrian selections. The themes were predictable and repetitive, with turkeys, pumpkins, and Pilgrims heading the list. Other recitations, exercises, and verse dealt with the Victorian themes of harvest, dyspeptic nightmares suffered by greedy little boys, adventures with hostile Indians (except these are resolved happily for all), humorous monologues in rural dialect, and contemporary holiday dinners. There were again exercises involving Mother Goose rhymes or personified Thanksgiving foodstuffs and allegorical figures. Unlike our contemporary trend of employing popular characters from TV cartoons or storybooks in Thanksgiving situations, the activities included in these collections almost always employed generic nursery-tale characterizations, except in the case of Pilgrims and Indians.

Much of the content was predictably sentimental or cute and perky, although it was at times less condescending than some of today's didactic

26. Thanksgiving exercise books for use in schools (1923–1940). Marie Irish, *Choice Thanksgiving Entertainments* (Dayton, Ohio: Paine Publishing Co., 1923); Mayme R. Bitney, *Thanksgiving in the Primary Grades* (Dayton, Ohio: Paine Publishing Co., 1924); Effa E. Preston, *The Children's Thanksgiving Book* (Lebanon, Ohio: March Brothers, 1928); Helen Ramsey et al., *"That Good" Thanksgiving Book* (Syracuse, N.Y.: Willis N. Bugbee Co., 1940); Lettie C. Van Derveer, *Thanksgiving Plays and Ways* (Franklin, Ohio: Eldridge Entertainment House, 1927); Corinne B. Jones et al., *Thanksgiving in the Schoolroom* (Chicago, Ill: Beckley-Cardy Co., 1937).

Thanksgiving lessons for children. The Progressive-era lessons neither denigrated the colonists as oppressors nor exalted the Indians as some sort of indigenous natural phenomena, but represented them as real people in conflict:

> The white man has taken the Indians' land
> And made him a homeless ranger.
> So sharpen your knives with a will
> And drive from our home every stranger.[20]

Idealization of the past was common, but it was balanced by verses such as "I'm Glad I Am Not a Pilgrim" ("To be a Pilgrim might have been / A noble thing to do. / But I'd hate to lead a life like theirs, — / Now tell me, wouldn't you?")[21] or by a positive description of the contemporary holiday in contrast to "over the river and through the wood," as in "A Modern Thanksgiving" of 1928:

> We take the trolley car and ride
> Our forty miles or so,
> Where grandpa meets us with his car,
> And we onward speeding go.
>
> At Grandpa's house we do not mind
> The winter's cold or storm,
> For it's heated by a furnace
> That keeps it toasty warm.
>
> The roast turkey is delicious,
> Which isn't at all strange,
> For it's cooked in a modern roaster,
> In a fine electric range.
>
> After dinner when we're so full
> That we feel inclined to rest,
> The phonograph entertains us
> With whatever suits us best.
>
> And because it's inconvenient
> For us to church to go,
> We hear a Thanksgiving sermon
> That's sent out by radio.
>
> I'm glad it still remains for us,
> On this modern holiday,

To return thanks for our blessings,
In the good, old-fashioned way.[22]

Similarly, not all the characters were unrelievedly uplifting, as "Aunt Dismal's" monologue demonstrates:

Well, good morning Mary, No, I can't stay more'n a minute; I jest run in to see how you're feelin'. [*Sadly*] Oh, you think you're better? Weel, that's fine—if it's true. You can't allus tell 'bout these sicknesses. . . . I said to Ezry, says I, I've got to take time to run over an' cheer Mary up a little; she's likely to be feelin' dreadful doleful, bein' sick with Thanksgivin' so near at hand. . . . Well, if you do set up to eat Thanksgivin' dinner, though I don't have no idee you can, the way you look—as bad accordin' to my notion, as Lizzie Skaggs did the last time I saw 'er, a day or so 'fore she died, an' her a-thinkin' too, that she was gettin' better—well, if you do set up to eat Thanksgivin' dinner with you folks, I hope you'll not be too thankful that you're better, 'cause it'd be awful easy for you to have a relapse, 'specially if you eat much.[23]

There was also room for fervently religious selections that would no longer be publicly acceptable, as in Novotnoy and Wolfe's *Standard Thanksgiving Book No. 1* (1937) "God Is Love" Thanksgiving drill for ten junior high students:

[Student] NUMBER TWO [*presenting placard with the letter* O]—
Thanksgiving to me means Obeying.
I'll try in my tasks every day
To do just as Jesus has shown me;
In this way my thanks I'll say.[24]

Through the use of materials such as these, teachers across the country instilled generations of schoolchildren with a familiarity of Thanksgiving that would deeply influence public opinion about the holiday's significance. The ideal was to educate through participatory activity to ensure a more lasting impression than was attainable through everyday schoolwork. Progressive educators believed that students enjoyed the break from routine and were able to recall their role in a small skit, or having their work of art mounted on the bulletin board, better than information from just another lesson. This certainly seems to be true, although students might not necessarily remember the object lesson associated with the activity as well as they did the activity itself.

The anthologies and booklets furnished only half of the holiday equation. While the exercise books might give detailed instructions for making costumes out of cheesecloth or crepe paper and provide stage directions for little dramas or pantomimes, they were limited to textual information (few had any illustrations). Equally important in communicating the holiday's significance were new visual images that evoked the emotional associations of Thanksgiving—the turkey, the pumpkin, and the Pilgrims. Holiday decorations, displays, music, and visual aids (ranging over time from the stereopticon and magic lantern to slide and film projectors) utilized illustrations from books and magazines and gave them a new role as independent emblems of holiday awareness.

Teachers acquired images from school supply houses and stationers to display among artworks produced by their pupils to create an evocative holiday atmosphere about the classroom. Possibly families decorated their homes with the seasonal Thanksgiving images as well, although I have not come across any examples. When the demand for Thanksgiving Pilgrims began, the same problem my colleagues and I at Plimoth Plantation later encountered in the search for Victorian Thanksgiving images made itself apparent to the Progressive-era educators—there were no appropriate Pilgrim Thanksgiving pictures available. Schools had to make do at first with existing art showing Pilgrims in other situations, such as George H. Boughton's *Pilgrims on Their Way to Church* and the various representations of John and Priscilla Alden.[25] An early Thanksgiving souvenir booklet marketed to teachers for distribution to pupils as early as 1903 (and for several years thereafter, with different dates printed on the cover) has a Boughton image of John and Priscilla on the cover. Inside there is a poem, "The Story of the Pilgrim," with several images including a rough version of the 1897 W. L. Taylor *First Thanksgiving* and a generic picture of Indians in western tepees.[26] The Aldens appear to be the basis for the most common classroom Thanksgiving Pilgrim decorations, a male and female couple of marriageable age (with a generic Indian or Indian couples added for balance). Even today, Pilgrim-costumed couples, including squirrels, bears, rabbits, children, and similar "charming" kitsch figures, remain the most popular Thanksgiving theme after the turkey. All of them are ultimately takeoffs based on John and Priscilla Alden. It is possible that the impetus for the open-air Thanksgiving dinner of 1621 scenes by Brownscombe and Ferris was in part the demand for illustrations of the famous dinner suitable for display.

The market for Pilgrim images, whether to signify Thanksgiving or some other theme, had already encouraged artists to adopt a visual shorthand for the first colonists to make them easily identifiable, like a commercial brand. The stereotype of the "Pilgrim"—tall black hats with buckles and blunderbusses, Dutch-boy haircuts, and belted frock coats for the men; caps and cloaks for the women; and elaborate collars, cuffs, and buckled shoes for both—became indelibly established in the American psyche

27. Pilgrim stereotypes: Interwoven Socks advertisement, *Saturday Evening Post*, November 20, 1920, p. 68. This holiday ad combines nearly all the standard Pilgrim stereotypes—log cabins, buckled hats and shoes, blunderbusses, somber clothes, "Dutch boy" haircuts—that have since been exploded.

(figure 27). While some of these elements had historical justification, the overall effect was caricature and humorous distortion. The Pilgrims may have been honored ancestors, but they were also quaint, old-fashioned, and slightly absurd. For their role as holiday representatives, the plaster saints had to be taken off their pedestals and rendered more approachable and amusing.

The blunderbuss, for example, represented quaintness and the inefficient naïveté of these preindustrial people, who might be virtuous but could not invent railroads, telegraphs, or repeating rifles. The fact that the blunderbuss was never known to have been carried by colonial hunters was less significant than the fond condescension this object extended to those innocents in the wilderness. The odd haircut was borrowed from caricatures of contemporary revivalists and reformers, as were the sober clothing colors. The men's tall, wide-brimmed hats were not historically inaccurate (although the buckles were), but the combination of these hats with mid-thigh-length black coats and exaggerated white collars and cuffs simply made the Pilgrims into caricatures of respectable top-hatted mid-Victorian gentlemen.

The one symbol in particular that stands out is the buckle. Pilgrims are known above all by their buckles. Buckles were anachronistically shown on hats, shoes, belted frock coats, and even on women's caps and dresses on occasion. To the Victorians, the buckle, or more specifically the shoe buckle, was a universally accepted sign for anything old-fashioned or outmoded, just as high-buttoned shoes were for their descendants in the twentieth century. "Small clothes" (breeches and stockings) and shoe buckles had quite quickly gone out of fashion after 1790.[27] Buckled shoes suggested the Revolutionary War generation with its knee breeches and tricorn hats, in contrast to the long trousers and newer fashions of the nineteenth century. Similarly, long belted coats were associated with ancient times and preindustrial life, as is shown in the belted tunics found in contemporary melodrama and pantomime costuming for everyone from ancient Romans to Robin Hood. The Pilgrims were thus grouped with other iconic figures with whom they shared these prominent buckles on their belts, shoes, and hats—Santa Claus, witches, leprechauns, Mother Goose, giants—all of whom were mythical entities. The buckles of the Pilgrims marked them not only as historical but also as legendary—transcending the scope of simple history to become immortal beings forever enjoying their autumnal festivities.

The association of the First Thanksgiving legend with young students became so strong as to dominate the way in which that narrative was presented. As we noted earlier, almost all books about the First Thanksgiving or the Pilgrims were written for children. The process was analogous to the earlier shift in which fairy stories and classical myths, in becoming a part of every American's youthful education, lost their role as serious adult fare for several generations. However, while Thanksgiving-themed books became children's fare, short stories for adults with a holiday or seasonal theme continued to appear in ever greater numbers as the number of popular magazines increased at the end of the nineteenth century. Most of these short stories were of the sentimental sort—not unlike those written for children—that Jackson Lears cites as an antirealistic evasion of the true nature of American life.[28]

The next step was the integration of these Progressive-era images and ideals into American culture in a more modern fashion—through advertising and mass production. While the textual approach to Thanksgiving continued in the same old grooves, an unprecedented visual approach to codifying the Thanksgiving holiday began to appear in the 1880s in advertisements and greeting cards. The commodification of the Thanksgiving holiday was about to begin in earnest.

Imaging the Holiday

While both conservative leaders and progressive reformers sought to unite the nation within a civic religion embodying patriotic pieties and a calendar of secular holidays, the burgeoning consumer culture at the end of the nineteenth century undertook to unite the American public for quite a different purpose. For commerce to prosper on a nationwide scale, it was essential that consumers extend their commercial relations beyond the local community. They needed to try new products, adopt new patterns of consumption, and embrace national brands. Taking advantage of new printing technologies and means of distribution, advertisers and other promoters of products or ideas unleashed an unprecedented flood of graphic imagery in magazines, trade cards, postcards, greeting cards, product labels, and posters with a public impact was comparable to that of film, television, and digital imagery today. The flood of accessible images occurred at a time when advertisers and intellectuals alike were becoming fascinated with the power of imagery and the psychodynamics of advertising and propaganda for manipulating public opinion. The new graphics permeated the contemporary culture, with special importance in those areas which, as Kitch observed, "[dealt] in ideals rather than reality" such as holiday symbolism.[1]

One graphic medium that quickly achieved the status of a national fad was the trade card or "scrap." Like other advertisements, trade cards sought to impress potential consumers—of the card as well as the product it stood in for—by the striking nature of the printed image. The publication of these colorful lithographed cards began in the 1870s, combining advertising with the engrossing appeal of what we now call "collectibles."[2] Earlier cards such as the religious "Rewards of Merit" (Protestant) and "Holy Cards" (Catholic) and pioneering Valentine and Christmas cards approximated the same format but lacked the commercial function and mass distribution of the trade card. Trade cards might be published with generic pictures, on the back of which retailers could add their name and line of merchandise, or by nationwide manufacturers with specific reference to their products on the printed side. The demand for decorative variety in scraps was so great that almost every sort of image was used, including simple floral designs, pretty pictures of children, scenes from daily life, contemporary ethnic or racial humor, and holiday themes. The cards were given to storekeepers by salesmen for distribution to customers, who could paste them into the new "scrap" books. Those distributed by patent medicine companies and large manufacturers carried high-quality illustrations and texts directly touting their products.

In addition to trade cards, a few printers such as Louis Prang of Boston and Raphael Tuck of New York began to publish high-quality holiday greeting cards. Most of these "bric-a-brac" cards were printed on single-thickness cardboard, but some opened like modern greeting cards, came with a string to hang them by, or might have a curious silk fringe around the edge. The interaction between image and text varied a great deal on these early cards. The pretty (or humorous) picture was intended primarily to catch the eye and please the recipient, just as the advertising "scraps" enticed the consumer by being collectible "gifts." What the picture actually represented was at first unimportant. Christmas or Thanksgiving cards of the time might have summer scenes or floral images that are somewhat puzzling to the modern eye. One Prang card, for example, wished the recipient a happy Thanksgiving with an illustration of a group of monkeys going through someone's belongings—an image not remotely associated with the holiday. Another Prang Thanksgiving card has a bunch of cherries, which are a summer fruit, while an anonymous Thanksgiving card of the 1880s was die-cut in the shape of a tambourine with a picture of a dark-haired girl (a gypsy?) and flowers (figure 28). Only the captions "A Happy Thanksgiving Day to You" and "Thanksgiving Greetings" reveal their intent. The holiday is brought to mind through the text alone, and the image serves solely as an aesthetic hook to attract attention. Over time, as both the designers and their audience internalized a visual grammar of Thanksgiving, such solecisms as gypsies or cherries for Thanksgiving ceased to appear. The "artful planting of certain clues in a picture . . . allow[ed artists to perform] an act of ventriloquism, an act which endow[ed] the picture with eloquence, and particularly with a nonvisual and verbal eloquence" that not only said "Thanksgiving" loud and clear but also reinforced a number of assumptions about the holiday and its social meaning.[3]

Picture postcards almost entirely superseded the trade and bric-a-brac cards at the turn of the twentieth century (figure 29). They became popular

28. Thanksgiving greeting card, Louis Prang & Co., 1885; anonymous "Thanksgiving Greetings" die-cut "scrap" or trade card. Lithographed cards such as these were the forerunners of holiday postcards and modern greeting cards.

29. Postcards illustrating early twentieth-century Thanksgiving imagery (1906–1920). *Left to right, from upper left*: cook, pumpkin, and turkey (Raphael Tuck & Co., ser. 123); Pilgrim hunter bringing home turkey (Raphael Tuck & Co., ser. 161); harvest scenes (P. Sander); "Indian Peace Dinner, Thanksgiving Day 1620" (John Winsch, 1912); humor, "Turning the Tables" (Ullman Mfg., ser. 85); charity, "Thanksgiving Day in the South 1912" (John Winsch, 1912); topical, "For Labor, Thanksgiving Greetings" (ca. 1914); Dutch, "May you a nice Thanksgiving get" (F. A. Owen Co.); children (Whitney-Made, ca. 1923); colonial, "A Peaceful Thanksgiving," John and Priscilla (ca. 1909); traditional cookery, by Frances Brundage (artist) (Thanksgiving series, card 130); Columbia and Uncle Sam (P. Sander, 1906); Dyspeptic nightmare, "Enjoy and well digest" (Louis Prang Co., 1883); 1621 Plymouth "Harvest Feast" (Geo. Keith Co., Walkover Shoes).

first in Europe; because the U.S. Post Office charged two cents to mail privately printed cards while only charging one cent for its own cards, their use was initially limited in the United States. The first American "souvenir cards" were apparently published in conjunction with the 1893 Columbian Exposition. Beginning in 1898, however, all American postcards could be mailed for one cent. This sparked an enormous new fad for sending and collecting postcards that peaked between 1905 and 1915. Until the First World War, Germany was the largest supplier of American cards. Literally millions of cards were bought and sent or collected:

The sheer number of postcards sent through the mails at the height of their popularity is staggering. In 1906 the *Post Card Dealer* reported that Germany's annual consumption was 1,161,000,000; the United States', 770,500,000; and Great Britain's 734,500,000. Official United States Post Office figures for the year ending June 30, 1908, cite 667,777,789 postcards mailed in this country. By 1913 the total had increased to over 968,000,000, and by this date the craze was reportedly on the decline.[4]

In view of the huge numbers of unmailed cards that survive today in collections, even these numbers do not represent the full extent of the postcard's popularity. Postcard publishers often issued cards in series or sets sharing a common motif or symbolism. Having to compose yet another unique and attractive picture of a turkey for a postcard when hundreds if not thousands of turkey cards had already been published might strain the skills of the most original artist. Still the illustrations' popularity and ubiquity, and the fact that many of these images still have cultural resonance today, suggest that the art of the time had an important role in determining the manner in which future generations would conceive of Thanksgiving. The illustrations were originally very much the expression of a particular period and culture, but through their very profusion they contributed to the public's stock of mental concepts to the extent of being treated as natural rather than conventional signs, conveying the timeless and essential nature of the holiday.

Thanksgiving has always been a relatively minor player in the proliferation of holiday trade or postcard imagery in comparison to Christmas, Valentine's Day, and Halloween, but the representations that appeared at this time established a popular decorative idiom for the holiday in a way that the illustrations of the nineteenth century did not. When Thanksgiving illustrations begin to involve figurative meaning in imaginary depictions instead of colonial families at dinner (or under attack), the contrast between wealthy holiday indulgence and the deprivations of poverty, or humorous caricatures of black families enjoying modest dinners and reunions, the process shifts from reportage to social symbolism. The new medium of chromolithography and print technology made it possible to flood the market with imagery identified with Thanksgiving, which in turn strongly influenced the way in which people conceived of the holiday. It was no longer just a matter of personal memories and stories. Through involvement with new print media, Americans came to internalize and share a scheme of symbols that collectively said, This is what Thanksgiving *is*. The imagery of the cards and advertisements made recognizable icons out of turkeys, Pilgrims, pumpkins, and harvest feasts that spoke directly to the public audience. These pictures, in their easily accessible material formats, reinforced the opinions of the time about what constituted a real Thanksgiving—and, through the strength and ubiquity of the media, the newer autumnal theme became the culturally dominant definition of the holiday. Commerce and boosterism might sully tradition, but they could also reinforce and strengthen public appreciation of the event's significance by providing attractive stories and images tied to the holiday.

Any attempt to survey this immense and diverse assortment of ephemeral images would be incomplete, but a sampling reveals how a few visual themes emerged to become widely accepted emblems of the American Thanksgiving holiday in the first decades of the twentieth century. The most common icon of Thanksgiving is of course the turkey, which was already the primary "interpretant" or conventional symbol for the holiday.[5] As synecdochic emblem of the holiday dinner, the turkey had been the first image to achieve universal recognition as a Thanksgiving icon. Even before the new media appeared, the bird was the most popular Thanksgiving image. Turkeys figure in the great majority of the Thanksgiving postcard images and are found on trade cards and in advertising media as well. While there are many instances of simple, realistic representations of the holiday pièce de résistance (in both senses of the term, as the special dish for a meal and a showpiece or collector's item), the turkey also appears in fanciful and emblematic arrangements. For example, a Prang greeting card of 1885 presents a fantastic image of a well-dressed small girl seated on a tree branch beside a turkey, and she is being handed an ax by an owl (see figure 28). The card benefits not only from its very obvious turkey but also from the ax in connecting with the holiday, lest anyone think the girl is simply roosting with a convenient bird. The captionless Prang card seeks to attract attention and intrigue the viewer by its impossible subject matter and impressive color printing, without context or explanation. Thanksgiving is evoked as a mystery, an aesthetic experience that can be consumed without a text.

The live male turkey is almost always depicted strutting in majestic display (which is actually done only for a few minutes at a time) with puffed feathers and spread tail. Sometimes female birds are shown as well. The alternative is the turkey in culinary splendor—roasting, being sliced and served, or in a preparatory state fetched by a hunter, hanging plucked in a butcher's shop or as part of a selection of holiday provisions. As the puffed-out bird is a more attractive image than the plucked carcass, artists occasionally show fully feathered turkeys being served on platters! While the turkey by itself could stand for the holiday, it was frequently used in concurrence with other icons to definitively identify the illustration as "Thanksgiving." Even after the Pilgrims became accepted holiday symbols, they were more often than not accompanied by a turkey. The ultimate reductive Thanksgiving symbol today is a turkey wearing a Pilgrim hat.

Turkeys are depicted as mounts with children riding on their backs, or pulling carriages, or even driving automobiles and flying airships. Pilgrims are shown hunting turkeys or carrying them home. Contemporary children are depicted either playing with or being intimidated by the large birds, especially as having second thoughts when they are carrying hatchets with intent. One card circa 1914 carries a message of American progress by including a small image of a blacksmith labeled "For Labor" surrounded with airships and a railroad. Another (as one of a series) presents the turkey with top hat and opera cloak as the chief actor that "starred on the bill" — the bill of fare, that is. One set of cards associates the turkey with the Pilgrims by positioning small colonial pictures on the bird's expanded tail feathers. Humorous cards show the turkey's revenge in a poulterer's shop, where anthropomorphic birds buy little people for an autumn dinner and (on an 1883 Prang greeting card) contemplate a boy's head protruding from a pie (see figure 29). A curious convention was to show the turkey with a ribbon as a leash or reins held by Pilgrims or children. The notion of the turkey as bearing the burden of the holiday may have suggested these representations.

The next-most-frequent holiday icon is the child, usually depicted in groups (sometimes as miniature Pilgrims and Indians) in association with turkeys and harvest decorations. Adult Pilgrims and Indians are next, most commonly appearing independently but sometimes jointly (but not at dinner). Harvest icons such as pumpkins, corncobs or shocks, autumn leaves, nuts, and flowers were popular by themselves or in combination with the other themes using the contemporary layered style of graphic design derived ultimately from the Japanese composite format adopted by the Aesthetic Movement artists just when the first cards appeared, which also influenced the use of "scraps" in amateur artistic arrangements.[6] The unabashed patriotism of the era resulted in a large number of Thanksgiving images involving flags, red-white-and-blue bunting, Uncle Sam, and "Columbia," the allegorical feminine representation of the United States, later replaced by the Statue of Liberty. African Americans and the Dutch are the only non-Anglo or Native communities to be frequently associated with the holiday on postcards. There is also a miscellany of other images depicting traditional associations of the holiday including acts of charity, family reunions and dinners, holiday cookery, dyspeptic nightmares, and prayer.

Representations of Pilgrims and/or Indians (including children dressed as these) feature men hunting or being pursued by turkeys, and women preparing or serving them. The old convention of colonial violence appears as well, with Indian and Pilgrim men fighting over a turkey, but in other examples Indians are shown presenting birds to colonists. Earlier Pilgrim representations including their landing from the *Mayflower* and Boughton's *John and Priscilla* or *Pilgrims on Their Way to Church* are given Thanksgiving associations by the addition of turkeys or harvest produce, or by being framed in a "wishbone." The turkey's wishbone and the custom of pulling it to make a wish appears in various designs of cards and magazine covers until the 1960s, when it seems to have lost its popularity as a Thanksgiving trope.

Foods representing harvest bounty, including pumpkins, corn, fruit, and nuts, are frequently depicted on Thanksgiving cards, often in their more attractive raw state but on occasion as pies or cooked dishes. Autumn leaves, vines, and the occasional cornucopia turn up as regular elements. Cranberries appear as well, but since they cannot be identified as easily as the former items, the berries are less often given prominence in art despite the fact that they ranked just below the turkey as markers of an authentic Thanksgiving dinner. As we mentioned earlier, one image that does not appear is the now-familiar outdoor 1621 Thanksgiving dinner with Pilgrims and Indians together. The dinners portrayed are single-family events, whether of Pilgrims, Indians, children, or contemporary households.

Patriotic symbolism involving red-white-and-blue shields, flags, bunting, and Uncle Sam is perhaps as common as that of the Pilgrims. Compositions include Uncle Sam accompanying a turkey, in football costume, and dining alone (he is not a family man, apparently, although he sometimes shares the table with Columbia). Children appear in "Uncle Sam" or military costumes, and there is even a 1908 turkey with an "Uncle Sam" head, and another with a boy's—the artist may have become desperate in trying to come up with yet another turkey image. There are representations of football on cards, but it is not as common a theme as blacks preparing for or celebrating the holiday, for example, and the players are generally boys rather than college-age men. The use of African American imagery, on the other hand, is fairly diverse. It runs from common stereotypes of blacks trying to steal turkeys or roosters for their holiday dinner and black cooks and servants to socially neutral or even favorable depictions of black and Caucasian children playing together with turkeys and black families enjoying their own family reunions. One popular card (judging by the number that have survived to appear on eBay) is a posed photograph of a poor black family and a tiny log cabin titled "Thanksgiving Morning in the South." This card first appeared as early as 1906 but was still being

30. Two versions of a Thanksgiving card from Germany, "S. B. Series 7013", ca. 1911, on one of which the faces of the children are overprinted in black.

mailed in the late 1920s. The association of blacks with the holiday was even strong enough to allow the overprinting of white children's faces as black, in an alternative version of one card of German origin (figure 30).

The Dutch figures on cards are almost always children clad in traditional costume. They are accompanied with dialect captions such as "I hope dot you vill haf all de goot t'ings for Thanksgifing" or "By Chimineddy: Vot a Peacefulness Thanksgiving I done already wish you." As many of these seem to date from the 'teens and 'twenties, one wonders whether the "Dutch" card was a way for German-American family sentiments to be expressed in an acceptable manner in the xenophobic atmosphere during and after World War I. Another possible explanation for the popularity of both black and Dutch figures is that they, along with the Anglo colonists and Native Americans, could be considered as part of the original, pre-industrial population of the country. With the turkey for an emblem and the Pilgrim harvest feast as its foundation myth, Thanksgiving emerged as a modern holiday with few commercial customs, but rich in its own decorative paraphernalia.

Although holiday postcards continued to be exchanged until World War II, competition from single-sided and French-fold greeting cards sent in envelopes began in the mid-1920s, and these eventually superseded the postcards. The images on the new greeting cards convey the same themes represented earlier on the trade cards and postcards, but they are usually simpler on the new cards, and more emphasis is put on the written senti-ment. Turkeys, fall themes, Pilgrims, and blacks were continued as favor-ites, to which were added chrysanthemums, "Dad" cards depicting ducks in flight, and humorous cards intended for young recipients. Thanksgiving failed to become a major card-mailing occasion comparable to Christmas, birthdays, Valentine's Day, Easter, Halloween, and St. Patrick's Day. Today there is always a modest selection of Thanksgiving and general autumnal cards and decorations available in stores, sandwiched between huge as-sortments of Halloween and "Xmas" sections, but the effort by greeting card publishers to capitalize on the holiday has not been an equal success.

Other Thanksgiving imprints appeared in the 1910s as schoolroom decorations, gummed stickers, bridge tallies, and crepe-paper nut cups and place cards for the holiday table (figure 31). The images one finds on these are almost always limited to the hard-core Thanksgiving sym-bols—turkeys, Pilgrims, Indians, and pumpkins. As with greeting cards, Thanksgiving ephemera were never as abundant as the comparable Hal-loween and Christmas materials. The die-cut or honeycomb-tissue turkey was among the first Thanksgiving home decorations. One example is a "Turkey Gobbler Centerpiece" patented in 1926. Papier-mâché turkey-shaped candy containers manufactured in Germany, which have since become valuable collectors' items, enjoyed seasons of popularity when not interrupted by wartime interdiction.[7] By the Second World War, these objects were a regular part of the holiday observation and the images they bore an accepted element of popular culture. Decorations made from paper, wax, glass, pottery, and fabric constituted a materialization of the holiday spirit.

Holidays were an obvious choice as vehicles for magazine advertising as well. Revolutionary advances in rotary press printing and color lithog-raphy at the end of the nineteenth century created the first modern mass

31. Holiday decorations, *center*: table decoration, Pilgrim couple, ca. 1920; *perimeter, clockwise from upper left*: bridge tally, Hallmark Cards, ca. 1925; mechanical card, Pilgrim vs. Indian turkey tug-of-war, ca. 1920; bridge tally, Indian maiden, ca. 1910; crepe-paper nut cups, "Yrrah" and "Eltrym" (Harry & Myrtle), E. A. Reed Co., ca. 1930; bridge tally, Pilgrim and turkey, ca. 1910.

medium, the mass-circulation popular magazine. Supported by advertising rather than sales, serials such as the *Saturday Evening Post, Ladies Home Journal, Munsey's,* and *McClure's* could afford to sell for only ten or fifteen cents an issue and achieve impressive circulation figures. They employed eye-catching pictorial ads to entice the reader and made liberal use of illustrations in the text, but their most impressive graphic feature was usually the cover illustration. The serious monthlies and some other serials retained traditional "text only" covers, but the new mass-market magazines employed striking cover art. Between 1880 and 1930, a period now commonly referred to as the "golden age of American illustration" (although the same advances took place in England, France, and elsewhere), magazines recruited some of the most successful artists of the day to the business of illustration, and magazine cover art achieved a greater cultural impact than at any time before or since. Skillful illustrators and artists were very well paid, and many became celebrities in their own right, including Howard Pyle, Charles Dana Gibson, A. B. Frost, Howard Chandler Christy, Jessie Wilcox Smith, J. C. Leyendecker, and later Maxfield Parrish, John Held, and Norman Rockwell. Magazine covers might use fanciful themes and stylized images, such as Leyendecker's turkey-carving cherub (*Saturday Evening Post*, November 13, 1909), and humorous cartoons of generic Puritans interacting with Indian maidens or in competition over the holiday turkey ("More Witchcraft," *Life*, November 1919, and *American Boy*, November 1927), but they as often presented realistic vignettes.

Thanksgiving magazine cover art was at best intermittent—few serials consistently used holiday symbolism on their November issue covers. Once realistic and photographic cover illustration became the norm in the 1930s, the practical difficulty of rendering Pilgrims or old-fashioned dinner preparation limited the field for some magazines to available images of turkeys (live and cooked), pumpkins, football, and contemporary dinner scenes. The child covetously eyeing the roast turkey during grace was one trope that flourished in midcentury magazine cover photos only to disappear in the shift of illustrative fashion to more realistic images in the 1960s. Putting a Pilgrim hat on models was another easy option, so that anyone from cartoon characters such as Dagwood or Donald Duck to the classic turkey itself might appear with this attribute on a holiday cover.

Children's magazines such as *Harper's Young People, Youth's Companion, Jack and Jill, Child Life, American Boy*, and *St. Nicholas* frequently used holiday cover art, as did humorous serials such as the old *Life* magazine, *Puck*, and *Judge*, although the latter covers were most often caricatures of a political nature. Later, *Mad Magazine* and *National Lampoon*, neither of which relied on photographs, occasionally used well-known themes in similar irreverent ways. Bimonthly and weekly titles such as *Liberty*, the *Saturday Evening Post, Collier's*, and the *New Yorker*, which went through more image ideas than the monthly magazines, found Thanksgiving a useful theme. Comic books regularly used Thanksgiving themes (sometimes without any accompanying holiday stories) of mostly Pilgrims and turkeys, even as early as the cover of *Fun Comics* (November 1937) on which a boy with a blunderbuss is overawed by a huge turkey. Women's magazines such as *Good Housekeeping, McCall's, Ladies Home Journal, Ladies' World*, and *Comfort* featured sentimental or humorous Thanksgiving images in the earlier part of the twentieth century, but by the 1960s they shifted to more mundane and photographical arrangements such as still lifes of the holiday dinner or cute kittens. *Country Gentleman* magazine often used Thanksgiving themes, perhaps because of their agrarian associations.

The same illustrative tropes turned up over and over again. The turkey, of course, in all its guises; Pilgrim and Indian men meeting during a turkey hunt or overindulging in a holiday dinner; the intimidation of women and children by enormous turkeys; bringing home the raw materials of a dinner; watching mother (or grandmother) prepare a pie or baste a roasting turkey; dinnertime prayers; looking covetously at the yet-uncarved turkey; pulling wishbones; and young wives struggling with dinner preparations—all these appear on many holiday covers. The *New Yorker* and *Saturday Evening Post* covers, on the other hand, presented more imaginative and varied holiday illustrations. One old favorite, in which children are seen providing poor families with baskets of food for a Thanksgiving dinner, faded away by the mid–twentieth century as charity became more formalized and impersonal donations to organizations replaced gifts in kind. Another popular image was of the "old-fashioned" Thanksgiving—harking back not to Pilgrim times, but to the childhood of the middle-aged people who were buying the magazine or products it advertised. In magazines published in the late nineteenth century, the scenes are from the 1820s to the 1840s (and occasionally earlier); by the 1920s, the 1880s were "olde tyme"; and from about 1930 to 1970, the "Gay Nineties" represented the nostalgic holiday past, in which cast-iron stoves and quaint turn-of-the-century costumes evoked the unspoiled traditions of the holiday. Today, the 1950s and 1960s appear to have become our contemporary nostalgic holiday past.

Thanksgiving advertising seems to have gotten a relatively late start— few items were presented with explicit Thanksgiving images until after 1920, in contrast to Christmas appeals, which appeared thirty or forty years earlier. Probably this was because there was very little commercial appeal to a holiday centered mainly on the consumption of a home-cooked meal. No traditional candy, floral, or gift exchange had evolved. An early example from the November 1904 issue of *Life* magazine simply frames an ad for the Equitable Insurance Company with a wishbone and a sentiment beginning "Wishes are good / When backed by deeds." By the mid-1920s, however, advertisers were designing special holiday ads, no matter how remote any logical connection between their product and Thanksgiving might have been.

Most of the ads were connected with food products, which had the most obvious connection with the culinary emphasis of the holiday, but other products used Thanksgiving imagery as well. Waterman's "Ideal Fountain

Pen" had a seasonally decorated ad with turkeys and corn in 1904,[8] and in 1951 Carter's "Trig" presented a man (with blunderbuss and Pilgrim hat pierced with an arrow) and boy (with feathers in his hair) clad only in their underwear following a turkey drum major. Interwoven Socks had Norman Rockwell do a "Thanksgiving violence" picture showing an appalled Pilgrim with blunderbuss amid a flock of fleeing turkeys and flying arrows in 1922.[9] Perhaps the long hose displayed by a man in knee breeches appealed to the Interwoven Advertising Department.

During World War II and after, Thanksgiving ads more often took the Pilgrims to be serious exemplars rather than figures of fun. As Jackson Lears notes, "The effort to ally advertising with the American Way of Life, begun in the dark day of the Great Depression, came to full fruition in the ideologically charged atmosphere of the Cold War."[10] The Cold War inspired INCO (International Nickel Company) to use a classic outdoor Pilgrim Thanksgiving scene (identified as 1623) in the *Saturday Evening Post* in November 1950 to advertise its support of the free-market system. The John Hancock Insurance Company published a "primitive" First Thanksgiving scene in the November 10, 1951, issue of the *Post* captioned "They showed us a secret of happiness," with similar political intent. The earthtoned scene includes one of the odder recurrent Thanksgiving images — the suspension of an entire unskinned deer by its legs over a fire. While the idea for this image may have originated from the practice of singeing bristles off a pig carcass, a deer hung in the fashion shown would not cook (as it would not revolve on the spit or supporting pole) but rather be immolated as a curiously impractical sacrifice.[11] One supposes that like the big cauldron that usually accompanies the suspended deer in these scenes, the image was intended to convey a primitive "ox-roast" sort of event, reinforcing, as the blunderbuss does, the virtuous naïveté of the poor Pilgrims. Some companies issued Thanksgiving advertising on other media. The C. D. Kenney Grocery Company produced a series of small, lithographed tin "tip plates" as holiday premiums for Thanksgiving in the 1910s. By the mid–twentieth century, however, coffee, cigarettes, Coca-Cola, wine, liquor, beer, TV dinners, canned goods, and Jell-O were all being offered as first-rate Thanksgiving staples, and the Pilgrim feast was presented as a shining example of American consumerism, courtesy of Madison Avenue.

It is not the medium but the evolution of the specific symbol system associated with Thanksgiving that is of importance here. Originally Thanksgiving was known to Americans only through personal experience of the holiday and its activities, or by verbal descriptions of the occasion. Turkeys were just wild or barnyard fowl fit for a feast — not icons — and the Pilgrims were not associated with the holiday at all. The first illustrations pertaining to Thanksgiving were simple depictions of family dinners or prayers and other scenes drawn from literary descriptions including homecomings, after-dinner amusements, home culinary preparation, and wartime dinner contrivances. These were all realistic rather than symbolic representations denoting what was generally understood to be characteristic of a standard Thanksgiving Day.

Americans internalized the stream of images and accompanying texts they encountered in schools, magazines, and stores so that it became their own personal comprehension of the holiday. As Salomon discusses, "similarity or dissimilarity pertains to the mentally-stored referent rather than to a 'real' one. Whether a film about ancient Rome is or is not a realistic depiction in one's eyes depends on what one knows already about the topic, the historical or archaeological faithfulness of the movie notwithstanding."[12] People usually judge the veracity of a representation by comparing it with preexisting conceptions—not some external, objective reference—and if those conceptions have been "stacked" by an unconscious adoption of what the media have shown, then media stereotypes are what appear genuine. New information is assimilated most easily if it can fit in with what has already been learned—that is, if it agrees with our preconceptions—so what we accept often tends to support what we already think. If our opinions of Thanksgiving were determined by the imagery we were exposed to in grade school, then those opinions (which derived from the illustrations and ideas of the time under discussion here) will always seem more real than alternatives we are offered later, such as those which criticize the common stereotypes. Unprecedented ideas take much more effort to assimilate, and if they are too strange or we are not particularly concerned with testing our prejudices, they are likely to be rejected whether they are more accurate or not.

Once the print media created a new, multifarious symbol system for the holiday, an "authentic" Thanksgiving had to involve turkey dinners, Pilgrims and Indians, family reunions, and autumnal associations, whatever an individual's earlier conception of it might have been. The old Thanksgiving, which was part of a New England holiday tradition that was contingent on events rather than fixed in time, and was associated with snowy early-winter days and regional or individual family custom (such as begging for handouts on Massachusetts' North Shore or in New York City), lost its claim on reality. The "real" holiday was now and *had always been* a harvest celebration that began with the 1621 "First Thanksgiving" and involved football, patriotism, and family values. Anything decked out with the well-known symbols of turkeys and Pilgrims, whether advertised, decorated, or simply referenced, was unquestionably "Thanksgiving-istic." This symbol system maintained its strong hegemonic status in American culture, despite occasional challenges, until the late 1960s. It also determined what was sought in the history of the holiday, making it impossible for researchers and writers to see the past in any other light regardless of the evidence.

Parades, Patriotism, and Consumption

A new holiday event emerged in the 1920s—the Thanksgiving Day parade. Strictly speaking, Thanksgiving parades are not about Thanksgiving at all but Christmas, yet they do provide a Thanksgiving Day activity that is enjoyed by millions of Americans in person or on TV. Initiated by downtown department stores to signal the "official" start of the Christmas shopping season, the parades were family-oriented events that became very popular in those cities that supported them. Going to see the holiday parade has become a tradition for many families, and after World War II televised Thanksgiving parades were eagerly enjoyed in living rooms across the country. Linda Young of the Flying Dreams website, who grew up in Cranston, Rhode Island, remembers watching televised parades in the early 1960s. "Back then, we didn't have a Walt Disney parade or one from Hawaii, but three others: Gimbel's parade from Philadelphia, J. L. Hudson's from Detroit, and the Eaton Santa Claus Parade in Toronto. Gimbel's parade was sure to have a smattering of mummers, and the Eaton's parade always featured storybook characters, including British ones that I'd never heard of except on the morning of the parade."[1] This sort of memory is shared by millions of Americans who grew up in the early days of television.

There had been parades on Thanksgiving in the nineteenth century, but these were the informal marches by groups of "Anticks" or "Fantastics" who also paraded on Christmas, New Year's, Washington's Birthday, and the Fourth of July.[2] "In New York City and Philadelphia, the Fantastics held elaborate parades, enlisting other groups and marching bands. In the late nineteenth century in lower Manhattan the event began at the call of a horn. Costumed men staggered out of saloons where they had been given free drinks. They mounted horses and carts for their parade. Along the way they would stop briefly to blow a horn into the ears of women spectators

32. *Street Gamins in Carnival Costume — Thanksgiving Day,* from *Outing,* January, 1904, p. 271. These Halloween-like disguises worn by children on Thanksgiving in New York City recall similar "anticks" on the North Shore in Massachusetts fifty years before.

crowded along the sidewalks. At the end of the parade they feasted on turkey and drink at an afternoon picnic, where fistfights often broke out. The evening ball that followed went on until the early morning."[3] These parades were accompanied by children dressed in rough costumes (figure 32) who begged for money in the manner of those on the North Shore of Massachusetts mentioned earlier.

These raucous events were considered a quaint and amusing custom until the labor troubles following the Chicago Haymarket Riot (1886) and other confrontations between protesting workers or unruly mobs and civic authorities unnerved public opinion, which quickly shifted to opprobrium, and the parades were denounced as occasions for dangerous violence. The child beggars survived for a while, but that custom eventually faded way— perhaps by being superseded by "trick or treat" activities at Halloween. Like so many other areas in American popular culture, Thanksgiving had become a "safe and sane" sentimental occasion.

Aimed at the hearts of children and the pocketbooks of their parents, Thanksgiving parades presented a fairy-tale atmosphere that had a minimum of Thanksgiving themes and imagery. They represented a sort of penance offered by a noncommercial holiday to the greater good of the nation's merchants. However, such parades quickly became as much a part of our modern Thanksgiving customs as football or family reunions. The first Thanksgiving parade was put on by the Gimbel Brothers Department Store in Philadelphia on November 25, 1920. It consisted of fifty people, fifteen cars, and a fireman dressed as Santa Claus who marched in the parade and then entered the Gimbels Toy Department by a ladder.[4] The central feature of the Gimbels Thanksgiving Parade, like all similar parades, was the "official arrival of Santa Claus" in his most marketable guise as patron saint of holiday commerce. The Philadelphia parade was sponsored until 1985 by Gimbels, which went out of business the following year. Sponsorship was then taken up by the local ABC-TV affiliate, WPVI–6, which has managed the event since then, taking on Boscov's Department Store as a partner in 1995.

The theme of children and toys was central to the early Thanksgiving parades, with many of the floats and costumed characters designed to represent nursery rhyme and fairy-tale settings. The Thanksgiving parade instituted by J. L. Hudson's Department Store in Detroit in 1924 was based on nursery rhyme and fairy-tale themes, with floats featuring "The Old Lady Who Lived in a Shoe" and Mother Goose herself. "Charles Wendel, display director at Hudson's, started the popular Detroit event after seeing festive carnival parades in Europe and Toronto. It was considered to be a benefit of working at Hudson's to be chosen to be among the parade marchers."[5]

Besides Santa, a favorite Thanksgiving parade figure was "Christmas Carol" (later known as "the girl with the patent-leather bangs").

Maureen Bailey, . . . a 15-year-old student at Little Flower High School in Birmingham, Michigan . . . created the legendary Detroit character of Christmas Carol. . . . Christmas Carol was designed to be Santa's helper. Her duties began on Thanksgiving day, when both she and Santa would accept the key to the city from Detroit mayor Al Cobo, at the end of the Hudson's Thanksgiving Day Parade. A special area on the 12th floor of Hudson's was created just for Christmas Carol to receive the children before their visit with Santa. Christmas Carol also got a chance to showcase her lovely singing voice by performing holiday songs for the youngsters. . . . Maureen played Christmas Carol from 1953 to 1955.[6]

The Hudson's parade grew in size and elaboration (there were eight brass bands and 1,008 characters in 1939), to become an annual tradition beloved of Detroiters (figure 33). "Hudson's remained the primary sponsor of the event until 1979, when the it was taken over by Detroit Renaissance. In 1983, the not-for-profit Michigan Thanksgiving Parade Foundation assumed the reins. The Parade Company, which was established as a subsidiary of the Foundation, has produced the parade since 1990. The Detroit parade is one of three major American parades [including those of New York and Philadelphia] that are nationally televised on Thanksgiving Day."[7] After a hiatus during World War II, the parade continued as before, first appearing on TV in 1948, and nationally broadcast from 1952.

In Chicago, the Thanksgiving parade was not originally the product of a department store but was introduced by the State Street Council in 1934 to help stir up sales during the depth of the Depression. The State Street Parade was taken over by the city in 1967, by McDonald's in 1984, and by Brach's Confections in 1990, becoming Marshall Field's Jingle Elf Parade in 1998, and it has been managed by Target Stores since 2002.[8] Some of its famous characters have been Weiboldt's "Cinnamon Bear"(1937), Montgomery Wards' "Rudolph the Red Nosed Reindeer" (1939), and Marshall Field's "Uncle Mistletoe" (1948).

Like Hudson's parade in Detroit, the most famous Thanksgiving parade of all also began in 1924, when the employees of Macy's Department Store volunteered to conduct a parade of costumed characters in New York. Now billed as "America's Parade," the Macy's parade has grown over the years into a spectacular media event and a continually changing mirror of popular culture. The first Macy's parade, in which the predominantly immigrant employees marched six miles down Manhattan from 145th Street to 34th Street, featured Santa Claus and Mother Goose, thirty-five clowns, and animals borrowed from the Central Park Zoo. It finished much as the

33. Thanksgiving parade sponsored by J. L. Hudson's Department Store, Detroit, ca. 1955. Obviously, the nineteenth-century ideal of a "white Thanksgiving" is still possible.

Gimbels parade had, with Santa entering the Toy Department via a ladder. Three years later the animals were replaced with inflated rubber figures (not true balloons) supported by handlers on poles and designed by puppeteer and illustrator Tony Sarg—"upside down marionettes," they were called. In 1928, Sarg designed the first true parade balloons, which were made with rubberized silk. These were maneuvered by rope guys as the modern ones are. When the parade finished, the balloons were released, but because helium expands with elevation, they burst even before they cleared the top of the Macy's building. The 1929 balloons had safety valves and sailed impressively away (there was a reward for returning them).[9] Macy's stopped releasing the balloons after one of them was demolished in a collision with an airplane in 1932.[10]

Like the Detroit parade, the Macy's parade evolved and increased in size, with floats, marchers, bands, and other attractions. In 1934, Walt Disney worked with Sarg to add his popular cartoon figures to the mix. The New York parade was also interrupted by the war but returned bigger than ever in 1945, when it was televised by NBC for local broadcasting, going national in 1948. The *Life* magazine history of the event declared: "It was about Christmas, yes, but in the oblique, even ecumenical, way that Mardi Gras is about Lent. Christmas gave Macy's a reason, but wasn't the only reason. Thanksgiving Day . . . was as central to the parade's ethos as Christmas. So the parade was energetic, spirited, showy, democratic, secular and non-secular. It looked like America."[11] Thanksgiving symbolism has always gotten short shrift, however. There have been turkey balloons and Indian and Pilgrim figures (although the latter was soon recycled as a football player), but the huge inflatables were far more often designed as toys, cartoon characters, and similar images. They followed fashion by going from Felix the Cat and Popeye in the early parades to newer characters such as Mickey Mouse, Superman, Underdog, Snoopy, Kermit the Frog, and Arthur the Aardvark. Santa has remained the central character and apparently deposed Mother Goose by claiming the huge goose throne on a float.

There are Thanksgiving parades in many communities today: Houston, Pittsburgh, Baltimore, Silver Springs, San Francisco, and even Hawaii. One of the newest traditions is the establishment of an annual Thanksgiving parade in Plymouth, Massachusetts. The Plymouth Rock Foundation now manages this parade, which was introduced following the 375th anniversary of the Pilgrims in 1995 largely through the efforts of Joseph McStowe, the owner of Isaac's Restaurant. It is not held on the holiday itself, when there is more than enough going on in town, but on the preceding Saturday. Unlike the more traditional events, it is resolutely focused on the meaning and significance of Thanksgiving and its place in the patriotic history of the country.

In addition to the parades, there were other developments in the American vision of Thanksgiving and the Pilgrims in the early twentieth century. The 1920s were a period in which romantic nostalgia for the colonial era was growing ever stronger. The middle class had embraced the aesthetics of the Colonial Revival, taken up antique collecting, and embraced Wallace Nutting's sentimental images. Americans painted their Victorian woodwork white, and new school buildings just *had* to be pseudo-Georgian in style. Meanwhile, intellectuals and trendsetters seized on Modernist art, architecture, and innovative design in furnishings. They too painted their trim white, and their walls as well. The stated objective of both parties was "honesty" and "simplicity." As Kammen puts it, "The crucial point is that the interwar decades were permeated by both modernism and nostalgia in a manner that may be best described as perversely symbiotic. That is, each one flourished, in part, as a critical response to the other. Most of the time, however, there was little if any recognition that an oxymoronic condition persisted: nostalgic modernism."[12] Rather like the contemporary college buildings that were built to a "streamlined gothic" metaphor, the era tended to blend past and present together. Despite or perhaps because of this cultural schizophrenia, Thanksgiving and its Pilgrim patrons continued to enjoy an uncritical popularity encompassing nostalgic feasting and family reunions. The now-conventional division between the Pilgrims and the Puritans allowed people to agree to laud the Plymouth contingent despite all efforts by critics to lump the two together in a genealogy of American woe. The social criticism of the period had little or no effect on the Thanksgiving holiday, in contrast to the effects that more recent vilification of colonists of all stripes, from Columbus on down, has had on our contemporary holiday observations.

A social complex that combined tendencies ranging from Babbittry to parlor Reds makes historical clarification of the mid–twentieth century tricky. For example, the visibility of the Popular Front and similar leftist initiatives has encouraged the notion that the country was leaning strongly toward that end of the political spectrum during the 1930s. Yet it was only the far ends of the political spectrum — the sanguine Left and the fearful Right — that actually anticipated imminent revolution:

This was not the Red Decade. Revolution was not in the air. A writer who traveled across the nation to learn what people were thinking concluded: "Only lawyers and bankers talk of revolution."[13]

Although the radicalism of the decade has become a commonplace in popular history, it mistakes the influence of an articulate (and often conflicted) minority for a major tendency in American opinion. There was certainly a broad current of radical thought and ambition among the intelligentsia that spurred artists and writers to try to make sense of the Depression and find some dramatic way to fix things. However, would-be revolutionaries and socially committed artists discovered unprecedented depths of suffering and confusion where they hoped to find anger and resistance. The fatalism and sense of failure that many poor people exhibited made it clear that "the people" were not about to rise up against capitalism.

The majority of Americans considered themselves middle class even during the depth of the Depression, and did not believe either socialism or communism had the answer to their problems.[14] Economically challenged, bewildered by the collapse of old certainties, and afraid for the future, they abandoned the easygoing manners and flirtation with radicalism of the 1920s in a search for security and the reinforcement of traditional American mores.[15] In fact, as Kammen observes, "By the mid-1930s, even the American left had joined [the] tradition-oriented bandwagon, albeit for its own political reasons. As Michael Gold wrote in the *Daily Worker* in 1935: 'The chief battleground in the defense of culture against fascist barbarism is in the question of the national tradition.' Some years later Esther Forbes, the New England novelist and folklorist, would look back and observe that

during the depression the United States became 'very curious about her
own past. . . . It was then the word "American" moved from the library
shelf to the cocktail lounge.'"[16]

One common element in the interwar search for affirmative history
was an emphasis on common people and everyday life in contrast to the
earlier tendency to single out elite culture and superior individuals. The
importance of folk culture was one thing that the Right and Left agreed
on, although it held very different meanings for each. The contemporary
interest in folklore, popular arts and crafts, and local customs that led to
revivals in folk songs, dance, crafts, and an expressed respect for "the common man" in progressive circles led more conservative groups to establish
historic houses and open-air museums such as Colonial Williamsburg
and Greenfield Village. The latter offered exhibits celebrating "rugged in-
dividualism," pioneer self-sufficiency, and American ingenuity alongside
elite artifacts and arts.

The most notorious example of the effect of commerce on the modern
holiday happened during Franklin Delano Roosevelt's administration. In
1939, the last Thursday in November was also the last day of the month. A
Thanksgiving this close to Christmas would considerably reduce the customary shopping season, a prospect that dismayed the members of the National Retail Dry Goods Association. President Roosevelt was petitioned
by the association to declare an earlier date for Thanksgiving to ensure
the commercial success of the crucial holiday shopping season. When the
last Thursday fell on November 30 in 1933, the association had made the
same appeal and had been refused, but this time the president listened. On
October 31, Roosevelt proclaimed Thursday, November 23, as the national
day of Thanksgiving. The result was a storm of protest.

A majority of Americans were dismayed by the apparent victory of
commerce over tradition — not to mention the confusion that this change
caused on college football schedules. The dispute carried over to the states
and cities, where some governors and mayors followed Washington while
others chose to keep the thirtieth as Thanksgiving in protest. In the end,
twenty-three states had Thanksgiving on November 23, twenty-three held
out for November 30, and two (Texas and Colorado) had two Thanksgivings that year. A similar division happened in 1940, when many states kept
their holiday on November 28 despite the fact that Roosevelt had declared
the twenty-first as Thanksgiving. In the spring of 1941, the president admitted that the effort had been a mistake (and a failure as well — there had
been no improvement in Christmas sales, perhaps owing to the confusion)
and announced that Thanksgiving would revert to its traditional date in
1942. The confusion was immortalized in the movie *Holiday Inn* (1942) in

a cartoon segment where a harried turkey has trouble figuring out which date to alight upon.

It was too late for 1941; calendars and schedules had already been prepared. In Plymouth, Massachusetts, the selectmen voted to go along with the November 20 date, which had been set by the president and the governor of the Commonwealth, despite the strong protest of Selectman James T. Frazier, "who declared that Plymouth, above all towns, being where Thanksgiving originated, should be consistent as of past years and not yield to an unwarranted proclamation."[17] Congress passed a law in November 1941 mandating the fourth Thursday in November as the permanent date for the Thanksgiving holiday. This was a compromise between the old "last Thursday" custom and the recent "Franksgiving" observances. After the few holdouts gave up their attempts to observe the day on the last Thursday regardless, the Thanksgiving holiday quietly assumed its place in the regular round of American holidays. The holiday was at last as Mrs. Hale had wished, legally sanctified and nationally guaranteed.[18]

During this same period, the association of Thanksgiving with Plymouth and the Pilgrims was fully realized. As we noted earlier, the connection was not yet dominant enough in 1920 to have the "First Thanksgiving" included among the scenes of Plymouth's massive Pilgrim Spirit pageant of 1921, and it only gradually gained ground thereafter. Separate, deeply rooted Pilgrim and Thanksgiving traditions existed in Plymouth as elsewhere in New England, against which the new holiday symbolism made slow headway. It might have been thought that Plymouth would jump at an opportunity to claim ownership of a national holiday, but such was not the case. In fact, the manner in which the First Thanksgiving slowly became part of the town's self-definition is an excellent parallel to the way the concept was adopted across America.

The Thanksgiving following the successful 1621 tercentenary celebration was not remarked on in the local newspaper, the *Old Colony Memorial*, although there were numerous ads for Thanksgiving provisions and a letter from Ada Brewster about the situation of Miss Charlotte Mitchell ("Princess Wontonekanaske"), a descendant of Massasoit. During the 1920s editorials noted that the "first Thanksgiving" had been celebrated by the Pilgrims at Plymouth, but this fact was given no more importance than it might have had anywhere in the country. At the same time, the appearance of Pilgrim images in ads or as decorations was increasing in the *Old Colony Memorial*. Plymouth had football games and Thanksgiving balls (sponsored by the local Girls' Club and other organizations), and its restaurants advertised Thanksgiving dinners without any effort to proclaim any unique local status of the holiday, and nothing of a historical nature was alluded to. In 1924 a large header had a classic Pilgrim man draped across the front page, but aside from the publication of the Massachusetts governor's proclamation (with an incidental reference to the Pilgrims), nothing was said about local associations with the holiday.

The first noteworthy event to focus attention on Plymouth's "Thanksgiving heritage" occurred in 1927, when Laurence Ellis of the Fox Film Company made a short feature in the historic Harlow House (1677) titled *New England's First Thanksgiving Day*, which was to be shown on Broadway on the Wednesday before the holiday and in Boston on Thanksgiving itself. It is significant that the motivation behind this project came from outside the community, where the association of Pilgrims with the holiday was strengthening and maturing. By 1930, Plymouth had begun to realize not only that the First Thanksgiving an important concept but also that its exploitation might be advantageous to the town. The *Old Colony Memorial* reflected this growing awareness in editorials that pointedly emphasized the Pilgrim claim and suggested that there should be a national Thanksgiving Day broadcast from the place where the holiday had begun. In 1932 the paper reprinted a classic account of the First Thanksgiving and its historical importance from America's oldest Catholic newspaper, *The Pilot* (Boston), which further attests to the growing acceptance of the story.

In 1933, WEEI of Boston in cooperation with the Plymouth Antiquarian Society (and Massachusetts governor Ely) broadcast a half-hour evening program of music and Pilgrim dramatizations across the national Red Network from the Harlow House. In 1934 Colonel DeBasil of the "Ballets Russe" came to Plymouth to study Pilgrim ideas and costuming. The following Thanksgiving was enlivened by an odd hoax in which President Roosevelt was ostensibly invited by "25 leading Plymouth businessmen" to come to a real Plymouth Thanksgiving dinner and discuss the New Deal. The president was reportedly insulted by the tone of this summons, and Plymouth leaders were quick to disavow any knowledge of such an invitation, although they did say the president would be welcome should he choose to grace the town with his presence on the holiday. Local Pilgrim descendants were joined by representatives of the Mashpee Wampanoag tribe bearing turkeys, ducks, and deer in a costumed event on Thanksgiving in 1938, and by 1939 the Thanksgiving broadcast and costumed pageant had increased in scope to last the entire day. This massive event was covered by all the major wire services and newsreel companies, constituting "the largest collection of newsmen anytime in the state."[19] The link between the Plymouth Pilgrims and Thanksgiving was now universally recognized, although this triumph did not go unchallenged by intellectuals who found the bourgeois holiday objectionable, or by other claimants to the "First Thanksgiving" title.

34. Anson Lowitz, *The Pilgrims Thought It Was Snowing*, from Sadyebeth and Anson Lowitz, *The Pilgrims' Party* (New York: Stein and Day, 1931 [1959]). The myth of popcorn being introduced at the "First Thanksgiving" was another contribution from Austin's *Standish of Standish* that has since been debunked but probably remains popular.

As representatives of the commonalty, the Pilgrims had a head start over both the Puritans of Boston and the adventurers of Virginia. Their historic economic and social inferiority to their contemporaries made them perfect representatives of the common man, and they were often thought of collectively rather than as individuals. Abandoning earlier misguided but resolute efforts to identify coats of arms and royal precedents for the *Mayflower* passengers, many of the Pilgrims' advocates were happy to embrace the comforting belief that their ancestors' virtue was one of democratic ordinariness. This can best be seen in George S. Willison's popular *Saints and Strangers* (1945), which divided the Pilgrims themselves between the puritanically inclined Leiden Separatists — or "Saints" as they called themselves — and the "Strangers" who were the other passengers on the *Mayflower*. The latter, Willison went to some lengths to demonstrate, were rowdy, colorful "Elizabethan" folk who provided a crucial secular leavening to the stiff Separatist stock and saved Plymouth from the fate of Massachusetts Bay.

Another example of the "folk" approach to the Pilgrims and Thanksgiving can be seen in Sadyebeth and Anson Lowitz's children's book *The Pilgrims' Party* (1931). The irreverent humor and disregard for historical niceties in both text and illustrations, which recall John Held, Jr.'s, "woodcut" style (figure 34), stand in contrast to the sedate and stereotypical depictions of the Plymouth colonists in school coloring and cutout packages[20] or children's books such as Margaret Pumphrey's *Stories of the Pilgrims* (1910, which was reprinted in the 1920s as a school text) and Esther Schenk's *Thanksgiving Time* (1932). It was at this time that *Mayflower* partisans (most particularly their documented descendants) began to take great pleasure in the discovery that the Pilgrims wore bright colors and drank beer. This, they believed, proved their ancestors were not the dark-clad, somber Puritan killjoys that contemporary essayists and cartoonists poked fun at. These same revelations have since been freshly discovered by each succeeding generation and are regularly cited to refute the taunt of "Puritanism." In popular art, the First Thanksgiving dinner became an example of not only intercultural harmony but also culinary indulgence and fun. The Pilgrims were jovial and "good sports," it was generally agreed (if not as fully as Willison or the Lowitzes might have it), and their very real religious commitment was sometimes ignored. Both conservatives and disillusioned leftists cited the Plymouth colonists' failed experiment with communal living as proof that communism would not work.

However, quibbles over Pilgrim and Puritan faults were swept away by the more urgent need for national consensus and unifying American traditions during World War II. In 1942 at Thanksgiving time, *Life* published a long, illustrated paean to the New England heritage called "The Puritan Spirit: It Is the Faith That Victory Comes from God." The Puritans (Plymouth Pilgrims and Massachusetts Bay Puritans alike) were now presented as the true progenitors of the American way and the font of inspirational strength that had sustained the nation throughout its existence. Fun was OK in peacetime, but it was now time for America to get serious, and the Puritans had a natural corner on that market. The article's introduction closes with a fervent assertion of the patriotic role of the Puritans/Pilgrims that would be uncritically echoed each Thanksgiving in postwar American culture:

Eventually the Puritans themselves died out and a new all-American type—the Yankee—took over New England. But the Puritan Spirit lived on and expanded and has always been a pervading influence in American life and in the individual American conscience. It was with the Minute Men at Lexington and Bunker Hill. It rode with the pioneers across the mountains to settle new lands in Ohio and Michigan and Illinois and Kansas. The Puritan Spirit was with John Brown at Harper's Ferry, and again it was with Marcus and Narcissa Whitman when those New England martyr-missionaries founded their school in the State of Washington, and were murdered by the Indians they wished to teach. It speaks from the pulpits and hearts of Americans today; the official statements of American leaders are filled with it. President Roosevelt might have been speaking for the Puritan Fathers on this page [the text was surrounded with portraits of Winthrop, Saltonstall, Cotton, Endicott, the Mathers, and Sewall] when he closed his first radio address on the war, on December 9, 1941, with the words that our cause and our hope were for "liberty under God."[21]

During World War II, Thanksgiving was understandably swept up in the hypertrophic patriotism of the time. As Baritz observes, World War II created the "stunning domestic facts" of 16,354,000 young Americans entering the military, and additional millions of civilians drawn into war work.[22] The war and its effects reached into every sector of American life. The media took on the duty of acting as national patriotic spokesmen for the duration, following on rather less than successful efforts of the Roosevelt administration's Office of War Information to engage the American public while avoiding the blatant propaganda that had characterized World War I. Advertisers made their every pitch to the public include something about the war, and of course rationing directly affected the entire population. Thanksgiving and its association with what we now call "family values" put the holiday right in tune with the officially sponsored patriotism of the home front and the theaters of war alike. Despite the widely publicized entry of women into the workforce and the "Rosie the Riveter" stereotype, the anxieties of both Depression and war brought out a latent yearning for "normal" family life. "Did deep societal values change [in World War II]?" historian D'Ann Campbell asks. So far as women are concerned, she gives an ironic but unimpeachable answer. "Yes, Americans emphasized more strongly the primacy of family and children in their lives than in previous eras."[23] The war brought to fruition the revival of patriotism in holiday observances (which had been mounting in the late 1930s) as it did in every other part of American life.

The Department of War, the Marine Corps, and the Navy Department had long observed Thanksgiving with particular care. There was a perceived need to strengthen morale at a time when the call of family and home was especially poignant. The military could not provide homecomings for all (particularly in time of war), but they could try to serve up acceptable substitute dinners. Surviving menus produced by every branch of the services since the beginning of the century demonstrate that military cooks aspired to the lavish traditional Thanksgiving dinner. The menus, often elaborately printed with the names of the company officers and sometimes even enlisted men (figure 35), have been preserved in great numbers, which attests to the importance of the occasion to the servicemen themselves. Many have autographs of the attendees, and returning veterans fondly preserved even crude mimeographed examples from the theater of war itself.

The two evident requirements for these dinners were a generous diver-

Menu
THANKSGIVING
DINNER

U. S. S. Monticello
THURSDAY, NOVEMBER 25, 1943

Menu
THANKSGIVING DINNER

CREAM OF TOMATO SOUP	CRACKERS
ROAST WESTERN TURKEY	
GIBLET GRAVY	CRANBERRY SAUCE
HEART OF CELERY	
MASHED POTATOES	CREAMED PEAS
OYSTER DRESSING	
OLIVES	APPLE PIE
MIXED NUTS	
ICE CREAM	CANDY
CIGARETTES	CIGARS
BREAD	BUTTER	COFFEE

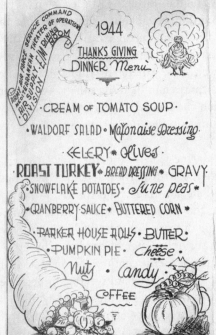

1944 THANKS GIVING DINNER Menu

ARMY AIR FORCE SERVICE COMMAND
MEDITERRANEAN THEATER OF OPERATION
AIR SUPPLY "I'M IN" DINING ROOM
DIVISION

· CREAM OF TOMATO SOUP ·
· WALDORF SALAD · Mayonaise Dressing ·
· CELERY * OLIVES ·
ROAST TURKEY * BREAD DRESSING * GRAVY ·
· SNOWFLAKE POTATOES · June peas *
· CRANBERRY SAUCE * BUTTERED CORN *
· PARKER HOUSE ROLLS · BUTTER ·
· PUMPKIN PIE · Cheese ·
Nuts · Candy ·
COFFEE

S/Sgt. EDWARD R. DICKERSON
"MESS SERGEANT"

"COOKS"

Sgt. HOWARD F. AKE —
Sgt. MISSOURI A. STROHL'TR
Cpl. RALPH F. HOUSEMYER
Cpl. ELWOOD S. McHENRY
PFC. WALTER L. LIBBY
PFC. WILBER H. MILBY
PVT. WOODROW W. FANNIN
PVT. DALE L. KELLY
PVT. JOHN S. SIGMAN

RAYMOND A. KINSER
2nd LT. AIR CORPS
MESS OFFICER

HERMAN STRASHEIM
MAJOR, AIR CORPS
· TROOP
COMMANDANT ·

35. Wartime menus: U.S.S. *Monticello*, November 25, 1943; Army Air Force, Air Supply, Mediterranean Theater of Operations, Thanksgiving 1944.

sity of foodstuffs and the iconic elements of a true Thanksgiving feast such as turkey and dressing, cranberry sauce, and pies.

The Thanksgiving menu of today remains surprisingly unchanged from those of the past. An analysis of 100 military menus, from 1917 to 1997 and from Boston to Saudi Arabia, show that 100% of the menus offer turkey, 98% offer dressing, 92% offer cranberry sauce, and 89% offer gravy. 96% of the menus offer pie, with 81% offering pumpkin pie. In the grand military Thanksgiving Day tradition, some things *do* remain the same![24]

Turkey continued to be the absolute requisite for Thanksgiving. It appears in every menu, even if it was just part of a confused mixture dropped into a mess kit.[25] World War II menus occasionally offer ham as well, and potatoes and candied sweet potatoes or yams are standard additions. Green peas, corn, and asparagus also turn up with some regularity — one assumes canned goods in these cases. Cakes as well as pies appear on the menus, and the dinner is more often than not finished off with cigarettes and cigars. Such creature comforts were welcome palliatives when one's immediate future was so unsure that long-term health was of slight concern.

A typical menu for companies stationed stateside might be like the one for the Battery "B" Eighth Coast Artillery in Fort McKinley, Maine (November 26, 1942):

Thanksgiving Menu

Fruit Cocktail   Olives and Celery
Roast Turkey   Cranberry Sauce
Apple and Raisin Dressing   Giblet Gravy
Mashed Potatoes   Candied Sweet Potatoes
Scalloped Corn   Brussels Sprouts
Lettuce and Tomato Salad
Parkerhouse Rolls   Butter
Mince Pie   Pumpkin Pie
Chocolate Cake with Whipped Cream   Ice Cream
Candies   Mixed Nuts   Grapes   Mixed Fruits
Milk   Coffee   Beer
Cigars   Cigarettes
After Dinner Mints

The menu is decorated with the company banner and several linecuts of Pilgrim subjects, and has autographs of those present. The inclusion of "butter" on a menu might seem odd today, but wartime shortages had rendered it a luxury. In the 1944 Thanksgiving edition of the *Jack Benny* radio show, Mary Livingston's maid Pauline tells her mistress that she has set the butter in the center of the table and surrounded it with consecutive barriers of saltshakers, pepper shakers, cream pitchers, and sugar bowls. When asked why, she says: "Well, we can't stop them from using the butter, but I thought we could slow them down a little."[26]

Out at sea, the spreads were scarcely less extensive. The U.S.S. *Monticello*, a transport ship doing duty on Thanksgiving in 1943, had an elegant restaurant-style menu (see figure 35) with card covers and blue tassel, which also included a characteristic wartime Thanksgiving message from the ship's chaplain, H. A. Wickersham:

When we think of *Thanksgiving* there comes to our minds turkey and football games. Less [*sic*] we forget, *Thanksgiving* came into being as a holiday in America when people who came from across the sea gathered to give thanks unto God. They were thankfull [*sic*] that they were safe after a sea voyage. There was food enough for all. Their potential enemies, the Indians, were their friends. They looked forward to freedom of worship which had been denied to them in their native country.

We on the *Monticello* have many reasons for giving thanks at this season. Just to mention a number of our blessings should invoke gratitude in our hearts. Among our many blessings are:

(1) We are alive. Our ship is afloat and serving the nation. What might have happened to us and our ship has not.

(2) We have hope of a final Victory. The successes of our armed forces during the past year cheer us and give us hope of Victory. The men and women which this ship has transported have played an important part in these successes.

(3) Our homes are safe. Not only has the soil of America been spared the ravages of war but our homes are being held together by those who are brave and true.

The spirit of gratitude of us on this ship is expressed in these words:

"Lord of life and death, we thank thee for the great adventure of life, with its untold possibilities, Its mighty opportunities."

"We thank thee if we have thee with us, there is no monotony or weariness in the world; But we go on forever exploring and adventuring across new seas where ship has never sailed before."

"We thank thee for that, for those who dwell with thee, each day opens new a continent of vivid experience, each day shows new a world to conquer; for thy love is new every morning, and life with thee is daily born again from its beginning."

The U.S.S. *Monticello* (A.P.-61) was originally an Italian ship, built in 1928 and interned in Brazil at the beginning of the war. It was bought by the U.S. government in 1942 and used as a troop transport, traveling in 1943 from Oran in Algeria to San Francisco via the Panama Canal. The vessel passed safely through the war and was returned to the Italian government in 1947.

A menu from the field might be less inclusive but still evoke the culinary spirit of the day, as, for example, an Army Air Force Service Command menu (which was issued as a hand-lettered eight-by-ten-inch photograph in lieu of printing) from the "Mediterranean Theater of Operations" in 1944. Soldiers who were actually on the front lines had to make do with what they could get, but even there effort was made to provide a proper Thanksgiving. Bill Shepard, who was in the 102nd Infantry Division ("Ozark Division"), U.S. Army, recalled such meals: "I remember the Thanksgiving dinners—there were always turkeys and pies and everything you would have at home. The food was often cold, if you were in the field [on Thanksgiving Day 1944, the Ozark Division had just broken through the Siegfried Line at Aachen], but it was Thanksgiving." In 1944, *Yank* (the armed services magazine) admitted, "There still isn't a helluva lot of turkey going around this year but you don't have to look in your mess kit to see who is winning the war. . . . In Italy you're freezing in the thick mud before the Po Valley just as you did last year before Venafro, and in Germany the Nazis are still holding on like hell past Aachen. But it does mean you can see the end, the end you sometimes wondered if you would see. Surer and surer we're building to the Thanksgiving we griped at missing in 1941."[27]

The observation of Thanksgiving by the armed services and the effort to make the day a pleasant break (when possible) from the rigors of the war and ordinary mess-hall fare was greatly appreciated, but what was probably more significant was that millions of young American men and women were being exposed to the standards of the official Thanksgiving dinner, possibly for the first time. Cliff Sampson of Plymouth, Massachusetts, serving in the navy on the U.S.S. YMS 84 yard minesweeper (which was blown up under him on July 3, 1945) in the Pacific observed about Thanksgiving military food: "But it was good food, I can't complain. Some of the food probably was better than a lot of people ever had before they were in the service. Some people came from poverty"—and had never seen a full Thanksgiving bill of fare before. It was inevitable that this would make a lasting impression, emphasizing both the significance of the day and what constituted an acceptable holiday dinner. Just as the labors of the New Deal, if not as fully effective as its architects had envisioned, brought throngs of previously marginal American families into the mainstream of American life, so the war widened the experience of countless thousands.[28] In this way a majority of Americans, moving in their own estimation toward membership in the American middle class, were instructed in the proper observation of one of that class's primary holy days.

Thanksgiving on the home front was marked by equal determination to celebrate the holiday in as traditional a fashion as possible while at the same time honoring or at least recognizing the rules of rationing and patriotic sacrifice. Dealing with shortages of turkeys and the other rationed culinary markers of the true Thanksgiving dinner (or shortages of desired military guests) was a familiar plot mechanism in wartime radio shows. Protagonists of both the working-class *Amos and Andy* and the middle-class *Great Gildersleeve* shows, for example, encounter humorous frustration and satisfaction in the dogged pursuit of a proper Thanksgiving dinner. For Thanksgiving in 1941 and 1942, the conniving water commissioner Throckmorton P. Gildersleeve struggles to obtain both turkeys and military guests (the immediacy of war and enlistment being a reality for Americans even before Pearl Harbor) at his table. In the 1942 subplot, his nephew Leroy is costumed as John Alden for the school play. In 1943, Andy Brown receives a series of letters from his nephew Jimmy announcing the arrival of an ever-increasing number of enlisted guests even as the Kingfish and the Ration Board thwart him from securing a turkey. However, this crisis is averted when the military guests are unexpectedly sent to their port of embarkation before they can get to Uncle Andy's in New York. In 1942 George Burns and Gracie Allen are confronted by wartime inflation and shortages when the turkey for which they budgeted $1.50 sells for 50 cents a pound—to someone else. The entertainment elite represented on the *Jack Benny Show* in 1944 are equally determined to celebrate a legitimate Thanksgiving despite everything, although it is more their own foibles rather than wartime conditions that make this difficult.[29]

In real-world America, rationing and shortages of such crucial ingredients as butter, sugar, coffee, fruits, vegetables, and meat made putting on a Thanksgiving dinner a challenge, so the shows rang true. In 1942 the American Cranberry Association ("Eatmor Brand") suggested that housewives use a cup of corn syrup—or of maple syrup, or half a cup of honey—and one cup of sugar for their sauce. Special cookbooks offered alternatives and substitutions. The challenge of the would-be patriotic host appears on a 1943 cover of the *New Yorker* in which one of Helen Hokinson's matrons, watched by an apprehensive butler and several guests in uniform, cautiously attempts to flame a plum pudding.[30] Patriotic advertising and articles furthered the association of Pilgrims with the holiday during the war. In 1944, *Parade* featured an article on the Barnes family of Plymouth, Massachusetts, titled "Sons and Daughters of the Pilgrim

Fathers Celebrate Thanksgiving." Pilgrims appear widely in ads, cartoons, and cover art. By the time the war was over, the Pilgrims could no longer be separated from Thanksgiving, for the two had become virtually interchangeable in popular culture.

Following the war, demobilization returned thousands of service personnel in a fairly short time, if not quickly enough for those involved. The understandable impatience is well illustrated in a *New Yorker* cartoon (November 24, 1945) that shows a young woman holding a pile of civilian clothing for a newly released soldier who is feverishly changing his clothes behind a tree just outside the gate of an army "Separation Center." Although rationing and price controls continued into 1946, peace and the return of prosperity ushered the nation into a period of optimism and assurance. David M. Kennedy summarized the tonic effect of the war: "As a thunder squall ionizes the sultry summer air, World War II left the American people energized, freshened and invigorated. Depression America had been a place of resignation, fear and torpor. America at war was quickened by confidence, hope and above all by empowerment."[31]

This and the advent of the Cold War sustained a widely held version of American history, now referred to as "consensus history," in which the sentiments of *Life* magazine's "Puritan Spirit" article and others like it ("the Puritan Spirit lived on and . . . has always been a pervading influence in American life") were given unqualified cultural approval.

"Consensus history," a term coined by the late Johns Hopkins historian John Higham, is commonly used by professional historians to refer to a view of American history that was dominant in the 1950s. Unlike the Progressive historians, such as Charles and Mary Beard, who preceded them, or the New Left historians who followed them, consensus historians saw in the American past more unity than conflict. Willing to posit distinctive national traits, they accepted notions of American exceptionalism and an American character. Some consensus historians, such as Daniel Boorstin, celebrated this unity, while others, such as Richard Hofstadter, lamented it. But they generally agreed on the possibility of writing master narratives about a unitary American people, focused on familiar highlights such as the American Revolution and the Civil War.[32]

This greatly benefited traditions such as the Thanksgiving holiday and its Pilgrim icons. Once again, the Thanksgiving image of everyone sitting down together in harmony and plenty perfectly fit the spirit of the times, and the Pilgrim story was celebrated as the first step in the onward and upward march of the American people.

The consensus view of the past simplified the complexity of history by constructing a single, uplifting narrative for popular consumption, following the imperatives of the 1945 hit song to "accentuate the positive, eliminate the negative."[33] The goal was to unite the American people as they had been united during the war by warding off the "pandemonium" of contentious diversity and the communist menace that was lurking in the wings. This vision of togetherness, now often enshrined in nostalgia for an era that was in fact rent by political insecurity and anxiety, capitalized on the unprecedented increase in economic opportunity that marked the postwar period. Starting in the primary grades, schoolchildren growing up in the 1940s and 1950s were imbued with this optimistic view of American history until the consensus broke down in the mid-1960s. Even today, many still retain a lingering conviction that what they learned in the third grade is more accurate than all the problematic interpretations that have arisen since.

Consensus and Competition
The Postwar Thanksgiving

After the war, America families continued to attend football games, prepare turkey dinners, and buy decorations to express holiday themes. The Hallmark Company and American Greetings Company produced several elaborate paper centerpieces for the dinner table illustrating the Thanksgiving theme, such as a pop-up *Mayflower* (with an onshore harvest depiction), a "Thanksgiving Centerpiece" consisting of two stylized Pilgrims, and a pop-up thatched log cabin, a tree with colorful fall foliage, and the Thanksgiving table surrounded by cheerful Pilgrims and (Plains) Indians. There were also the long-popular "honeycomb" turkeys and pumpkins. The Gurley Novelty Company of Buffalo, New York, which made rather corny figural candles for holidays, turned out large numbers of cute Pilgrims, Indians, and turkeys (many of which appear to have survived unburnt) for households across the country. Classrooms were hung with Pilgrim images whose features and haircuts changed in time with contemporary styles, courtesy of the Beistle and Dennison companies. Childish art was festooned on blackboards (or now perhaps green boards), and the sound of childish voices singing "We Gather Together" was heard throughout the land. The hiatus between the candy-and-costume commerce of Halloween and the full-scale consumer rush of Christmas was not yet as narrow as it is today. Thanksgiving enjoyed a largely unblemished popularity.

A particularly straightforward illustration of the Cold War view of the meaning of Thanksgiving is contained in the twelve-minute educational film *A Day of Thanksgiving* (1951). In this didactic film, the Johnson family is obliged to celebrate Thanksgiving without a turkey for dinner. In contrast to many educational films, *A Day of Thanksgiving* depicts the possibility of poverty in America, but with the purpose of making the family members—Dick, Tommy, Susan, Baby Janet, "Mother" (she has no other name), and father Bill Johnson—contemplate the many things they are thankful for because they live in America: plentiful food, free libraries, sufficient clothing, freedom of religion, public education, the chance to play ("it's fun to grow up in America"), cleanliness, personal safety, modern conveniences (such as washing machines, hot water, telephones, and automobiles), access to suitable work, housing, newspapers, and voting with no fear of a midnight knock on the door. Even in a Thanksgiving sans turkey, the central element of the annual American civic eucharist, the partakers can experience an epiphany of the American way of life.

Cold War fears and pieties aside, the dominant American mood was positive. The Depression was over, the war had been won, and despite the need for vigilance to prevent any such reoccurrence, America had emerged into a bright new, efficient, and sanitized world. This triumph was attributed to the vigor of the American way, which was in part the consequence of the sacrifices and perseverance of the Pilgrims and other forefathers. The lessons of the past were inculcated in schools and the popular media through an improved, streamlined version of American history that had all the corners rounded off. Earlier discontinuities and debates were smoothed over and hidden beneath the polished surface of postwar culture.

During these years Thanksgiving was often presented in the American media each November as if it were a sort of "holiday in dreamtime," located in a timeless golden autumn afternoon of Pilgrim dreaming. Like the "Dreamtime" of the Australian aborigines, Thanksgiving was shaped by storytelling between generations, but the environment around which it was constructed was more often one of graphic imagery and decorative objects rather than geographical location (except in the case of Plymouth itself). Access to the eternal nature of the holiday was sought through the nostalgic evocation of old-time holiday scenes and pilgrimages to one's childhood home or Plymouth itself. Whether the timeless First Thanksgiving of the Pilgrims or nostalgic images of "Gay Nineties" kitchens and country households of the prewar era, history was repeatedly evoked to awaken a holiday spirit through which all Americans could share in the transcendent reality of the 1621 Pilgrim event.[1] The belief in a direct connection between the First Thanksgiving and the present was firmly fixed in the American psyche.

Plymouth, Massachusetts, had discontinued its Thanksgiving broadcasts and elaborate pageantry during World War II; in 1945 it once again hosted a holiday broadcast. There was a fifteen-minute radio presentation from the Harlow House by WBZ announcer Milton Bacon followed by a half-hour broadcast of the choir of the Unitarian First Parish Church. This was of course one Thanksgiving when the whole country had plenty to be thankful about. Although the practice of nationwide broadcasts was later abandoned, the town continued to do what it could to bolster its identification with the holiday. Earlier in the day there was a football game among returning veterans and a Union church service at the First Baptist Church.

Since the local woolen mills and tack factories were declining or going out of business, tourism was now recognized to be an increasingly important part of the Plymouth economy. The Thanksgiving link with the Pilgrims was no longer slighted, and tourism was seen in a new light. (In 1925 the *Brockton Enterprise* had noted that Plymouth tended to rest on its laurels and do little to promote itself as a tourist town.)[2] The town began an annual practice of distributing free cider and donuts—and one year, free Pilgrim hats—to the public at the historic houses and other venues on Thanksgiving Day. The "Pilgrim Progress," a march of fifty-one costumed volunteers representing the Pilgrims who survived the first winter, took place about ten o'clock each Thanksgiving morning, followed by a Union church service. On one or two occasions, a Pilgrim tableau vivant program that had originally appeared in 1921 was restaged in Plymouth's Memorial Hall. However, a new player was about to join in the Plymouth celebration that in time would overshadow these civic celebrations.

In December 1945, Mr. Ralph Hornblower, Sr., a Boston investment broker, gave the Pilgrim Society $20,000 to acquire the land and plans necessary to support the creation of an outdoor museum dedicated to the history of the Pilgrims and their Indian contemporaries. The creation of such reservations of the past, with their collections of historic houses and re-created communities, was still a new impulse in the American museum world, and Plymouth was seen to be a place where such an institution would be very welcome. The town was, after all, one of America's oldest national shrines—a place to which tourists had made pilgrimages to experience the sense of place where "It All Began" since the earliest days of the Republic.

Plymouth had always been a difficult place to achieve a sense of the past. Unlike Williamsburg, Mount Vernon, or even Philadelphia, there was very little of a physical nature surviving that could evoke the town's historic significance. The chief focus of pious respect for the Pilgrims had long been Plymouth Rock, but it required a considerable exercise in imagination to connect this venerable icon with the dramatic adventure of the first settlers. A thorough preparation in the written history of the Pilgrims was needed before the Rock could have any meaning. Like the formless "aniconic" stone idols of the ancient Romans that were thrown into the shade by the realistic statuary of the Greeks, the Rock could not easily compete with the more vivid attractions of other American twentieth-century cultural spectacles.

None of the primitive structures that had first housed the Pilgrims survived, and those of the second period of settlement that had been turned into historic houses were not really evocative of the 1620s, the focal point of the Pilgrim story. The few actual relics of the Pilgrims were collected together in Pilgrim Hall, itself a museum piece. The hall had been built in 1824 by the Pilgrim Society and was one of the very earliest museums in the nation. However, the old swords, books, and chairs protected by velvet ropes or glass cases and Victorian art depicting the Pilgrim Fathers did not necessarily speak to the sophistication of postwar Americans, especially those of the younger generation.

President Ellis Brewster presented the idea of a new, outdoor museum in a letter to the Pilgrim Society on December 3, 1945:

The thought is to begin the erection of a Pilgrim and Indian Village, which would include not only replicas of Pilgrim houses and of Indian tepees, but also a museum where Indian relics might be displayed. . . . Mr. Hornblower wishes to discuss the project with his son, one of our trustees, who only just got back from War Service Saturday. Henry is a recognized authority on such a project . . . and should have a large part in it—possibly being employed in its development.[3]

A "Pilgrim Memorial Village" was, Mr. Hornblower said, an idea he had long envisioned, and he hoped that the funds he was donating would make it possible for the Pilgrim Society or a subsidiary organization to make it a reality. The genesis of this dream had come from the inspired imagination of his son, Henry (Harry) Hornblower II. Although the Hornblowers were neither native Plymoutheans nor Pilgrim descendants, they had summered in Plymouth for many years and had developed a great affection for the town and its history.

An agreement was signed by the principals on September 21, 1947, and on October 2 Plimoth Plantation, Inc., was incorporated, to serve as a "memorial to the Pilgrim Fathers" to further "the historical education of the public with respect to the struggles of the early settlers in the Town of Plymouth, with the expansion of that settlement and the influence of the Pilgrim Fathers throughout the world."[4] The statement of purpose reflects two popular assumptions about the Pilgrim story that were widely accepted at the time. The first was that suffering and perseverance validated the Pilgrims' role as exemplars of the human condition. The privations that the Pilgrims had suffered in their emigration to the New World were understood to be so central to that experience that they typified the traditional celebration of individual and group effort in the struggle for survival against both the hostile natural environment and rival groups. Objectively, other groups might have suffered more deeply, or have fought against greater odds, but the pious flight out of England and the victorious establishment of a family-centered settlement unsullied by motives of greed or imperialism marked the Pilgrims as the first "Real Americans."

The second assumption was that the Pilgrim story, like the American way of life, spoke to a universal need throughout the world. The experiences of this small band of white, middle-status English immigrants were thought to be inspirational not just to Plymoutheans or New Englanders or Americans but to all peoples. While it was true that the Pilgrims' story could conceivably have meaning for people everywhere, the assumption that it not only was of great interest but also had, already, international significance was naïve. It was a revealing statement of the postwar American intellectual climate, a time when the triumph of "Western Civilization" was unconsciously accepted as the basis for evaluating the history of the entire world.

From these assumptions it followed that an improved vehicle for the communication of the Pilgrim message was an important aspiration. The war to save the democratic way of life had been won, and it was time to reaffirm the national values that had made that victory possible, at home and abroad. The story of the Pilgrims at Plymouth was a valuable tool by which American virtues could be promulgated in the struggle to "make the world safe for democracy." Ultimately the belief became a self-fulfilling prophecy, for Cold War efforts to bring the American message to the world did carry the Pilgrim story to many countries including Japan and Germany, where it was embraced in an effort to understand what had made the United States the victorious international power it had become. As Thanksgiving and the Pilgrim story were now inextricably entwined, increased interest in one enhanced the other as well.

The Plantation in its early stages was largely the physical expression of commonly shared impressions of the Pilgrims, of which Thanksgiving was only a part. The Pilgrims had become so well established in the popular mind over the past century or so that everyone "knew" what they looked like, what their story meant, and how they "would have" lived. Yet there was also an acute awareness that the subject was ridden with stereotypes, sentimental inaccuracies, and nonsense. The Plantation's founders took their task seriously and were determined to not perpetuate myths or errors, nor to pander to the public's less accurate preconceptions of the Pilgrim story. For example, recent research had demonstrated that the clothes the Plymouth settlers wore were not all blacks, whites, and grays but the colorful dress of their Jacobean English contemporaries, and that they did not build log cabins in the stereotypical frontier mode but timber-framed English houses. Such discoveries were eagerly adopted by the new organization and instituted in the face of criticism from outraged "experts" or dismayed visitors who did not find their preconceptions realized. Later criticism of those initial attempts may have been justified in the light of more accurate scholarship, but it should not be overlooked that the original plan for Plimoth Plantation reflected the best information and most honest opinions then available.

While most of the literature introducing Plimoth Plantation dealt with the broader symbolism of the Pilgrim story, the first publicity shots of the "First House" on the Plymouth waterfront in 1948 depicted a Thanksgiving image: a costumed Pilgrim (descendant Spencer Brewster) carrying a musket and a turkey home to his young family. Thanksgiving was a natural vehicle for attracting media coverage and encouraging public visitation, so the museum stayed open each fall until the end of November and did what it could to strengthen the association of the Pilgrims with the holiday. It reprinted selections dealing with Plymouth from Ralph and Adelin Linton's *We Gather Together: The Story of Thanksgiving* (1949) as *The Pilgrim Thanksgiving: The Story of the Most American of Our National Holidays Adapted from Contemporary Records, 1621 and 1623* in 1951 to help boost this understanding. In 1953 the Plantation cooperated with Jordan Marsh, the Boston department store, in installing an impressive Thanksgiving display using costumes for eight Pilgrim men, seven boys, six women, and three girls together with an impressive number of actual Indian artifacts borrowed from the collections of the Peabody Museum at Harvard. Unfortunately some of the latter, such as a necklace made of dogs' teeth, were damaged in the process.

In November 1957, the *Mayflower II*, which had first arrived in Plymouth on its fifty-five-day voyage from England on June 13, returned from a trip to New York to be officially handed over to Plimoth Plantation. The Thanksgiving Day media extravaganza included a three-hour televised segment of Dave Garroway on the *Today Show* in the re-created Fort Meetinghouse on the Plymouth waterfront in which actual Thanksgiving content was overshadowed by an extensive sales pitch for the new Pilgrim Village, turning the event into a publicity campaign for the museum. On Saturday, November 11, 1959, in cooperation with the National Council of Churches, three hundred recent refugees were invited to attend religious services and a Thanksgiving dinner (a classic Cold War initiative) at the new Eel River Pilgrim Village site. The Plantation also put on a reenactment of the "First Thanksgiving" with costumed volunteers (including a hundred boy scouts) playing various colonial and Indian roles. The guests and the public were entertained with various colonial "games" and a set piece depicting the famous treaty between Massasoit and the colonial leaders. All these events strengthened the Plantation's lock on the holiday (figure 36). When the Plantation filmed a movie version of the Pilgrim

36. "The Day the Pilgrims Feasted" provides an example of Plimoth Plantation's early, naïve re-creations of the "First Thanksgiving."

story, titled *Plymouth Colony: The First Year,* in cooperation with educational filmmaker Coronet Films in the fall of 1960, the results had "a great deal about Thanksgiving it," as education director Arthur Pyle observed.

When one looks back at the postwar media treatment of Thanksgiving throughout America, the immediate impression is of cheerful optimism and commercial abundance. The public was strongly advised to include in its holiday celebrations beer ("In this friendly, freedom-loving land of ours—beer belongs. . . . Enjoy it!"), liquor, cigarettes, soda, or whatever nontraditional product was on offer. Advertisers such as the United States Brewers' Foundation (today's Beer Institute) presented large ads depicting jovial and well-dressed American families gathering for their turkey dinners. Other companies exulted over the convenience contemporary housewives had in canned, packaged, and frozen foods, including the new frozen "TV dinners." "In those days when the corn or spinach or pear crop was harvested, there was a surplus of the particular food in season—and people would eat it until they were sick of it. But just a few months later they would have given anything for the same summer food to break the monotony of their winter meals. Today, all Americans have to do to enjoy any of dozens of fruits and vegetables is to open a can."[5] The pleasant, conventional scenes that accompanied these ads promoted the holiday itself as much as they did any particular product. The implication was that Thanksgiving was central to aspirations to be part of this successful and prosperous way of life in which everyone was depicted as happy, well fed, WASP, and middle-class.

At the same time, there was an undercurrent of anxiety that is sometimes overlooked in the nostalgia for the period, which drew strongly on this same hyperbolical imagery. Certain advertisers took the holiday opportunity to warn their patrons about the dangers threatening the world the Pilgrims made. The International Nickel Company inserted a full-page ad headlined "There was plenty for ALL, only when men were <u>Free</u> to work for <u>themselves</u>" in magazines such as the *Saturday Evening Post* in 1950. It actually ignores the 1621 harvest festival ("Even after the 1621 harvest was gathered, the daily ration was only a quarter of a pound of bread for each person") and locates the significant Pilgrim Thanksgiving in 1623, citing the abandonment of communal labor that year as the reason for prosperity: "And so, in 1623, they turned away from governmental dictation and gave each family a parcel of land for its own use. . . . No wonder they gave up for all time their sharing of poverty . . . [*sic*] their belief that it was good for all to suffer scarcity together. They found that it is better for each man to work for himself to produce *plenty*, because that benefits everyone." Take that, you New Dealers and Commies!

In 1951, the John Hancock Insurance Company asserted, "They [the Pilgrims] showed us a secret of happiness" (figure 37). The secret was hard work and the satisfaction found in simple things: "And then we think back—back to some personal wilderness we have all been through in our time. Perhaps there was once a day when simply to feel the sun again, to smell another morning's freshness, to hear a child laugh again was miracle enough. . . . They had freedom, too. . . . They owned themselves; no man owns more." The accompanying illustration of the First Thanksgiving was done in a folk-primitive style in autumnal earth tones to emphasize the trope of innocent simplicity. It includes an example of the odd "deer immolation" image sometimes found in Thanksgiving representations. Like the blunderbuss and the buckles, this signals the innocent simple-mindedness of the poor Pilgrims.

Republic Steel's large 1952 newspaper ad listed the blessings of Americans: "Freedom ('God's richest gift and today the lingering hope of the oppressed in other lands'), Courage ('To defend the Cause of Freedom'), Memories ('We do not forget American bravery and sacrifice at Valley

They showed us a secret of happiness

They came as strangers to a wild land, and none of them knew which day would be the last.

Never in the old country had they known such a winter: the wind so cold, the food so scarce, the enemy night so filled with dread.

Never had they worked so hard, paying with aching backs for every shelter raised against the cutting wind.

Everywhere they went, Famine and Death watched them with pale expectant eyes. And by the end of that bitter year, there was hardly one among them who had not lost to the cold earth someone he could not live without.

Then these men and women who had nothing sat down to a hearty feast, filled with gratitude for what they had.

We who follow them sometimes wonder why. Did they know some secret of happiness, denied to us, that made them so glad for so little?

And then we think back—back to some personal wilderness we have all been through in our time. Perhaps there was once a day when simply to feel the sun again, to smell another morning's freshness, to hear a child laugh again was miracle enough—a time when just to find oneself alive was a gift beyond belief. They had their lives; no man has more.

They had freedom, too. They were where they wanted to be. They could go where they chose to go. All the days ahead were theirs to use as they pleased. They owned themselves; no man owns more.

Remembering this, we join their feast, brothers to all the wise men whom trouble has taught to look at what they have, and not at what they lack.

John Hancock MUTUAL LIFE INSURANCE COMPANY
BOSTON, MASSACHUSETTS

37. "They showed us a secret of happiness," John Hancock Insurance Company advertising offprint, 1951, with a painting by Doris Lee. Visions of primitive virtue and simplicity for a postwar audience. Courtesy of the Doris Lee Estate.

Forge, Tripoli, the Alamo, Gettysburg, San Juan Hill, the Argonne, Normandy beaches, Iwo Jima and Korea'), Faith ('In God in nations in man and in ourselves'), Hope ('That all peoples of God's world will be united in everlasting Peace'), the Bell ('The Liberty Bell whose inspiring chimes now echo on foreign shores and whose Song of Freedom Is drowning out the bloody dirge of communism'), Unity ('At any real threat to our Freedom a *united* America rises in her might'), Wisdom ('To know that there are many enemies at home who seek stealthily to take our freedoms from us, from our children and our children's children'). And so we pray. . . ." The illustrations are of a Pilgrim family praying at their family dinner (rather than a communal event) and a modern American family doing the same.

Predictably, Plymouth's Thanksgiving public-relations gold mine inspired envy and competition among those communities that felt they might have a better claim to "America's First Thanksgiving." These challenges led to a perennial debate over where the first Thanksgiving actually took place. Serious historians had never lost the issues raised in this book, although they may have chosen to overlook them, and they provided satisfactory ammunition for would-be challengers. The relatively late date in early colonial history of Plymouth's 1621 event, the weakness of any claim to historical continuity, and the absence of documented religious content was seized upon by rival claimants who then offered alternative candidates for the coveted honor of hosting the real "First American Thanksgiving." John J. Wicker, Jr., a politician from Virginia who became the champion for the Berkeley Plantation claim, headed the most significant and determined challenge. In 1958 Wicker founded the "Richmond Thanksgiving Festival," an organization dedicated to having the probable Berkeley Thanksgiving of December 4, 1619 (Old Style) supersede Plymouth's 1621 example in popular recognition and acquiring the coveted First Thanksgiving attribution for Virginia.[6] The Berkeley Plantation Thanksgiving of 1619, like the 1621 Plymouth event, had long been forgotten, and it was not rediscovered until the late nineteenth century. The recovered records of the Berkeley Hundred particular plantation were first published in the *Bulletin of the New York Public Library* in 1899. Lyon G. Tyler, president of William and Mary College and a fervent advocate for the South's precedence in American history in opposition to popular assumptions favoring New England, found this reference in 1931 on a trip to New York. It was Wicker's espousal of the cause, however, that led to its widespread recognition.

Perhaps there was an element of the old Jamestown versus Plymouth competition or a holdover from Civil War sectional animosity in this claim. As Wesley Frank Craven observed, the first Virginian historians had rather dropped the ball in the eighteenth century when they focused on the more respectable post-1624 history of Jamestown and failed to stress the point that Virginia preceded Plymouth.[7] It did not help that Jamestown had long been abandoned and there was no one there to fight for its recognition. New England had picked up that ball and run with it, positioning Plymouth in popular culture as "the first permanent settlement." By the time Virginia caught on as the bicentennial approached in 1807, it was too late. No amount of rightfully indignant protest on the part of Virginia's actual thirteen-year lead in the race to colonize America has been able to seriously dent Plymouth's questionable title as the birthplace of British North America. Adding insult to injury, Plymouth continued to scoop Virginia in the mass media from time to time, an example being the highly visible voyage of the *Mayflower II* in 1957, the year of Virginia's 350th Jamestown anniversary celebration. Wicker accused Massachusetts of envying Virginia's status as the first colony and Virginia's ownership of the first Thanksgiving as well, but it was really the other way round.

The following year Wicker began his campaign, and the *Saturday Evening Post* (November 28, 1958) published two articles under the rubric of "Let's Have a Little Less Nonsense About Those Pilgrims." The first, "That Mythical 'First Thanksgiving'" by Virginius Dabney, editor of the *Richmond Times-Dispatch*, quite reasonably presented Virginia's claims to Thanksgiving for recorded observances at Jamestown in 1607 and 1610, but went on to discuss in some detail why the 1619 Thanksgiving at Berkeley Hundred was the superior candidate. He incidentally noted that Abraham Lincoln visited Berkeley in 1862 to consult with General McClellan—a visit Wicker would later inflate into "official recognition" of the yet-to-be-discovered Thanksgiving reference. The second article was by Maine author John Gould, titled "Who Says They Were First?" Gould discussed possible earlier Thanksgivings by explorers and settlers who arrived in Maine and points north before the Puritans reached Massachusetts—both French and English. His favored candidate for a "first" was the Popham colony's thanksgiving service in 1607. He complained that the Pilgrims' fame had long obscured the early history of the New England/Maritime Canada region, yet closed with a loyal Yankee's "Hooray for the Pilgrims, but—." What was clear was that Plymouth's claim had now become a matter of dispute.

In 1962, President Kennedy issued a Thanksgiving proclamation that gave credit to the Plymouth colonists for establishing the holiday custom.[8] Wicker quickly sent off a telegram protesting the Pilgrim origin as an error, and demanded a correction.[9] The matter was addressed by the president's special assistant Arthur Schlesinger, Jr., who, after consulting with historians such as Samuel Eliot Morison, returned a reply acknowledging the alleged error and promised that it "will not be repeated in the future."[10] Plimoth Plantation then got into the act. Harry Hornblower wrote to Schlesinger (whom he knew) about this affair. Harry did not dispute that there had been earlier "thanksgivings" in America but urged critics to consider the example of Florida's potential claims in this matter and in particular that of Rene Laudonniere's account of Ribault's 1562 expedition. "All of this makes for marvelous nonsense, but I think it only fair that Florida have a chance to get in the game."[11]

This tempest in a beanpot did not settle the matter, nor did it dampen enthusiasm for the debate. Numerous other claimants rose to the bait, such as El Paso, Texas, which has used Don Juan Oñate's service in April 1598 as a public-relations vehicle in friendly competition with Plymouth since the 1990s. It is, after all, just a game, as Harry Hornblower said. There indubitably was a first Christian "thanksgiving" in America. It was a Sunday service in Spanish in the Caribbean, Mexico, or wherever, and probably has yet to be identified. For those who like Guinness record book–style "firsts," the best candidate *on record* within the present boundaries of the United States is probably the one Harry cited, which would give the Thanksgiving laurels to Jacksonville, Florida, where Fort Caroline was built by the French Huguenots (therefore Calvinists like the Pilgrims) on the St. Johns River. Today, Fort Caroline National Memorial is located near the intersection of Monument Road and Fort Caroline Road, approximately fourteen miles northeast of downtown Jacksonville. The Huguenot connection suggests the possibility of a Calvinist Thanksgiving resembling the New England model.[12]

Plimoth Plantation could afford to magnanimously relinquish Plymouth's title of "First Thanksgiving" for two reasons. First, its historians knew that the 1621 event was neither a Thanksgiving nor any sort of religious occasion but more probably a harvest celebration drawing on English secular (or at least as secular as any activity might be in the seventeenth century) customs and precedents. Second, it mattered very little what either the defenders or the opponents of the Plymouth claim said, anyhow. The Pilgrim identification with Thanksgiving was firmly embedded in the American psyche and would remain so. The 1621 event had so strongly defined the parameters of an acceptable First Thanksgiving that even when rival claimants made their pitches, they felt it necessary to include open-air dining, turkeys, harvest symbolism, and sometimes Indian guests to legitimize their claims. When the Richmond (or Virginia) Thanksgiving Festival presented a huge holiday reenactment at Berkeley Plantation in 1967 for eight hundred people, it included an outdoor turkey (and Virginia ham) dinner, traditional Thanksgiving autumnal decorations, and costumed activities that looked for all the world like a typical Plimoth Plantation event. The episode they were ostensibly commemorating was, by contrast, a simple early December church service that had involved none of these things. The settlers did not even have a harvest in December 1619, let alone a gala "colonists and Indians" feast.

Ultimately, the first instance in America of any event that might be identified as a "thanksgiving" was historically irrelevant — such concerns were only part of the public-relations game Harry Hornblower had identified. With the exception of Berkeley and perhaps Fort Caroline, each of the other alternative claims was a standard thanksgiving service held on a Sunday in normal Catholic or Anglican fashion, and equally immaterial to the history of the American holiday. Even more beside the point were traditions of harvest customs and celebrations, whether Christian, Native American, Roman, Greek, Egyptian, or Chinese. The harvest tradition is pertinent only to the 1621 Plymouth event and its inclusion in the Thanksgiving repertoire in the nineteenth century. Yet while harvest customs might be irrelevant in the historical origins of Thanksgiving, they are central to any understanding of the 1621 Plymouth celebration and that event's ultimate influence on the American holiday. For this reason, Plimoth Plantation would focus most of its resources in playing up the harvest-festival angle. The Lintons' book, which presents Thanksgiving as the evolutionary result of harvest traditions, provided important support for Plymouth's claim. If the 1621 event at Plymouth was to retain the title of the "First Thanksgiving," it would be through its ownership of harvest-festival attributes and Indian guests rather than any association with the historic Calvinist Thanksgiving holiday.

Each year during the 1960s, Plimoth Plantation put on some sort of Thanksgiving program that gave modern pilgrims to Plymouth a chance to immerse themselves in the contemporary harvest-time ambience of the Pilgrim story. Some of the museum's heaviest daily attendance of the year took place on Thanksgiving Day and the Friday following, as visitor and local families entertaining guests and relations sought out something "Thanksgiving-y" to do when dining was not their primary activity. By 1963, the museum had published several newsletter articles, a teachers' guide, and a classroom play called *Mr. Bradford's Story* that emphasized both Thanksgiving's harvest-festival character and the accepted history of the holiday. The "firsts" controversy was neither avoided nor accorded any importance. One of the activities in the *Thanksgiving Day Observance* teachers' guide was to "Trace the history of early 'Thanksgivings' along the Atlantic coast prior to the arrival of the Pilgrims." Other activities included study of the Cherokee "Green Corn Dance," reporting to the class with a list of "common misconceptions related to the Pilgrims' First Thanksgiving," and comparing George Washington's 1789 proclamation with Lincoln's 1863 example. The subsequent history of the holiday was condensed in the *Pilgrim Times* newsletter:

Although other days of thanksgiving are recorded, what is not generally understood is that these were frequently days of a solemn and penitential nature not to be confused with the harvest festival atmosphere of the thanksgiving of 1621. Such "Thanksgiving" days were declared at various times by Pilgrims, by George Washington and by various state governors. The first nationwide celebration of the holiday as we know it today really obtained its impetus from the untiring efforts of Mrs. Sarah Josepha Hale, whose novel "Northwood" in 1827 described "pumpkin pie" and "good and true Yankee Thanksgiving" and who later in 1846 started a systematic campaign in her famous "Godey's Lady's Book" of Philadelphia, to have a national celebration proclaimed by the President.

Her efforts bore fruit with President Lincoln, who in 1863 proclaimed the first of our modern Thanksgiving holidays.

The article also stated, "No research has found recorded dates for the 1621 Thanksgiving, but it is generally believed to have been closer to the September–October harvest time than late November."[13] These oft-repeated mileposts in the generalized history of the holiday, while neither fully accurate nor historically inclusive, were satisfactory to everyone involved and formed the basis of the official pronouncements.

Plimoth Plantation has been particularly influential in determining the contemporary visual representation of the Pilgrims and their holiday. The museum has no original buildings or antiques in its re-creation of the early Plymouth settlement, and therefore cannot claim the numinous "historical authenticity" for its exhibits that a collection of historic artifacts possesses. Instead, it approaches intellectual legitimacy through the "historical accuracy" of its reproductions of seventeenth-century material culture, sparing no effort or expense in the replication of period clothing, architecture, livestock, and furnishings. These often very expensive accoutrements are used in the public representation of period life, which provide the re-creations the soiling and wear of actual historical artifacts. This striving after verisimilitude is quite similar to the way that Merchant Ivory and other serious historical filmmakers have recently taken great pains to evoke a sense of the past through meticulous attention to the tangible (if not the cultural) representation of historical eras.

Thanksgiving may not be as child centered in its observation today as Halloween, Christmas, or Easter (there being no custom of presents, candy, or party activities associated with it in American families), but its historical and commemorative basis has been thoroughly infantilized. This is also one of the most significant areas in which the holiday has been incorporated into contemporary "consumer culture," the object of consumption being the commercial images, shows, and stories that are turned out for the holiday market. Although Thanksgiving customs such as sending greeting cards, holding family reunions, and hosting the holiday turkey dinner are still adult practices, the holiday's symbolic basis—the 1621 First Thanksgiving and the Pilgrim story in which it is embedded—is now almost entirely child centered. Like fairy tales and myths that were originally socially significant for adults before they were relegated to children, the Pilgrims and their holiday story have been commodified in the twentieth century to serve a juvenile market.

The veritable flood of Thanksgiving and Pilgrim titles that have appeared since the 1960s are primarily aimed at youthful readers at the preschool through grade school level. These can be divided into three varieties: historical accounts, contemporary holiday descriptions, and character tie-ins. Historical titles generally focus on the Pilgrim origin of the holiday, although there are also books about how Thanksgiving was celebrated in American history by immigrants, pioneers, or old-fashioned families. Contemporary descriptions are generally didactic stories about how this or that family—animal or human—celebrates the holiday, with some moral or example of social redemption being provided. Tie-ins are a particularly popular variety of holiday story, in which some already established cartoon or literary series character adds a Thanksgiving experience to his, her, or its other adventures.

Many historical accounts of the Pilgrim "First Thanksgiving" show Plimoth Plantation's influence in their illustrations in particular (at least when the images are realistic enough to make a judgment). Some are focused entirely on the harvest celebration, while others include the First Thanksgiving as the climactic event in the overall story of Pilgrim immigration and settlement. Log cabins have just about disappeared in children's books, and the clothing of the characters generally resembles that of the Plantation's costumed staff rather than the stereotypes of the pre–World War II period. The thatched, clapboarded houses, daub baking ovens, dirt-floor interiors, and furnishings reflect the Plantation's Pilgrim Village exhibit at the time when the books were published (these change from time to time as houses are replaced and styles modified by successive curators). Many also have taken advantage of the museum's research into what may have been served at the famous feast, what the "re-creations" may have been, and what the 140-odd attendees may have done during the event.

Other authors use the classic images of Jennie Brownscombe (see figure 1), J.L.G. Ferris, or other artists and illustrators as well as Plantation imagery. *N. C. Wyeth's Pilgrims* relies entirely on Wyeth's fourteen-panel mural of the early Pilgrim years, done for the Metropolitan Life Insurance Company building in the early 1940s, and presents the feast in a manner contemporary with the illustrations.[14] Author-illustrator Richard Scarry's little anthropomorphic animals in *First Thanksgiving of Low Leaf Worm* mix Plimoth Plantation imagery with English popular impressions about seventeenth-century costume and architecture. The narratives that accompany the pictures commonly present the story from a child's point of view, which usually involves anachronistic adventures involving Squanto or fictional Indian children and colonial children "helping" by gathering nuts and berries (despite the seasonal absence of the latter) and firewood or, in the case of girls, helping the women prepare the feast. A great many American children form their first impressions of the holiday's historical meaning from these books, and they are therefore of considerable importance in decisively shaping popular conceptions of the holiday.

Recent examples of the historical genre that do not focus on the Pilgrims include *Rivka's First Thanksgiving* (in which a 1910-period Jewish family from Poland struggles with the appropriateness of the American holiday), *Milly and the Macy's Parade* (the story of another Polish immigrant girl and the beginning of the famous parade in 1924), *A Strawbeater's Thanksgiving* (in which a slave boy, Jess, fights to win the right to assist in playing music at a harvest celebration), *An Outlaw Thanksgiving* (in which Butch Cassidy rescues a girl and her mother from a stalled train and takes them to the Hole in the Wall ranch for a holiday celebration, allegedly based on a real incident), and *Molly's Pilgrim* (in which a Russian immigrant girl finds that a doll made by her mother helps her assimilate her first Thanksgiving experience in America).[15]

Thanksgiving stories depicting modern families (or cartoon characters) celebrating the holiday generally have the same themes as their predecessors concerning issues of family reunion and conflict, charity and selfishness, toleration and assimilation, as well as more contemporary concerns about ethnicity, gender, and nutrition. These often involve nontraditional ethnic groups or recent immigrants, as in *How Many Days to America*, which parallels the arrival of the Pilgrims with an account of a boatload of refugees from Cuba or Haiti being welcomed on Thanksgiving Day. *The Thanksgiving Door* begins with an elderly wife burning the turkey so that an old couple goes out to eat on Thanksgiving Day. They select a restaurant (which is actually closed) in which the immigrant owners' family is eating dinner, but the family decides to invite them in as their guests. In *Amber Brown Is Feeling Blue*, a fourth-grade schoolgirl has to decide whether to have her holiday with her divorced mother in Washington State, with her father in New York, or with her new friend. Ann Rockwell's preschool-level *Thanksgiving Day* depicts the traditional classroom portrayal of the holiday with children dressing up as Pilgrims, Wampanoag Indians, and even as the *Mayflower*. A review of this title on Amazon.com by Emilie Coulter observes, "There's no room for cynicism in this genuinely warm, honest book about a time that, for a while anyway, was peaceful, with people who were capable of friendly coexistence." In comic titles featuring anthropomorphic animals or humorous humans, a common trope is to have the turkey as a guest and eat vegetables, as in *A Turkey for Thanksgiving, Silly Tilly's Thanksgiving Dinner, The Tasty Thanksgiving Feast, Gra-*

cias, the Thanksgiving Turkey, or *The Know-Nothings Talk Turkey*, which exploit this particular modern sentiment.[16]

The other major category is that of the character tie-in, in which well-known cartoon protagonists, from Charles M. Schulz's *Peanuts* crew or Walt Disney's *Winnie the Pooh* (in which any resemblance to A. A. Milne's and E. H. Shepard's characters is purely fortuitous) to Marc Brown's *Arthur the Aardvark*, Stan and Jan Berenstain's *Berenstain Bears*, Sarah Willson's *Dora the Explorer*, and Norman Bridwell's *Clifford the Big Red Dog*, have some sort of Thanksgiving adventure and overcome some difficulty and/or attain an appropriate moral enlightenment. While all the children's books have a commercial intent, the tie-ins largely capitalize on the holiday themes of dinner, family, and inclusion for just another redundant seasonal plotline rather than a significant interest in Thanksgiving's history and meaning. On the other hand children who are exposed to these stories at a susceptible age will presumably incorporate something from these inconsequential tales into their personal identification of the Thanksgiving holiday just as previous generations did with the ephemeral stories found in the holiday anthologies of the first half of the twentieth century. The same can be said for the inclusion of the holiday in most television series and movies. For example, *A Charley Brown Thanksgiving* (1973), *B.C. — The First Thanksgiving* (1984), and *A Rugrats Thanksgiving* (1993) all present varying contemporary takes on the modern holiday as a matter of entertainment.

In films such as *The Gold Rush* (1925), the holiday simply offers poignancy to the famous sequence of Chaplin and Mack Swain ("Big Jim McKay") trying to eat the shoe, without having any further relevance to the holiday. In *Alice's Restaurant* (1969), the holiday dinner enjoyed by the countercultural contingent in the former church in Stockbridge, Massachusetts, which leads to Arlo Guthrie's arrest for littering, is secondary to the larger issues of the draft and the Vietnam War. It does show the strength of a tradition that is happily embraced by decidedly nontraditional types despite the absence of the standard middle-class trappings. Similarly in *Planes, Trains and Automobiles* (1987), the holiday family reunion is just a "McGuffin" that drives the frantic efforts of Steve Martin ("Neal Page") and John Candy ("Del Griffith") to get home through the comedy of errors that begins with a canceled flight between New York and Chicago. Thanksgiving itself is incidental. The denouement, however, does evoke the standard trope of holiday redemption in which reunion is achieved and Page is reconciled with the bumbling but kindhearted Griffith.

Despite the momentous changes occurring in American society in the 1960s, the middle class strove to hang on to the unified postwar vision of the Thanksgiving holiday and maintain and pass on the traditions of its

childhood. The mass media and most American households were still willing to stop for a moment and once again summon up the ghosts of Thanksgiving past. Even among the rebellious young, modernized Thanksgiving
graphics on rock posters, communal rather than familial dinners, and a
sentimental honoring of Native Americans were reversals rather than re-
jections of their parents' holiday. Arlo Guthrie's Thanksgiving saga was a
classic holiday story fully appreciable by a modern audience for whom the
old Victorian tales had lost savor. Yet the deep cultural challenges of the
period were about to make their mark on Thanksgiving as well.

Today, the challenge to the standard historical understanding of
Thanksgiving and its significance comes not so much from the rival "firsts"
(although these continue to be put forward from time to time) but from a
division between the Pilgrim-centered and Indian-based interpretations
of the holiday. Once Thanksgiving became a focal point for Native protest
and activism, an entirely new view of the holiday began to emerge in the
public consciousness.

New Myths for Old—
Thanksgiving under Siege

The essentially peaceful nature of the Pilgrim and Wampanoag festival has been a central tenet of the American holiday since the "First Thanksgiving" achieved national prominence. Social harmony has played a fundamental role in the modern representation of Thanksgiving in art and literature and established the day as a model of egalitarian and interracial fellowship. The symbolic violence that characterized depictions of the colonial holiday after the Civil War had largely been forgotten by World War II, for that imagery no longer made cultural sense, even in the humorous context in which it had survived the longest. However, this began to change when a group of Indian students met in Plymouth in 1969 to protest the holiday, which they found indicative of the cultural disregard of the age-old plight of Native Americans in the United States.

On the Wednesday before Thanksgiving 1969, two hundred protesters against the Vietnam War began a thirty-six-hour "fast for peace" at Plymouth Rock, then dispersed to complete their action at Boston, Providence, Washington, D.C., and elsewhere.[1] "A fast in protest of the war [was] organized by Rev. John E. Cuples of Boston, Geo. Wald of Harvard, Dick Gregory, Mrs. Helen Chase of Plymouth, and sponsored by Boston Area Clergy and Laymen Concerned about Vietnam" and "a half-dozen other peace and religious groups. Thomas F. Quinn, an attorney, is a leader of the local [Plymouth] laymen joining in the protest which also included Rev. Gerry Krick [First Parish Church, Unitarian], Rev. Woodbury [retired Baptist minister], Rev. John Scorzone [St. Peters' Catholic Church, assistant pastor], Rev. William W. Williams II of First Baptist Church. . . . Jim West, a Cheyenne Indian from Oklahoma, now a student at Andover Newton Theological School [and brother of W. Richard West, current (2005) director of the Smithsonian's National Museum of the American Indian], will help conduct today's anti-war protest and join in the Thanksgiving fast."[2]

A UPI release described the Thanksgiving protest on November 28, 1969:

50 Indians Demonstrate in Plymouth Rock March

Plymouth, Mass. (UPI) — Indians feasted with the white man at the first Thanksgiving here in 1621. Thursday, 50 Indians returned to demonstrate against the holiday.

"We say Indians have nothing to be thankful for," Michael Benson, 19, Navaho from Shiprock, N.M. and a student at Wesleyan University in Middletown, Conn., said. "Thanksgiving is a mockery for us."

The Indians, all students, marched around historic Plymouth Rock where the Pilgrims landed. Dressed in full Indian regalia, they carried signs reading, "What happened to the War on Poverty?" and "Support Native Americans."

The celebration in 1621, described by Pilgrim Edward Winson [sic] in a letter, had "many of the Indians coming amongst us, amongst the rest, their greatest king, Massasoit, with some 90 men, whom for three days we entertained and feasted.

"And they went out and killed five deer which they brought to the plantation and bestowed upon our governor and upon the captain and others," Winslow wrote.

Benson, president of the Organization of Native American Students, said the government has taken little action to relieve the Indians' plight and his group decided to take its plea to the public.

They picketed for an hour and dispersed.

Over 12,000 persons jammed Plymouth during the holiday, visiting the rock and Plimouth [sic] Plantation, a replica of an early Pilgrim settlement where Mayflower II is docked.

The *Boston Globe* further reported: "Among the crowd was a group of 50 young Indians from east coast colleges and prep schools. John Quaderer, a spokesman from the group, the Organization of Native American Students, (ONAS) addressed audiences at the Mayflower and Plymouth Rock. 'We want to make people realize that while turkey is in abundance in the east today, our tribes in Dakota are starving,' Quaderer said."[3]

It was an era in which political protest and confrontation over civil rights or the Vietnam War was a common occurrence, but the Plymouth protests were something more. They just happened to take place when the nascent American Indian movement achieved one of its most signal victories — the occupation of Alcatraz Island in San Francisco Bay. After an abortive attempt to seize the island on November 9 (there had been an earlier attempt in 1964), "The real invasion took place on November 20, 1969. At about 2 a.m., nearly eighty American Indians from more than twenty tribes pulled up to the island's eastern shore in three boats that

San Francisco Chronicle reporter Tim Findley had secured through his friend Peter Bowman, of the No Name Bar. The bar was a local hangout for journalists and other so-called 'intellectuals,' and Bowman agreed to take the Indians to the island after he got off work after midnight. Findley rode over with them to cover the landing. When they stepped ashore, the group's noisy cheers awakened Alcatraz's only caretaker, Glenn Dodson, who—claiming to be one-eighth Cherokee—offered them the deserted three-story warden's residence."[4]

This takeover would last nineteen months, and galvanize American Indians across the country to join in the contemporary struggle for rights and justice. As photographer Ilka Hartmann, who witnessed the siege, observed, it was part of the wider atmosphere of protest at the time: "There had been the Civil Rights Movement in the South, then the Black Power Movement. The Panthers had been formed in Oakland. The United Farmworkers, led by Cesar Chavez and Dolores Huerta, were organizing in the San Joaquin Valley. At San Francisco State University and UC Berkeley, home of the Free Speech Movement and Peoples Park, there had been 'Third World Strikes.' Students had demanded and clashed with the police for ethnic studies—Black Study Programs, Chicano-, Asian- and Native American Studies."[5] The time was ripe for Indian political action, and the seizure of Alcatraz was the result. News of this exploit quite probably helped spur on the events in Massachusetts. Simultaneous with the Plymouth protest, "hundreds of Native Americans and their supporters came to Alcatraz to celebrate a day of victory and to express their renewed pride in Indian identity" at an event they dubbed "un-Thanksgiving Day."[6] Although the 1969 protest attracted little interest in Plymouth, from that day forward the American Thanksgiving holiday would never be the same.

A second Indian Thanksgiving protest took place the following year, but 1970 was not just another year—it was the 350th anniversary of the landing of the Pilgrims. Pilgrim advocates in both Plymouth and Provincetown (where the *Mayflower* first made landfall a month before the more celebrated arrival at Plymouth Rock) were eager to make the once-in-a-generation anniversary a success, but things did not go as smoothly as they had for the 1920/21 tercentenary. The early 1970s were a singularly inauspicious time for the veneration of historic traditions and values. Neither the federal nor the state governments were as forthcoming with support and funding as they had been fifty years earlier, and even in the town of Plymouth political factionalism resulted in failure to substantially fund 350th-anniversary events. The spirit of the times was typified by revolt against established institutions, not their celebration.

Frank James, a Wampanoag teacher and president of the Federated Eastern Indian League, had been invited by the 350th Anniversary Committee to deliver a speech from the Native point of view as part of the anniversary activities. He sent a preliminary copy of his remarks to the committee, but although the speech was historically accurate and fairly moderate in tone, it was not laudatory enough for the committee. James criticized the effects of colonialism and commented on the subsequent plight of the Wampanoag, expressing only guarded optimism for the future. The committee found his talk "enflamatory," and the invitation was withdrawn. Consequently Mr. James worked with leaders of the Wampanoag and Narragansett communities and, with the approval of the Plymouth selectmen, organized a protest fast for Thanksgiving Day, which was called the "Day of Mourning" to "focus attention on Indian 'repression' in a 'dignified and responsible manner.'"[7] The intent was to communicate the concerns of the Indian community through prayers and meditation during an "anti-Thanksgiving" staged by people who had less to be thankful for amid the general commemoration of the Pilgrims and their legacy.

Accordingly, on the morning of Thanksgiving Day 1970, about two hundred people gathered on Cole's Hill around the statue of Massasoit overlooking the Plymouth waterfront and Plymouth Rock. The event did not quite go according to the original intentions of the organizers. They had invited members of the newly formed American Indian Movement (AIM), including Claude Belcourte, Edward Benton, and Russell Means, to attend, which had a momentous effect on how the protest turned out. The program that local tribes had put together was overshadowed by the actions of activists who ignored the printed schedule of events and instigated a far more militant (and probably more effective) series of measures. Following rousing speeches by Means and others, the activists and younger members of the crowd stormed down from Cole's Hill and boarded *Mayflower II*, where they proceeded to climb the rigging (against the protests of the Plimoth Plantation staff) and rip down the English flags. They threw a small replica cannon and a manikin representing Captain Jones into the harbor before returning to Cole's Hill for further speeches by Indian representatives from across the country and Canada. They threw sand on Plymouth Rock to symbolically bury the symbol of Pilgrim occupation. The Day of Mourning participants had been invited to partake of a traditional Thanksgiving dinner at Plimoth Plantation, but after marching the three miles to the Pilgrim Village site, they rejected the invitation, overturned the tables of food, and carried off the cooked turkeys that had been provided. Later, at a dinner provided by the Bourne Sports Club, "an Indian representative said they were happy with the 'Day of Mourning' because it gave them what they were seeking, a nationally-publicized protest which made more people aware of the Indian plight."[8]

Although this dramatic turn of events may have surprised the organizers, it did reveal an undercurrent of resentment that had long simmered in the Wampanoag community. In 1921, representatives of tribes from Maine rather than Cape Cod had provided most of the Indian participation during the tercentenary. "Miss Charlotte L. Mitchell (Princess Wontonskanuske) voiced what was apparently common opinion among the Wampanoag Indians in the *Boston Globe* after the 1921 Plymouth Tercentenary: 'The fandangoes at Plymouth this summer were a farce. It was a celebration of the anniversary of the killing of the owners of the New England hills and plains,—the Indians. Why should I have been dragged to Plymouth to celebrate such an event? Massasoit, my grandfather, eight times removed, should have killed the so-called Pilgrims instead of helping them.'" She did go, nevertheless, to meet President Harding. She was not particularly impressed.[9] The "Day of Mourning" now established an annual Native alternative to the message of traditional Thanksgiving symbolism, and an occasion for similar protests in the future.

The 1971 Day of Mourning was a much less dramatic event due to heavy rains that day, but as time went on the protest against the popular image of the Pilgrims (and in particular the Thanksgiving Day Pilgrim Progress march) became more assured and focused, and local Native spokespeople became more outspoken. The following year protesters (organized by Frank James' new organization, the United American Indians of New England) indulged in another raid on *Mayflower II*'s flags, which they replaced with their own blue banner (with a "red teepee" on it), and several young men climbed down and spat on Plymouth Rock. It was cold and raw in 1973, which again discouraged much activity. On Thanksgiving, November 29, 1974, James led a "raid" on Pilgrim Hall. The bones of a young Indian woman had been on exhibit for many years along with the crushed copper kettle in which they had been found on Cape Cod. The bones had been removed from exhibition years before, but James and the protesters demanded their release, which the director agreed to. Frank James and UAINE continued the annual observance of the "Day of Mourning" with few contentious incidents until 1994, when some of the old radicalism re-emerged. Their diligence may not have made headlines, but it did establish the seriousness of the Indian intent and kept the issue in the public eye.

Far from causing insult, the Indian dissent aroused a spirit of sympathy among the Plimoth Plantation staff. There had already been a major shift away from the traditional Pilgrim filiopietism to a more disinterested historical approach at the museum in 1969, when the earlier exhibits of antiques, signs, demonstrations, and manikin displays were replaced with the "living history" approach, which has since characterized the institution. Representatives of the local Indian community were invited to join the Plantation Board of Governors and to participate in the management of a new "American Indian Studies" program, with the creation of a new Indian Summer Camp exhibit on Eel River.

More significantly, the traditional Thanksgiving Day program was reconsidered, and in 1971 no particular historical activities or events were scheduled. Instead, a special "harvest supper" with period cuisine was held in the Pilgrim Village on the evening of September 16 to reinforce the increasing emphasis on the harvest-festival rather than the thanksgiving character of the 1621 event. In 1973, an entirely new public three-day "Harvest Festival" was initiated on Columbus Day weekend, while Thanksgiving Day itself was nothing more than a normal late-fall day with no special activities. The museum publicized the historical plausibility of the earlier seasonal occurrence and the secular nature of what had happened in 1621 by including English harvest activities such as games, folk dancing, and harvest processions in the new celebration. In 1977 Plimoth Plantation installed a major exhibit on Thanksgiving in the Fort-Meetinghouse that concentrated on the 1621 harvest celebration and the evolution of the holiday from the nineteenth century on.

The perception that the "First Thanksgiving" had in actuality been a harvest festival and the belief that the modern American holiday was yet somehow derived from the events in Plymouth in the early autumn of 1621 was now a matter of historical orthodoxy. Thanksgiving had finally achieved a commemorative role in keeping with many other holidays. Consequently, the exact nature of the 1621 event — including the probable bill of fare, the particular role of the Wampanoag participants, the number of attendees (as well as their ages, genders, and racial identification), and similar minutiae — became a matter of intense concern. Everyone wanted to be sure that they had an accurate impression of what had happened on that momentous occasion at Plymouth. The result was that a continual series of inquiries and requests for editing arrived at Plimoth Plantation and Pilgrim Hall, which were the recognized authorities on the holiday.

In 1987 the Plimoth Plantation Research Department published *The Thanksgiving Primer*, a collection of articles containing answers to the past decade's most often received requests for information. The *Primer* began with a short history of the holiday based on an earlier press release, which had by then become a standard informational piece. The second section described the Pilgrims as actual historical characters, in order to address the various stereotypes that had grown up around them. Many people were interested in reenacting authentic "Pilgrim worship services," so a chapter on their religious beliefs and practices was included. A discussion on seventeenth-century cuisine and examples of contemporary English recipes were included to correct misconceptions about what was most likely served (or not served) at the famous feast. This also answered the needs of those who wanted to prepare a real "Pilgrim" dinner. The perennial question of what constituted accurate Pilgrim clothing was addressed in a chapter on period dress, and suggestions were provided for the simple construction of appropriate costumes. The last section attempted to explode the more pernicious Thanksgiving myths and errors. It included an illustration depicting the most egregious examples such as buckled hats, popcorn, blunderbusses, log cabins, immolated deer, Plains Indian costumes, and so forth. A bibliography of useful sources was also provided. With Plimoth Plantation taking the lead, the standard view of the First Thanksgiving was coalescing to what it is today in American culture.

The Plantation's interpretation did not please everyone. Conservative opinion, unwilling to relinquish the traditional conception of the holiday as a religious Thanksgiving, criticized the harvest-festival interpretation as "revisionism" pandering to the fashionable secularism of the Left. The radical Left, on the other hand, denounced any commemoration of the Pilgrims as the glorification of racism and imperialism. After a period of relative quiescence following the decline of 1960s activism, the furor that surrounded the five-hundredth anniversary of Columbus' voyage to America reignited the interpretive issue in the Native American community and made early European/American colonialism yet another of the many "ism" targets of the contemporary Left (figure 38). In Boston, the Associated Press reported a mass protest gathering on October 12, 1992:

Christopher Columbus' landing in the Americas got as much attention Monday from Indians who were mourning Europe's conquest of the New World as it did for traditional celebrations of the voyage.

Thousands of people crowded into a huge communal Indian gathering in Boston to watch a dance exhibition, eat raccoon stew and corn bread and mingle with descendants of the people who lived in Massachusetts 9,000 years before the Pilgrims landed.

"The whole event is to emphasize the point that we're not celebrating 500 years of discovery for people who didn't need to be discovered," said Jeremy Alliger, director of *Dance Umbrella*, a co-sponsor of the powwow.[10]

Widespread disagreement among Americans over the appropriate manner in which to observe the Columbus anniversary spilled over into the Thanksgiving debate. In 1994, the annual Day of Mourning protest in Plymouth took a new turn. Frank James, who had organized the event since its inception, stepped down and turned over the direction of the Day of Mourning to his son, Roland (Moonanum) James, and his son's wife, Mahtowin Munro. The new leaders mobilized a contingent from the permanent protest culture in Cambridge, Massachusetts (including the

38. "Should the Indians Have Killed the Pilgrims?" *Village Voice*, December 3, 1996. Seventeen people responded to the question, and while opinions varied, it is clear that young hip New Yorkers have little use for the Pilgrims. Cover image by Robin Holland; reproduced with permission of the artist.

All-Peoples Congress, the Workers World Party, Revolutionary Youth, and Cape Cod-ers Against Racism) to join in the event. This resulted in an escalation of tactics that brought the Mourning sympathizers in direct confrontation with the Pilgrim Progress marchers. As reported in a December 1 press release from the "Worker's World Service,"

On Nov. 24, a group of Native people and their supporters disrupted the "Pilgrims Progress Parade." Chanting, "Thou shall not kill," "Thou shall not steal," and "Pilgrim bigots we say no, racism has got to go!" the activists blocked the parade participants with their bodies and a banner that read: "You Are on Indian Land."

The Pilgrims Progress Parade is held every year in Plymouth, Mass., on Thanksgiving Day to commemorate the 51 Pilgrims who survived their first winter in the "New World." According to Moonanum James (Wampanoag), Sachem of United American Indians of New England (UAINE), the parade "is an insult to our people. It perpetuates the myth that Native people gave up our lands willingly to the European colonists and that everyone lived happily ever after. It is nothing but a glorification of genocide."

For the experienced urban protestors or anyone (such as the Boston police) familiar with the usual occurrences during similar protests, the temporary scuffle in which the banner-bearing, slogan-shouting protesters attempted to block the path of the Pilgrim Progress on its way to the ecumenical service in the First Parish Church was nothing out of the ordinary. The Progress marchers, however, found it terrifyingly intimidating. They were just ordinary local, middle-class volunteers—men, women, and children—who had signed up for the traditional sedate march, not frontline action in America's culture wars. Eventually both marchers and protestors crowded their way into the church, before disbanding. The annual ecumenical service subsequently barred either group from attending in the future.

In 1995, which happened to be the 375th anniversary of the Pilgrim landing, the protesters again symbolically "buried" Plymouth Rock and ritually denounced the Pilgrims and the Progress, but no confrontation took place. That year had seen a successful townwide celebration involving both Native and colonial-historical commemorations and events, which perhaps inhibited the radical element in some fashion. In 1996, however, hundreds of Mourning sympathizers managed to get ahead of the fifty-one Pilgrim Progress marchers (the Progress had been unfortunately scheduled earlier than usual and coincided with the conclusion of the protest events) and forced them (at the suggestion of the Plymouth police) to turn north onto Main Street rather than entering Town Square. Heckling protestors pursued them as they straggled back to the Mayflower Society House on North Street. The anger, fear, and resentment of the Plymouth marchers at this imposition and the failure of the Plymouth police to defend local citizens from the obstreperous and insulting behavior of the out-of-town protestors led to a great deal of unfavorable commentary in the local paper and in civic circles.

Smarting under what they felt was unwarranted criticism for their efforts to peacefully broker a difficult situation, the Plymouth police determined that this sort of thing would not happen again. Accordingly, when the Day of Mourning crowd attempted to march up to Town Square on Thanksgiving 1997, it was met with a large number of state and local police (the Progress had been prudently scheduled for later in the day). Rather than accommodating the protest as they had in the past, the police forcibly broke up the march. Although it must have been frightening at the time, this was the best thing the protesters could have hoped for—a "police riot," which was recorded by the large contingent of press people who had come to Plymouth in hopes something dramatic would occur. The sense of self-righteous triumph is evident in the UAINE press release of December 11 (for further information from UAINE, see appendix 3):

Plymouth Rocked by Police Riot

Cops brutally assault Native people & supporters at Nat'l Day of Mourning

Police attacked a peaceful march of several hundred Native people and our supporters in Plymouth, Mass., on "Thanksgiving" day. More than 150 cops—latter-day descendants of Custer and the U.S. Cavalry—descended on women, children, elders and men who were merely attempting to march on a side street of Plymouth. The cops attacked without warning and with no provocation. . . . Several hundred Native people and their supporters had gathered in Plymouth for the 28th Annual National Day of Mourning. Since 1970, UAINE has organized the National Day of Mourning, a protest against the U.S. celebration of the mythology of Thanksgiving and against the racist "Pilgrim Progress Parade." Before the police assault on the attempted march, there was a speak-out on Cole's Hill. Native people representing the Maya, Yaqui, Inuit, Wampanoag, Lakota and other nations spoke. UAINE chose not to disrupt the parade this year. [It was not there to be attacked, this time.] The police attacked anyway. Why? Because the government is afraid of the people's movement we have been building at the National Day of Mourning. We have been able to bring people of all races and ages and genders and sexual orientations, together like one fist. This is the oppressors' worst nightmare.[11]

"It's all on videotape!" they exclaimed gleefully—and accurately. Richmond Talbot, a Plymouthean vacationing in Thailand at the time, saw it on the news there as events unfolded half a world away. Plymouth became for an instant the focus of some rather unwelcome publicity. As is usual in these cases of official overreaction and civic embarrassment, the Town of Plymouth dropped all charges, agreed to guarantee to allow marches on future Days of Mourning, and agreed to the installation of two bronze plaques, one on Cole's Hill explaining the annual Day of Mourning and another in Town Square where the head of King Philip, the Wampanoag chief killed by colonial forces in 1676, had been placed on view for many years. The text of the Cole's Hill plaque (which is still resented by many Plymoutheans and Pilgrim supporters) was in the end a relatively painless way in which to resolve the dispute:

Since 1970, Native Americans have gathered at noon on Cole's Hill in Plymouth to commemorate a National Day of Mourning on the US Thanksgiving holiday. Many Native Americans do not celebrate the arrival of the Pilgrims and other European settlers. To them, Thanksgiving Day is a reminder of the genocide of millions of their people, the theft of their lands, and the relentless assault on their culture. Participants in a National Day of Mourning honor Native ancestors and the struggles of Native peoples to survive today. It is a day of remembrance and spiritual connection as well as a protest of the racism and oppression which Native Americans continue to experience.

On Thanksgiving Day 1998, huge numbers of jubilant protesters and sympathizers flocked to Plymouth with accompanying media coverage, but the drama was over, and nothing untoward (or newsworthy) occurred. Since that time, the Day of Mourning has been held annually without incident. However, a rival Plymouth Wampanoag presence below the hill south of Plymouth Rock, led by Rodney P. Joseph, sachem of the Federation of Old Plimoth Indian Tribes, now presents an alternative, more positive view of the Pilgrim-Indian story.

The struggle over the true significance of the Thanksgiving holiday has not been limited to the town of Plymouth. A similar challenge has been occurring in the nation's classrooms, where some teachers whose liberal sympathies far outstrip their historical sophistication believe, in the spirit of the 1960s, that it is time to redress the wrongs done to the Native Americans. This urge to reenvision history in the cause of moral justice, which Jonathan Keats describes as "that particular set of Anglo-Saxon attitudes, amounting to universal guilt and embarrassment, with which modern cultural decorum requires us to confront the past"[12] is strong in modern American educational circles. As in the case of Forrest Carter's popular but fraudulent *Education of Little Tree* (1976), the nostalgically contrived "Speech of Chief Seattle" (best known in the admittedly fictional movie version written by Ted Perry in the late 1970s), or the books of Carlos Castañeda, the American past is lovingly distorted to suit the longings and desires of the present. One of the most influential examples is "Teaching About Thanksgiving," introduced by Chuck Larsen and apparently written by Cathy Ross, Mary Robertson, and Roger Fernandes of the Highline School District in Washington State in 1986. It is a highly inventive, revisionist version of the First Thanksgiving story, glorifying the Wampanoag and defaming the Pilgrims, that has since been excerpted, augmented, and spread across the World Wide Web by like-minded advocates, such as Mitchel Cohen, S. Brian Willson, John Two-Hawks, and Daniel N. Paul.[13] The relevant sections are as follows:

The Pilgrims were not in good condition. They were living in dirt-covered shelters, there was a shortage of food, and nearly half of them had died during the winter. They obviously needed help and the two men [Samoset and Squanto] were a welcome sight. Squanto, who probably knew more English than any other Indian in North America at that time, decided to stay with the Pilgrims for the next few months and teach them how to survive in this new place. He brought them deer meat and beaver skins. He taught them how to cultivate corn and other new vegetables and how to build Indian-style houses. He pointed out poisonous plants and showed how other plants could be used as medicine. He explained how to dig and cook clams, how to get sap from the maple trees, use fish for fertilizer, and dozens of other skills needed for their survival.

By the time fall arrived things were going much better for the Pilgrims, thanks to the help they had received. The corn they planted had grown well. There was enough food to last the winter. They were living comfortably in their Indian-style wigwams and had also managed to build one European-style building out of squared logs. This was their church. They were now in better health, and they knew more about surviving in this new land. The Pilgrims decided to have a thanksgiving feast to celebrate their good fortune. They had observed thanksgiving feasts in November as religious obligations in England for many years before coming to the New World. . . .

Captain Miles Standish, the leader of the Pilgrims, invited Squanto, Samoset, Massasoit (the leader of the Wampanoag), and their immediate families to join them for a celebration, but they had no idea how big Indian families could be. As the Thanksgiving feast began, the Pilgrims were overwhelmed at the large turnout of ninety relatives that Squanto and Samoset brought with them. The Pilgrims were not prepared to feed a gathering of people that large for three days. Seeing this, Massasoit gave orders to his men within the first hour of his arrival to go home and get more food. Thus it happened that the Indians supplied the majority of the food: Five deer, many wild turkeys, fish, beans, squash, corn soup, corn bread, and berries. Captain Standish sat at one end of a long table and the Clan Chief Massasoit sat at the other end. For the first time the Wampanoag people were sitting at a table to eat instead of on mats or furs spread on the ground. The Indian women sat together with the Indian men to eat. The Pilgrim women, however, stood quietly behind the table and waited until after their men had eaten, since that was their custom.

For three days the Wampanoags feasted with the Pilgrims. It was a special time of friendship between two very different groups of people. A peace and friendship agreement was made between Massasoit and Miles Standish giving the Pilgrims the clearing in the forest where the old Patuxet village once stood to build their new town of Plymouth.

This admixture of fact, opinion, and gratuitous nonsense has been critiqued and refuted by Dr. Jeremy Bangs[14] and Caleb Johnson,[15] but it continues to flourish as a "New Thanksgiving Myth." As Ronald Wright observed, "there is a pervasive cultural attitude in America that the past, if not altogether irrelevant, is as malleable as the future, as subject to the will as the present."[16] The new myth aspires to supersede the older First Thanksgiving myth by standing the traditional story on its head, making the Indians the chief players and benefactors at that event in 1621 instead of the Pilgrims. The most important tropes that have grown out of this silliness are that the Pilgrims were entirely incapable of farming, fishing, or building for themselves, and that they were starving their first year and survived only because the Wampanoag fed them. The truth of the matter, as can be seen in their own accounts, is that as ordinary English country folk, they were quite competent in these matters, and Squanto's actual invaluable if more limited contribution was advice on planting the new crop, maize, and his role as translator. As for "starvation," there was plenty of food that first year in the supplies they had brought with them, for half the company was soon no longer there to consume it. Tough times came later, and then the Pilgrims did depend on corn supplied by the Indians—through trade rather than charity—yet even with the dearth they experienced in 1622–1623, there was no "starving time" with fatalities, as there was in Virginia. Some of the blame for this confusion rests with Samuel Eliot Morison, who inserted "The Starving Time" as a section head for the segment about death from exposure and infectious disease in chapter 11, "1620," in his 1952 edition of Bradford's *Plymouth Plantation*.

In a related Web-borne myth courtesy of Mr. Larsen, a Puritan villain new to history, "Thomas Mather the Elder," is introduced:

[The Puritans'] rigid fundamentalism was transmitted to America by the Plymouth colonists, and it sheds a very different light on the "Pilgrim" image we have of them. This is best illustrated in the written text of the Thanksgiving sermon delivered at Plymouth in 1623 by "Mather the Elder." In it, Mather the Elder gave special thanks to God for the devastating plague of smallpox which wiped out the majority of the Wampanoag Indians who had been their benefactors. He praised God for destroying "chiefly young men and children, the very seeds of increase, thus clearing the forests to make way for a better growth," i.e., the Pilgrims. In as much as these Indians were the Pilgrim's [*sic*] benefactors, and Squanto, in particular, was the instrument of their salvation that first year, how are we to interpret this apparent callousness towards their misfortune?[17]

We can interpret this as the fiction it is. There never was any such person or sermon, of course. The quote is actually from Edward Johnson's *Wonder-Working Providence* (1653) and speaks to the plague of 1618, which did decimate the coastal tribes, but has nothing to do with the Pilgrims in 1623. As Jane Kamensky observed in her article "Thankstaking" about the UAINE victory, the game is not historical accuracy but political advantage:

Is it "true history" that Thanksgiving Day celebrates European "genocide," theft, and the "relentless assaults" Plymouth's English migrants visited upon indigenous culture? The settlement [of a lawsuit between protesters and the town of

Plymouth] establishes that no less an authority than the Massachusetts Historical Society will "confirm the accuracy of the facts set forth in [*sic*] the [Cole's Hill] plaque." But, the agreement continues: "No higher level of accuracy for the ancient facts set forth on the plaque will be demanded than has been required for representations that are made in the Town of Plymouth" about its own early history. The Indians' Thanksgiving needs only to meet the standard of truth set by that of the Pilgrims' eighteenth-century descendants. Turnabout, in other words, is fair play."[18]

Since the loss of innocence about the Pilgrims and the Thanksgiving holiday tradition, various efforts have been made to correct public perception. On one hand, the conservative evangelical community has waged a spirited defense of the classic First Thanksgiving story and the traditional significance of the Pilgrims in American society. As a probable majority of Americans became familiar with the Thanksgiving story in grade school, such support for the traditional preconceptions is unremarkable. At the other extreme, however, the Native American community and its allies have continued their attack on the Thanksgiving myth to the extent of attempting to establish a new myth in place of the older one. Turning around Samuel Eliot Morison's observation that the Pilgrims have become the "spiritual ancestors of all Americans," the new perspective proposes that it is the Native peoples who are the true "spiritual ancestors" of the American people, and that the American Thanksgiving holiday should rightly celebrate Native American traditions of giving thanks rather than continue to focus on what is portrayed as a dishonest and unworthy Puritan Thanksgiving tradition.

Spokesmen for this alternative viewpoint have hinted darkly that the origins of the New England Thanksgiving are not based in Christian charity but derive instead from a chauvinist and racist celebration of the destruction of Native America. Citing the well-publicized problems in interpreting the "First Thanksgiving," the alternative view asserts that the actual "first" New England Thanksgiving was declared in 1637 after bloodthirsty Pilgrims returned from massacring the Pequot community at Mystic, Connecticut. In actual fact, the Plymouth colonists did not get their act together in time to participate in the Pequot War, although they did join in the celebration of colonial victory. The next real Thanksgiving, the new myth continues, was in 1676 at the conclusion of "King Philip's (or Metacomet's) War," which resulted in Native subjugation, slavery, and death following the disastrous defeat of the Native peoples' attempt to stem the tide of colonization. While these results are quite true, this ignores the suffering that took place on the colonial side—but of course in the essentialism of the protesters, there can be only black or white, heroes or villains, and all are redeemed or damned by their political group identity. Even the account of the 1621 Plymouth celebration has been recast as an event at which the local Wampanoag were the hosts and suppliers of most of the food to an inept and treacherous colonial community, whose survival depended solely on the aid and forbearance of the Native population.[19] Unfortunately, none of the hyperbole and invention is really necessary, as the case for the tragic result of colonization on the Native peoples is sufficiently damning without exaggeration, even if it has nothing to do with the tradition of Thanksgiving.

As historical interpretation, all this is mere rhetorical nonsense, but such rhetoric is a potent source of new myth. Like the deep reverence for the Anglo-American past that the First Thanksgiving myth inspired in our predecessors, the new Thanksgiving myth evokes concern about the tragic consequences of that same Anglo-American expansion held by a sizable portion of the American public. Today's contemporary cultural climate provides fertile ground for this alternative fiction just as Victorian fears led to the Thanksgiving myth of colonial violence. In fact, the new myth may prove a far more effective approach to abolishing the First Thanksgiving myth than all the reasoned criticism that has been directed against it.

Conscientious scholars have sought for years to exorcise the First Thanksgiving myth by painstakingly exposing its various historical inaccuracies and anachronisms. Also, not all the efforts to present the Native perspective have been beset by myth, as Karen Nelte's careful analysis demonstrates.[20] The American public has been told repeatedly that there are flaws in the traditional conception of the First Thanksgiving, that the Pilgrims did not eat cranberry sauce, that buckles and huge white collars were not a Plymouth fashion, and that turkeys are not mentioned in the more important of the two references to the event. Yet these very iconic elements turn up in classrooms and popular culture every November without fail, regardless. To attempt to explode a myth by carping about the minute details of its narrative is to attack the symptoms, not the disease. Myth is not a rational but an expressive understanding of history, a matter of unconscious belief rather than intellectual conviction, and is all but immune to objective criticism.

The new "noble savage" Thanksgiving, on the other hand, fights fire with fire. It seeks not so much to debunk as to supplant the earlier beliefs. The emotional appeal the revisionist Thanksgiving story has among its intended audience is understandable, given the lingering frustrations of a long-suppressed minority, but the attack has not stopped there. The new Thanksgiving myth, often shorn of its more obvious absurdities and rhetorical excesses, has also found a receptive audience among liberal segments of the American public eager to expose old hypocrisies and redress the wrongs of the past. Curricula drawing on the new Thanksgiving myth have appeared in schools seeking to downplay the old civic pieties concerning the Pilgrims and to privilege a Native perspective of the holiday. In general, the new myth has been successful in gaining these converts because it speaks effectively to our present hopes and fears, but the inroads it has made have so far been scattered and numerically insignificant.

Neither the conservative defenders nor the reformist opposition have had much effect beyond their own partisans and sympathizers. The general public remains unconcerned with the failings of the traditional Thanksgiving story. They continue to enjoy their decorative be-buckled Pilgrims and warbonneted Indians while consuming turkey and cranberry sauce in the perfect confidence that they are maintaining a tradition that began in 1621. They may also be aware of the cultural battles surrounding Thanksgiving and give intellectual allegiance to one version or the other, but as with the contest between Santa Claus and Christ's Nativity, this cognitive dissonance has no effect on their habitual practices and tastes.

Should the traditional Thanksgiving myth then be regarded as a false but harmless part of popular culture, which is irritating only to stuffy experts and humorless activists? After all, the central event, the 1621 harvest festival, is a rare and inspiring example of how two cultures could meet in harmony and peace, if only for a moment in an otherwise grim struggle for political supremacy. Does it matter that it was not technically a Puritan Thanksgiving, or the beginning of an unbroken tradition? I would suggest that it does, for while the festive decorations may be innocuous, the larger influence of this one-dimensional representation of the past effectively obscures the real history of America. Like any myth, the First Thanksgiving is a stereotypical answer to a far more complex reality. Like most stereotypes, the First Thanksgiving myth contains a core of historical reality, just as the new Thanksgiving myth does. The problem is that each myth presents a dangerously partial view that prevents any true appreciation of the issues involved. The more strenuously that partisans of each extreme insist that their perspective is the only entirely truthful one despite clear evidence to the contrary, the more likely it will be that the American public will feel free to ignore them. This serves only to negate the real lessons that our Thanksgiving tradition can provide.

For Native Americans, the fact that their only appearance in the annual round of remembrance that our American holiday cycle provides should be as bit players in a saccharine tale of an autumn dinner party is a bitter irony. The centuries of violence and neglect that their cultures suffered before and after 1621 are trivialized and ignored in the glow of this single mythological moment. Yet the current effort to substitute a more satisfying myth for the older tradition is no answer. It simply puts the injustice on a different footing and does not honestly confront the real problem, which is that popular history continues to overlook their story in all its lights and shadows. As permanent residents in Thanksgiving Land, be they the aboriginal heroes or mere straight men for the Pilgrims, the Native Americans can never transcend the limitations that stereotypes impose. The ideal solution might be to institute an entirely separate holiday that is focused on their real heroes alone and escape as far as possible from the confines of the Thanksgiving table. After all, if the First Thanksgiving was not one at all, why should they accept a Pyrrhic victory that mythically binds them to an irrelevant event?

The benefit of a release from the Thanksgiving table would perhaps be even greater for the Plymouth colonists. It is not always appreciated that the burden of a favorable stereotype can have as harmful consequences as a negative one. It becomes cultural typecasting, dooming the recipient to a one-dimensional character role that allows neither for interpretive growth nor for a balanced presentation of a community's history. In the case of the Pilgrims, they have been essentially turned into mythical figures, the Ghosts of Thanksgiving Past, whose predetermined role is restricted to a brief, strictly scripted appearance each fall and regarded as irrelevant during the rest of the year, at least outside Plymouth, Massachusetts. It is true that they still command respect for the rest of the 1620–1621 story, but like the myths of Greece and Rome, these once-leading exemplars of American society have been reduced to actors in a children's story, with little importance beyond their seasonal advent in advertising and on greeting cards.

The Plymouth colonists would greatly benefit if they could be freed from this fond fiction. They could be once again seen as real people rather than historical may[flower]flies who sprang to life and had their brief bright moment of glory before disappearing off the stage of history in an autumnal haze. Plymouth Colony lasted more than seventy years after the harvest dishes were washed, and there are many more important things that can be found in the Pilgrims' history if it is returned to them. If they are to be given a symbolic role at all, let it be once again as the representatives of all New England and its contributions, for good and ill, to the American nation and the world.

However, as it is highly unlikely that either the Wampanoag or the Plymouth Pilgrims will ever entirely shake themselves free of Thanksgiving, there is another way in which they can take advantage of the cultural baggage they bear. Once all the problems and difficulties with the First Thanksgiving have been confronted, there remains the poignant and inspiring fact that, as in Camelot, there once was a time when, with the best intentions, two very different cultures came together in that autumn celebration. We can and should acknowledge that it was a brief, fleeting, doomed event that has been greatly disserved by advocates and detractors alike, and cherish it as an image of hope and trust in the future. Although Thanksgiving's potential has been squandered over the years, its message is still one that all Americans can share—that through a respect for diversity and cooperation, the society the Pilgrims and the Wampanoag prefigured can thrive and grow.

Thanksgiving Now, Then, and Forever

Not all contemporary redefinitions of Thanksgiving have been negative or reactionary. Some have wanted to enhance the affirmative and progressive nature of the celebration. The holiday now has its own permanent memorial in the "Chapel of Thanksgiving" in Thanks-giving Square in Dallas, Texas. Opened in 1976, the chapel

is an international resource devoted to gathering and sharing the thanksgivings of the United States and the world. The Thanks-Giving Foundation was established on May 29, 1964. Serving as a national resource for the 200-year-old traditions of prayer and thanksgiving in America, The Center's primary purpose is to:
- Gather and share the thanksgivings of the world
- Provide a place of honor for the great American and world traditions
- Conduct research about gratitude in all religions and cultures
- Promote thanksgiving globally

The foundation was also instrumental in the "revival of the long-dormant National Day of Prayer which begins as President Ronald Reagan restores it to its traditional spring date based on Thanks-Giving Square research. Congress unanimously confirms the action in 1988."[1] Even Thanksgiving's old partner, the Fast day, is represented.

On a smaller scale, California author Victor Villaseñor was inspired by a vision of a flock of snow geese in 1992 to propose an extension to the Thanksgiving holiday that would "become a world holiday of brotherhood." He accompanied forty or so sympathetic associates to Spain to initiate this new annual event, which was called the "Snow Goose Global Thanksgiving." There was a spontaneous ceremony involving a sombrero that had belonged to his father (a Mexican immigrant to the United States) and a flag with a design of a snow goose flying across an outline of a heart on a blue field. During the ceremony he described his dream for extending the goodwill of the American holiday with an additional communal gathering on the Sunday preceding the holiday. The flag image was later reproduced on the cover of a small, self-published book outlining Villaseñor's dream vision and his crusade for a Thanksgiving-related occasion emphasizing world peace and social harmony. In the booklet he addresses the contemporary grievance-oriented protests and dissent by telling people who see themselves as victims that they need to forgive and move on (just as the perpetrators are usually happily getting on with their lives), citing his father's adoption of "living well is the best revenge" philosophy. Villaseñor traveled to Plymouth, Massachusetts, to arrange for a second celebration in 1993, but although some individuals expressed interest, he was unfortunately unable to secure town support for the event. Since then Villaseñor's holiday has been observed annually in Oceanside, California, and in other locations such as Alpine, Texas; Albuquerque, New Mexico; the Rosebud Reservation in South Dakota; and in Indianapolis, Indiana. Defined as "a day for people to put aside their political, racial, and socio-economic differences and to come together with a sense of community,"[2] the Snow Goose Global Thanksgiving is one example of how Thanksgiving's irenic and inclusionary premise can be reworked for a modern audience.

A similar tendency is evident in another little book, *The Thanksgiving Ceremony* (2003), by media executive Edward Bleier. Also a son of immigrants, Bleier felt that Americans were missing out on Thanksgiving's inspirational potential, and that some sort of simple structured ritual would be useful to strengthen the holiday tradition. "Over the years, as my wife and I prepared and celebrated Thanksgiving dinners by ourselves or with our friends, I became fixated on the idea of celebrating in a more formal and meaningful way. For at least twenty-five years I have dreamed about developing a formal ceremony that any family or collection of friends could celebrate during the traditional meal."[3] The resulting book includes a potted history of the holiday and the Pilgrims (including contemporary exaggerations concerning the Native contribution, but presented in a positive light), a twenty-minute participatory ceremony that resembles a cross between the Passover seder and a pre–World War II classroom exercise, and a diverse collection of inspirational quotes and poems on the Thanksgiving theme. It would be interesting to know how many families found in this earnest and touching little book a useful pattern for conscious reflection on Thanksgiving's symbolic significance, which is often absent from the modern holiday observance. There are celebrity blurbs on the book—these may be attributed to Bleier's wide circle of acquaintance—and thirteen positive reader reviews on Amazon.com, two of which mention buying multiple copies to distribute. A review by "A Reader from Atlanta"

(November 11, 2004) shows that the book did fulfill its author's goal in at least one instance:

I have just discovered this very charming book The Thanksgiving Ceremony. In these extraordinary times "new traditions for America's Family Feast" is a glowing jewel. I am reminded that "it" is not about polished silver, starched linens, the right amount of sage in the stuffing, the side dishes, desserts or wine selections, who gets to carve, and whether or not you-know-who will embarrass everyone. "It" is about our past and our future, fellowship, commitment, joy, perseverance and progress. And about faithful thanksgiving — every day. Thank you — Ed Bleier — for writing this book. Our family will read it together on Thanksgiving Day.[4]

Another "reader" (October 13, 2003) observed, "After years of being vaguely disturbed that Thanksgiving had descended into a football-food orgy at my house, and at the homes of relatives, with little to no recognition being given to the origin of the day, I *love* this book." Although such sentiments are not as widely disseminated as the polemics discussed in the preceding chapter, I suspect there is a broad undercurrent of support for the traditional holiday that is neither overtly conservative nor progressive. Most Americans who care about the significance of the holiday, as opposed to the majority who take it for granted, do not want to reverse or destroy the holiday's traditional associations, but to derive what pleasure they can from them.

Another attempt to put new life into an old holiday was the introduction of a Thanksgiving parade in "Thanksgiving's hometown" — Plymouth, Massachusetts — in 1996. The parade is held not on Thanksgiving Day but on the preceding Saturday, for there is plenty of local activity on the holiday already. The parade was the brainchild of Joe McStowe, owner of Isaac's Restaurant on Plymouth's waterfront. McStowe wanted the town to do something special for Thanksgiving to carry forward the good feelings generated from the 1995 anniversary celebration, during which there had been a North Plymouth neighborhood parade on Thanksgiving. As McStowe was knowledgeable about Drum and Bugle Corps competitions (one of which was scheduled in Plymouth the following summer), he was able to recruit a number of units for the new parade. His most important contribution, however, was Isaac's Restaurant's sponsorship of the event. He also installed unexpectedly dramatic fuchsia-colored banners along the parade route. The November 23, 1997, parade, which was followed by a Drum and Bugle Corps competition that evening in Plymouth's Memorial Hall, was a great success. McStowe and the town collaborated on the event for the next four years, but conflicts over expenses (Isaac's could not continue to contribute as much as it had) and McStowe's management style led to a parting of the ways in 2002. The organization of the parade was taken over by the Plymouth Rock Foundation, a local Christian group that had previously assumed responsibility for the Pilgrim Progress after the Mayflower Society was unable to maintain it. McStowe claimed that part of the difficulty between him and the town was a result of his homosexual orientation. "As an openly gay man," Stowe told the *Boston Globe,* "they had a problem with my [choice of the parade's representative] color. I never thought the color pink would scare people. It has been my favorite color since I was a kid." The new parade director, Ollie DeMacedo, said, "It just wasn't a Thanksgiving *color.* I never associated it with a gay thing. I think Joe is grasping at straws," which seems more to have been the case.[5]

Unlike the older holiday parades, the Plymouth parade does not have a strong Christmas orientation but is a celebration of Thanksgiving itself and the traditions that surround it (figure 39): "Under new sponsorship a parade committee was formed representing the diversity of the Plymouth community. New leadership birthed new ideas and a new direction. As a Plymouth Rock event, America's Hometown Thanksgiving Celebration focused on the historical aspects of Thanksgiving and our nation. Since the mission of Plymouth Rock Foundation is to preserve the integrity of the Pilgrim story, committee members decided to expand from the Pilgrim story to the legacy of Pilgrim character and principles. Thus the theme 'America Gives Thanks through the Years' was decided upon. This theme provided the structure and each year brings new content."[6] A series of floats representing symbolic milestones in the history of the Pilgrims and the United States were constructed, and a greater variety of bands and participating groups joined in the parade, which is now a popular and integral part of Plymouth's Thanksgiving season.

Such idealistic efforts have even transcended the United States. In 1997, the General Assembly of the United Nations, by Resolution 52/16 of November 20, 1997, proclaimed 2000 the "International Year of Thanksgiving."

The Economic and Social Council

Considering that the dedication of a year to the act of giving thanks gives us the opportunity to remember the fundamental importance of cultural diversity in the development of a rich and harmonious international life and that one of the purposes of the United Nations, as expressed in its Charter, is to achieve international cooperation in solving international problems in economic, social, cultural and humanitarian areas without creating any distinctions based on race, sex, language or religion,

Convinced that the observance of the year 2000 as an international year of thanksgiving within the United Nations will bring together the efforts of nations to achieve full tolerance and strengthen universal peace,

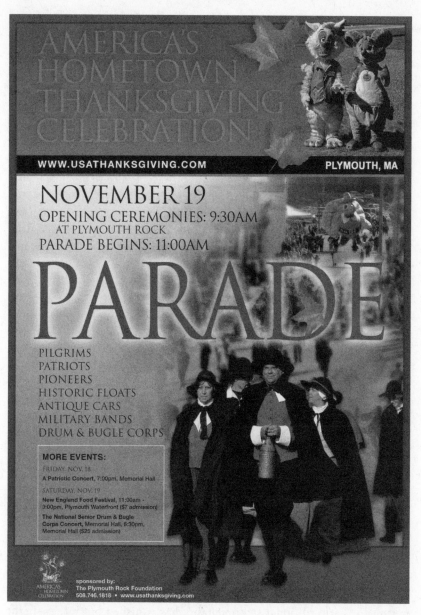

39. Handbill for "America's Hometown Thanksgiving Celebration" parade in Plymouth, Mass. (scheduled for the Saturday before the holiday), 2005.

Mindful that the preamble to the Charter of the United Nations includes the practice of tolerance as one of the principles that need to be applied to prevent war and maintain peace,

Affirming that this initiative will contribute to international cooperation by creating an awareness among peoples and Governments of the importance of gratitude as much in the personal and civic life of every human being as in the relations between the countries and cultures of the world,

Affirming also that the proposal to begin the twenty-first century and the new millennium with an international year of thanksgiving to celebrate the gift of life as the most noble expression of the human spirit is intended to promote friendship and solidarity between nations, [the Economic and Social Council]

1. Reaffirms that such an expression of gratitude will bring together national and international efforts to achieve full tolerance and strengthen universal peace and international cooperation;
2. Recommends that the General Assembly, at its fifty-second session, proclaim the year 2000 as International Year of Thanksgiving;
3. Invites all Member States and interested intergovernmental and non-governmental organizations to do whatever they can in their respective areas of expertise to contribute to the preparations for the Year and to publicizing it.[7]

However, in America the fine words resulted in very little beyond a commemorative postage stamp depicting the spiraling stained glass "Glory Window" in the Dallas Chapel of Thanksgiving and a few pious references to the U.N. "year." As with Villaseñor's and Bleier's books, these positive sentiments lacked the power to influence events, for they were out of touch with a broad spectrum of American and international opinion that is either hostile to sentimentality in general or anxious not to be seen as naïve or "uncool." The Modernist fashion for "hipness," irony, and cynicism has greatly dampened the appeal of holiday sentiment over the past forty years.

Elizabeth Pleck has postulated that we are in fact living in a "postsentimental" age in which the intelligentsia regards openly affirmative or patriotic sentiments as embarrassing, unfashionable, and immature. This does not mean that traditional sentimentality has vanished but rather that it has become déclassé. "Framed often as a reaction to what was perceived as the excess of sentimentality, the postsentimental approach to holiday celebration recognizes, if not celebrates, family diversity as well as ethnic and racial pluralism. . . . [Yet b]ecause the postsentimental approach depends on parody or critique of American sentimentality, it requires the continued existence of sentimentalism. In the postsentimental era of celebration, sentimentality has not disappeared, but instead has become a subject of debate."[8] As a holiday, Thanksgiving is traditionally relegated to the sentimental rather than the "cool" side of the cultural divide, where Halloween or New Year's Eve can be found. This apparent binary opposition between saccharine sentiment and worldly sophistication, which is also a trope in holiday anecdotes and stories, has been operative since the advent of Modernism over a century ago. Families gathered around the Thanksgiving table engage in this debate to accommodate conflicting generational or individual attitudes toward the celebration of Thanksgiving. What is more significant, however, is that apparently very few simply give up and ignore the holiday or fail to observe it in some fashion. Evidently Thanksgiving continues to be valued in spite of the questions it raises, and some kind of observance is almost universally thought to be worth the effort.

However, sentimentality in a broader sense is not solely a characteristic of the traditional side of the debate. "Sentimentalism" is defined in the Oxford English Dictionary as "the disposition to attribute undue importance to sentimental considerations, or to be governed by sentiment in opposition to reason," and this could be said to be as true of the Left's veneration of cosmopolitan ideals and privileging "oppressed" segments of society as it is of the Right's reverence for traditional families and conventional religious or patriotic beliefs. Progressive pieties that celebrate "diversity" and "pluralism" can be as full of credulous subjectivity and emotional affectation as the conservative patriotism or "family values" they attack. Like most of the "post-" this-and-that tendencies we come across in contemporary discourse, postsentimentality is more the continuation of a cultural tug-of-war that has been going on for a long time than any real break with the past.

If anything, the debate is between opposing holiday sentiments rather an attack on sentiment itself, and it has become more vigorous of late. In films, the cliché has long been for hip young people to offer snappy, ironic dissent to their parents' bland, bourgeois sentimentality, but now such scenes are as often a send-up of the callow pseudo-rebel, who renders him- or herself ridiculous by chattering platitudes about Indian martyrdom or vegetarian orthodoxy. After years of defensive opposition by conservatives against the self-assured and fashionable agenda of reformers and progressives, traditionalists are now exhibiting new strengths and have succeeded in almost leveling the cultural playing field. This has resulted in a sort of stalemate in which the American public vacillates between wanting to be sophisticated and "cool" or earnest and "square" — or both simultaneously — on this important occasion. The sentimentality debate may appear at first to be a simple binary opposition, but for many people it is characterized by Derridean ambivalence, occupying an "undecidable" intermediary ground that rejects either fixed position. They simply want to enjoy the holiday—sometimes in concert with holiday traditions and sometimes in opposition to them.

One illustration of this is the manner in which Thanksgiving is represented now in the movies. Unlike children's books, which are the principal vehicle for prescribing Thanksgiving attitudes, films are not always didactic or reductive. Films that play directly to the stereotypes of the stresses of modern middle-class family life or incompatible personal values by way of slapstick exaggeration—earnest suburbanites meeting New Age flakes (*National Lampoon Holiday Reunion*, 2003) or uptight businessman becoming entangled with infuriating, good-natured klutz (*Planes, Trains and Automobiles*, 1987)—have little interpretive value, but those that employ the holiday more incidentally reflect the ways in which American families actually assess and interpret Thanksgiving. Or rather, they reflect how our cultural purveyors *believe* they do. The story lines are often little more than updated versions of the Victorian tropes of reunion, conflict, reconciliation, and redemption, but the incidental handling of holiday symbolism and signification reveals the perceptions authors and directors have of Americans' contemporary Thanksgiving values.

For example, in *Pieces of April* (2003), April Burns, an estranged bohemian daughter, invites her embittered, dying mother and the rest of her suburban family to Thanksgiving dinner in a shabby Lower East Side apartment. The plot involves two major areas of dramatic tension: April's frantic and inept attempts to prepare her turkey dinner (after she discovers that her oven does not work) and the chaotic interaction of the Burns family on the drive to New York. Insight into holiday attitudes is found most clearly in the former. April's good-natured black boyfriend, Bobby, registers a middle-class regard for the family occasion. In addition to getting a new, conservative suit for the visit, he undertakes to decorate the apartment in good Thanksgiving style, buying a kitschy, turkey-shaped salt and pepper set (which April, reminded of her old bourgeois life, pitches but then resurrects from the trash) and putting up decorations to evoke the spirit of the day. April's diverse neighbors both help and hinder—an older black couple lend her an oven for a while, instruct her in proper Thanksgiving cookery, and make homemade cranberry sauce for her, while a helpful if bewildered Chinese family finally completes the roasting of the turkey. On the other hand, a vegan neighbor reneges on the use of her oven ("I won't cook anything that had a face"), and a gay tenant reluctantly lends her the use of his new stove only to balk later when she will not accommodate whatever social interaction he has in mind. Here we see positive and negative tropes of "neighborliness" that by implication denote the Thanksgiving holiday spirit.

The commemorative nature of the day is made plain (in addition to the decorations) by April's attempts to explain what the holiday is all about to the (non-English-speaking) Chinese parents. She begins by trying to describe the Pilgrim experience with earnest, grade school simplicity— "it was a *really* hard first year"—but then reconsiders as she remembers the alternative version and begins again from the "cool" perspective by describing how the Pilgrims "stole most of the land and killed most of [the Indians]"—then stops again, and in a sudden epiphany, blurts out the message of the film—that the two contrasting groups did come together, for on "this one day, they knew for certain that they couldn't do it alone." Although the holiday message of the family's station wagon ride is less explicit, the very fact that the ill, bitter mother and well-intentioned father (along with April's teenage siblings and a grandmother named "Dottie" suffering from dementia) persevere through all obstacles and misapprehensions in their effort to bridge the long-standing familial divide in Thanksgiving's name reveals the cultural weight of the holiday. The movie ends with the standard happy denouement and reconciliation, but it is the earlier revelations about what Americans believe constitutes an authentic Thanksgiving that are important.

What's Cooking (2000) is a film depicting four simultaneous suburban Thanksgiving celebrations in Los Angeles' Fairfax district. The Williams (African American), Avila (Hispanic), Nguyen (Vietnamese), and Seelig (American Jewish) households each prepare a turkey dinner, with variations on the family conflict theme that cover many of the standard problems faced by modern American holiday gatherings. The movie opens with a traditional Thanksgiving school play attended by Mrs. Williams, in which the children, including her daughter (who later initiates a game of "Pilgrims" at home), are decked out in elaborate paper Pilgrim and Indian costumes and carry a paper turkey among other seasonal holiday props. The only other reference to the historical roots of the holiday is a brief sarcastic "grace" offered by the goth daughter of a white couple visiting with the Williamses, who remarks on the plight of the Indians—the loss of land and the introduction of measles—labeling the event a "Thanks-taking" rather than a Thanksgiving. This is quickly passed over by everyone else present in the well-to-do home except for rebellious son Michael.

Each family prepares a requisite turkey in its own way (unsuccessfully in the case of the Nguyens, where it burns and Kentucky Fried Chicken is substituted). Pumpkin pies are present in the Nguyen, Avila, and Seelig households (and perhaps at the Williamses' as well, but it is hard to tell). Cranberry sauce—homemade in the Avila, Williams, and Seelig examples, and canned for the Nguyens (it remains uneaten)—completes the iconic culinary markers of the feast. Otherwise, the menus reflect the ethnic heritage of each family. The most traditional American Thanksgiving meals are seen in the Williams and Seelig homes. There is competition between the gourmet tastes of housewife Alma Williams and the traditional preferences of her mother-in-law, and the addition of polenta by Mrs. Seelig for her Italian (?) daughter-in-law to an otherwise down-to-earth postwar menu, which includes sweet potatoes with little marshmallows. Except for the obligatory turkey, cranberry sauce, and pumpkin pies, the Avilas' and the Nguyens' dinners consist of their own ethnic cuisines. Each family delivers its own version of a dinner grace, with a contribution from each guest at the Williamses', while the youngest son in the Nguyen family offers a standard Americanized list of thanks — and future wants.

The individual plots for each household's holiday involve typical examples of family conflict, with no particular Thanksgiving association beyond the fundamental theme of the problems posed by family reunions. The Williamses' prosperous sophistication is challenged by husband Ron's recent affair, wife Audrey's unease (exacerbated by her mother-in-law's carping), and son Michael's involvement in throwing white paint over the conservative state governor, for whom Ron and his guests work. The Avilas' conflict is based on the parents' separation. Lizzie's erring husband, invited against her wishes by her son, shows up only to be confronted with her new boyfriend. Their college-aged daughter invites her boyfriend, Jimmy Nguyen (who has led his strictly traditional family to believe he is staying on campus), and he is welcomed without difficulty by the exuberant extended Avila family. The complication for the elderly Seeligs is the lesbian relationship of daughter Rachael and her partner, Carla, complicated by earnest, naïve hints about marriage from Rachael's aunt and the revelation of Rachael's pregnancy (with a gay donor, Jerry, who is also present). The Nguyens' problems begin with Americanized daughter Jennie's white boyfriend and the discovery of a condom in her coat pocket, but this is overshadowed by Jennie's discovery that her brother Greg is hiding a gun for a friend. This family is perhaps the least wealthy, least acclimated, and most traditional of the lot, with the usual Asian concerns for achievement, dutiful children, and filial loyalty. The climax of the film comes when Greg's little brother accidentally fires the pistol while the rest of the family is agonizing over their dilemmas. We later discover that he was not hurt, but the gunshot and its shattering of a window reveal that all four families live on a single intersection in suburbia, underlining an assumed similarity of America's isolated middle-class lives.

Home for the Holidays (2005) presents an embarrassingly dysfunctional family holiday beset with plot complications. A just-fired single mother, Claudia Larson, is driven to the airport by daughter Kit (who announces her intention to have sex with the boyfriend whose family she is visiting for Thanksgiving) and flies from Chicago to suburban Maryland to join her family for the holiday. Her parents still live in Claudia's childhood home in cluttered, slightly outdated bourgeois expansiveness. Here the tension is provided by the outrageous interaction between the various family members. Gay brother Tommy—whose partner (or rather "spouse," as it comes out that they have married) is back in Boston—arrives in the middle of the night with his friend/employee Leo and stages a mock break-in. Uptight younger sister Joanne (who brings a competing cooked turkey for the dinner) and her conservative yuppie family arrive with obvious apprehension. Loopy Aunt Gladys insists on revealing a long-past infatuation with her host and brother-in-law. All are greeted by Claudia's affectionately bickering parents—cynical but practical mother Adele and impish, affable father Henry. The assumption is that not only have the rather over-the-top characters been misbehaving in a similar fashion for years (and expect to do so again come Christmas) but that the sometimes mean-tempered behavior has become their normal way of relating. Only Joanne's husband, Walter, has any real problem with this. The Larsons feel no need for decorations to legitimize the event, but they obviously accept the cultural imperative to gather together despite the chaos and ill feelings their gathering engenders. Henry is puzzled by this (in his "benediction" he muses inchoately, "Everything is changing too damn fast; give me those old-fashioned, pain-in-the-ass traditions like Thanksgiving, which really mean something to us, although, goddamn it, we couldn't tell what it is") but accepts it as a given.

A suburban Thanksgiving of yet another sort is depicted in *The Ice Storm* (1997). Here the holiday is incidental to the movie's depressing round of bored, upper-middle-class sexual indulgence and adolescent confusion in the decadent 1970s, so that the holiday dinner scene is more interesting for what it omits than what it includes. There is no extended family or crazed kinfolk. Grandpop, who inspired "yelling and hysteria," has passed on—"we do miss him," father Ben Hood adds with pious insincerity. The turkey dinner for a nuclear family of four is modern and fashionable, like the household itself, but perfunctory. The Hoods dutifully celebrate Thanksgiving because "that's what done," but the event has atrophied and become empty of meaning for the family. An incongruous nod to tradition comes when Ben asks daughter Wendy to deliver a grace, which is obviously not normal mealtime practice. After surprised hesitation, fourteen-year-old Wendy comes up with an appropriately cynical "grace": "Dear Lord, we thank you for this Thanksgiving holiday weekend, and for letting us white people kill all the Indians and steal their land, and stuff ourselves like pigs, and napalm children in—" before she is interrupted. The idea is clearly to mock the hypocritical appeal to tradition among well-to-do Connecticut sophisticates (although if the Indian part is an anachronism reflective of 1990s attitudes, that would not have been in the social vocabulary of a fourteen-year-old in 1973). Even so, no one balks or questions the keeping up of appearances, which is a major preoccupation of this dysfunctional family.

Turning from these conflicted suburban families to accounts of Jewish clans celebrating Thanksgiving in Woody Allen's *Hannah and Her Sisters* (1986) and Barry Levinson's *Avalon* (1990), we see another side of the holiday's role in American life. Lacking the option of Christmas reunions, these families gather around the nondenominational Thanksgiving table to catch up on relationships and rehearse the various burdens of family history. In both cases, the Thanksgiving reunion serves as a device to punctuate the passing years and changing situations of the family and individuals associated with it. Three Thanksgivings mark the beginning, middle, and end of the various threads of the story in *Hannah and Her Sisters*—all of which are very modern and urban without any explicit evocation of the holiday's historical significance. In *Avalon*, the Krichinsky family is shown at four widely spaced Thanksgivings over half a century. The first two dinners are crowded with relations, reflecting the traditional family unity of the immigrant brothers and their wives and children. Thanksgiving at first is still a new American concept, met with amused observations: "the Pilgrims started it, whoever they were," and "It's a strange kind of holiday." As the movie progresses, the Old World familial cohesion fitfully breaks down under the pressures of modern life. Two of the more prosperous second-generation couples move to the suburbs, leaving the others in downtown Baltimore, after which family meetings and holiday reunions wind down. On the third Thanksgiving, we see first-generation Sam Krichinsky as a widower, living in suburbia with his son Jules' family (whose surname, "Kaye," like their lives, has been Americanized); they are watching television and dining alone as an American nuclear family. The final holiday depicts a brief visit by grandson Michael Kaye and his young son to Sam on Thanksgiving in a nursing home in the 1960s, by which time the original extended family has become only a memory. Thanksgiving remains a constant, but it has become a hollow modern exercise emptied of tradition and history in a fissiparous national culture.

What we can deduce from these movie themes is that Thanksgiving is above all a middle-class imperative, that the federal holiday makes it possible to travel to join with family members for the eucharistic consumption of turkey and cranberry sauce at an old-fashioned midday dinner hour, and that the historic links are dutifully inculcated in children but then only erratically remembered, should the occasion arise. Most importantly, the holiday and its requirements are internalized to the point that, above a certain social level, its observance simply cannot be omitted.

Surveying films, articles, and websites to learn what Americans think

Thanksgiving is about, we conclude that, despite the efforts of various parties to redefine the holiday in a specific direction, the American Thanksgiving progresses in much the same way it has for the last century. The holiday has steadily become more broadly humanistic, so that the primary observation is not commemoration or contemplation but family reunion and dinner, to which the custom of watching parades or football games is often added. Rituals such as Christian benedictions or secular recitations of things to be thankful for may occupy families briefly, but they soon fall upon the American feast of turkey and cranberry sauce with materialistic gusto. There can be no doubt that Thanksgiving will continue to be an important social ritual in the American civic calendar whether the old pieties are abandoned or not, and that it will evade capture by political extremism or, for that matter, commercial exploitation.

Consumerism has become a prevalent intellectual anxiety nowadays, but the effect of commerce is less an issue with Thanksgiving than with Christmas or Halloween, and even so, "[r]esisting the machinations of merchants [is] not particularly important to most people most of the time. Whatever humbug, exploitation, or imposture resided in modern celebrations (and there was plenty), alienation [is] only one leitmotif in a larger chorus of affirmation."[9] The traditional dinner does not lend itself to commercial excess, and there has never been a successful attempt to make it an occasion for buying candy, flowers, or gifts. The use of greeting cards is modest, and the holiday has not undergone "child centering," which is a relief. Knickknacks and decorations are one aspect of commercial affirmation that Thanksgiving involves. Many families enjoy buying and displaying holiday decorations, perhaps to capture a holiday spirit they can no longer find in abstract traditions with which they feel no personal connection. Having an accumulation of Thanksgiving and harvest-themed objects around the house reinforces the sentimental (as well as the symbolic and historical) side of the holiday, and also legitimizes the celebration amid otherwise quotidian surroundings, as Bobby and April attempt in *Pieces of April*. The use of topical decorations is also part of a wider trend toward "dressing up" homes with flags, inflatable figures, "shelf-sitters," miniature figurines, and similar topical gewgaws. In his study of American holidays, Jack Santino noted, "people [now] hang decorations throughout the year, changing them according to the months and the holidays."[10] There has been a steady increase in the importance accorded American Indians in holiday symbolism—both affirmative and critical—while Ellis Island, with its focus on ethnic difference, is now as potent a symbol of America's origins as Plymouth Rock. Yet, if the Pilgrims are relinquishing some of their iconic significance, they are by no means losing their ornamental role as sentimental holiday symbols.

The continued use of Pilgrim and Indian imagery attests to a widely diffused curiosity about and enthusiasm for the historical/symbolic foundation of the holiday—sketchy and confused as these impulses may be. The commemoration of the Pilgrim feast, which was largely a twentieth-century construct, has receded somewhat, leaving the Plymouth colonists and their Indian guests serving more as logos of the holiday than as its tributary heroes. As Barry Schwartz observed in his study of the Abraham Lincoln legend,

> Generations like our own, that celebrate "cultural diversity" are not attracted to national heroes. . . . Instead of admiring Lincoln, America's ethnic communities document their own accomplishments, and insist on their rightful place in American history—such is the multiculturalist argument. Multiculturalism is hostile to national heroes because it distinguishes so sharply the identity of the nation from its constituent communities and assumes that the latter see historical actors like Lincoln [or the Pilgrims] as strangers with whom they would have nothing to do were it not for the dominant culture's influence. The multicultural perspective defines the state's assertion of national ideals as ethnic genocide.[11]

But multiculturalism is only one way in which Americans approach history and commemorative holidays. The continued popularity of sentimental First Thanksgiving imagery indicates that the holiday is still an occasion for quaint representations of the past, and it is firmly anchored on the nostalgic side of the "sentimental versus cool" debate for most Americans.

What does the future portend for Thanksgiving? It would be gratifying to be able to assert that the documented history of Thanksgiving's origins and evolution as presented in this book should be the correct way in which to view the subject, and that Thanksgiving will hereafter be liberated from the inaccurate and misleading accounts that begin with the unexamined assumption that it all began with the Pilgrims—or with Mrs. Hale and President Lincoln—but matters of history, heritage, and belief are not that simple. What actually happened in the past is often less influential than what has been believed to have happened. The erroneous concepts that have in fact shaped our understanding of Thanksgiving's history and determined the manner in which the holiday has evolved since the late nineteenth century have a significance that cannot be overlooked or explained away. The perception that Thanksgiving owes a great debt to the Pilgrim story may be, like that story itself, a myth, but that myth is inextricable from both the history of the holiday and Thanksgiving's actual significance in American life. As R. I. Moore has cogently observed, the antithesis between the "teleological" history . . . meaning (I think) inquiry primarily shaped by perceived outcomes, and the reconstruction of the past in its own terms—*wie es eigentlich gewesen* in Ranke's phrase—is a false one. Historians have to live with Heisenbergian uncertainty: they cannot simultaneously plot position and trajectory without distortion.[12]

Acknowledging this "uncertainty" and the ambiguity it involves, we will close by viewing the situation from a different point of view.

We began this study of Thanksgiving with the discovery that popular history, which claims a direct line of descent for Thanksgiving from the 1621 Plymouth harvest festival and from harvest customs in general, was mistaken. Neither the Plymouth colonists and the Wampanoag Indians nor ancient harvest festivals were the historical progenitors of the American Thanksgiving. The holiday's true genealogy stretches back through New England Puritanism to the providential holy days of Calvinism in England and Europe. Thanksgiving was not an American holiday by birth, but rather a naturalized immigrant tradition. In the interests of historical accuracy, we need to acknowledge Thanksgiving's true historical origin and accurately explain its evolution as a fundamental American tradition. However, after having made this thesis the central argument of the book, I would now like to acknowledge that the accident of birth does not trump all other factors in questions of heritage. Our modern Thanksgiving did not originate in Plymouth in 1621, but for all practical purposes, *it may as well have.* The Pilgrims, with their legendary "First Thanksgiving," have become, by adoption as it were, the real patrons of the American Thanksgiving. Karen L. King has identified an important factor in intellectual history that she calls "the fallacy of equating origin with essence, or the assumption that the original form of something was automatically its true, essential form forever after."[13] What Thanksgiving was in the early New England colonies is no longer central to its identity. Over the years, the holiday has grown, matured, and been transformed into something quite different. What began as a strict Puritan day of worship that suffered "no servile Labor, and such Recreation, as, though at other Times innocent, [being] unbecoming . . . on so solemn an Occasion"[14] has, over its four centuries of observance, become a civic ritual that embodies secular recreations and family gatherings, and celebrates the spirit of the harvest in the tradition of the Hebrew Feast of Tabernacles, American Indian thanksgivings, and agricultural celebrations around the world.

Today, Thanksgiving's collateral descent from the 1621 Plymouth festival is its defining characteristic. The Pilgrims' and the Wampanoag's mythic gathering has become for better or for worse the principal emblem of the holiday. The holiday we enjoy today may have far deeper historical roots, but it is the tradition that began with President Lincoln in 1863 that marks the birth of *our* American Thanksgiving. What was at one time an early winter event for summing up the providential results of the entire year has been transformed into an aesthetic autumnal harvest celebration symbolic of the agrarian society from which our nation evolved. Engaged partisans may debate the respective symbolic roles of the Pilgrims and the Wampanoag, the appropriateness of commercial holiday exploitation, or the relative merit of the sentiments of tradition against the sentiments of sophistication, but it is the existing myth of Thanksgiving that continues to shape the public understanding of the holiday's meaning, history notwithstanding. Like all living myths, the Thanksgiving story is genuinely empowering for those who believe in it and, as in other matters of faith, is not amenable to arguments of reason.

The holiday's cultural vigor is actually demonstrated by the very conflicts and debates that surround it, for if Thanksgiving was no longer an important factor in American life, there would be no motivation to dispute its meaning or observation. Like the fact that the holiday retains its unique Thursday position in the national calendar and has not been shifted to a Monday or some other more convenient time slot, the arguments and ambiguity are actually reassuring. Any tradition that can be modified at will, or narrowly defined without dispute, has in fact lost its cultural vitality. It has become a lifeless social artifact, with importance perhaps to some narrow constituency or cultural historians but not the general public. Debate indicates relevance, and the dispute over the appropriate role of Thanksgiving in American life demonstrates that the holiday is very much alive and still evolving. As Barry Schwartz observes,

No legacy, however, is equally appealing to all parts of American society. Some Americans question or disparage national memories rather than embrace them; others wish to modify or replace the existing legacy, in part or whole, with another. The nation, then, is not a common legacy of memories fixed once and for all; it is a common movement, a common quest whereby communities seek their own understanding of the past, cherish it, come to grips with it, or deliberately use it in their own way.[15]

Liberal arguments involving the politics of memory that seek to challenge the Pilgrims' iconic position as the honorary ancestors of all Americans, or showcase the tribulations of the American Indians under colonialism, or acknowledge the separate experiences of subsequent immigrants are all potential factors in the future interpretation of the holiday. Alternately, the recent political turn to the Right and the increased influence of conservative Christian opinion in American life may have a different effect and tip the scales toward a more traditional interpretation of the holiday. All that can be said with certainty is that Thanksgiving will continue to be polysemic, in that it will signify different things to different people, and even different things to the same people in different circumstances.

However, for the majority of Americans, these issues are of peripheral interest if any at all. The quibbles of historians and activists have little real effect on the way in which Americans observe the holiday. Turkey dinners and family reunions or watching parades and football matches do not require historical expiation or explanation. Similarly, the use of decorations, whether of Pilgrims, turkeys, Indians, or generic harvest-season scenes, need not evoke debates over the exact nature of the 1621 "First Thanksgiving." And this is as it should be—not everything about a holiday needs to be interrogated, worried over, and debated. If the American Thanksgiving did not come about in quite the way most people think it did, we hope that those who are interested in such things can find answers to their questions here and get a clearer understanding of the problem. For the rest, and for everyone in due season, it will be enough simply to embrace the holiday and have a happy Thanksgiving.

A Thanksgiving Poem by Henry Bliss

From Henry Bliss, *Thanksgiving, A Poem, In Two Parts* (Pittsfield, Mass.: Phinæhas Allen, 1815), pp. 2–11.

Part One

Behold! Where pleasure bids her votaries rise,
Wide as the Genius of Thanksgiving flies,
O'er "Massachusetts' hundred hills" she calls
For sports and feasts, for riots and for balls,
From hobbling age to sprightly childhood steer,
And lists her thousands in her gay career.
Such daily works of preparation made,
Such ways and means of luxury display'd,
To fancy's eye 'twould certainly appear
That Nature had her frolicks once a year;
Or that the states by fits 'twas plain,
Had lost their reason and become insane.

All other business now lay aside,
Save what for this best holiday provide,
While toiling thousands in the work are found,
Butchers and cooks and tailors hurried round,
As if 'twas meant on this auspicious day,
To reach the goal where every pleasure lay;
Or that its end had only been designed
To feast the body, not improve the mind;
Or set apart to see who most outvied
In scenes of vain extravagance and pride.
Not so the brutal tribes, poor harmless race,
Whose blood must pay for Massachusetts grace,
To them the day rolled on by gloomy fate,
Is ushered in by slaughter through the state.
E'en now I hear, or seem to hear from far,
The mingled groans from this *New-England war*!
Borne in the breeze the cries of dying swine,
The bleeding lambkins and the slaughtered kine,
By hecatombs they tumble through the state,

Each hour is murder and each moment fate.
Geese, turkies, ducks and pullets now are found
In fluttering heaps laid gasping on the ground.
No town nor village known, or proud or mean,
But now takes part in this inglorious scene;
No rank, no family, so high or low,
But makes a feast or makes a festive show,
Proud wealth contributes to the cheering day,
And full-fed poverty looks plump and gay,
For every cottage boy with hurried pace,
Bears home his offering with a smiling face,
And fancies while he muses on his way,
Some happy scene to crown th' approaching day.

The Cookery now goes on, the baking's laid,
And many a mammoth pie and pudding's made,
Roast meat and gingerbread and custards rare,
Are seen and smelt and tasted everywhere,
Plumb-cakes and sweet-meats of all kinds abound,
The country floats with dainties fit for kings,
An inundation of the choicest things.

See the poor family whose toil and care
Can scarce procure life's comforts through the year,
Ev'n for one rich repast on this blest day,
Will turn and shift and straiten every way,
Oft when the groaning oven is releas'd,
And cakes and pastries on the table plac'd,
The children snatch them, while with bawling notes
They cram the red-hot victuals down their throats.
Dogs too and cats are gorg'd with flesh and bones,
The day brings surfeits and the night brings groans.

Some now from country shops or markets come,
Bring much fresh news with spice and brandy home,
The farmer thriving in these plodding climes,
Raves loud against the hardness of the times,
The merchant who his double profit takes,
Exclaims against th' unrighteous price he makes,
Or while he slyly feeds Columbia's foes,
Grows rich and fattens on his country's woes,
Condemns her rulers, feigning to abhor
The dire effects of an unrighteous war.

But see the long anticipated day
That bears its thousands down the world's broad way,

Again arrives its splendors to reveal,
To save its custards and its cleric zeal,
And while its brilliant crowds it now arrays,
Far more of pride than piety displays;
Too many seen at church now know no more
The preacher's words than what they knew before;
Three-fourths at least some other object calls,
To see new bonnets and to talk of balls!
Some go for news, and some to learn the price
Of beef and cheese, or when they'll have a rise;
Some go to hear the Parson preach and pray,
Some find no faith in what he has to say.
New gowns, new coats, new fashions now appear,
Pride in the front and envy in the rear;
The day is short, the meeting is soon done,
The worship closes much as it begun,
Save here and there some worthier being found,
Urg'd on by duty and with virtue crown'd,
Who sees through all creation spread abroad,
The vast exuberant bounties of a God!
Sees him in Providence our views above,
Or hails his mercies in Redeeming Love;
Sees Him all good, all glorious in His ways,
And feels his bosom glow with love and praise,
Ev'n while he views His kind indulgent hand,
That showers His blessings on our guilty land,
The sacred theme while pleasing to pursue,
He sings of mercies and of judgments too;
Sees how long fed by heaven's peculiar care,
Her wayward sons His blessings could not bear,
Like Israel murmuring, 'till a righteous God
Permits their wrongs and sends His scourging rod,
Suffers their guilty foes with haughty scorn
Their wealth to plunder and their rights to spurn.

From church dismiss'd where pleasure leads the way,
Her votaries follow and her crowds obey,
Let loose to pastimes, mirth and social joy,
Balls, feasts and visits now their hours employ,
And oft the revel roar still louder rings,
While Folly fiddles on her lowest strings;
And much too oft in taverns gather'd round,
The impious order of the day is found,
Breaks out from vulgar groups who there resort,
Loud raving riot and delirious sport,

The laugh, the shout, the oath blasphemous heard,
The wreck of morals and the God unfear'd

Thus 'tis in this or some such impious way,
Vain thoughtless thousands keep Thanksgiving Day;
Thus o'er the banquet and the flowing bowl,
Deform the nobler beauties of the soul;
Carousing at the taverns and the feast,
Unconscious as the viands which they taste;
Not e'en one thought of gratitude they show
To Him from whom their numerous blessings flow.
Not so the circles where the expanding heart
More polish'd scenes of pleasure can impart,
And such there are in every country town,
Of virtuous habits and of fair renown,
Whose minds unwarp'd by dissipation's fires,
No low pursuit nor vulgar theme inspires,
Form'd for society that's more refin'd,
Which mends the morals and improves the mind,
Their souls arise on philosophic wing,
From man, from nature, up to Heaven's King;
And while they soar all earth-born themes above,
Hail HIM the fountain of Eternal Love!
To such the day a nobler banquet brings,
To such it opens all its sacred springs,
Nor this alone, all days alike impart,
His gifts and claim the homage of the heart.
Or if adverting to their country's cause,
Its wrongs, its insults, and its righteous laws,
With liberal candor they the theme pursue,
Nor hate the friend who differs from their view.

Thus round the social fire their evening hours
Improve their being and exalt their powers,
While trifling crowds in revelry delight,
And plunge in giddy pleasures of the night,
'till morn return'd in gay amusement leads
The sister holyday that now succeeds.
Dancing goes on, no care their bliss controls,
Throng'd ball-rooms shake while soft'ning music rolls;
Now beaux and fops so modish and so fine,
Like insects fluttering in the sun-beams shine,
While swarming belles in buxom charms so gay,
Swim in the dance and flutter in the play,

While some in cards and dice their hours employ,
Or in carousals catch the passing joy;
Love, Courtships, Weddings too are carried on,
And much of social visiting is done,
And oft where malice marks her victim's doom,
The slanderous tale runs whispering around the room,
And oft some flight of wit the humor pours,
'till all the table with loud laughter roars.
Now the rich banquet spreads its dainty store,
'till hungry Epicures can eat no more;
Now every child through all the country round,
With puddings, cakes, and gingerbread is crown'd;
And many a slattern's brat may now be seen,
Who ev'n for once a year is scrubbed and clean.

Lo! arm'd for sport, whose whole troop of men and boys,
Elate and merry with expected joys,
Now to th' appointed rendezvous repair,
To form jovial shooting matches there.
At measur'd distance plac'd and tied with care,
The feather'd victim bides the unequal war;
'till one more skillful or more lucky found,
Lays the poor prisoner bleeding on the ground,
And in proud triumph bears his game away,
Whose price, perhaps, a dozen scarce could pay.
At once another fowl his place supplies,
And many a marksman now his utmost tries,
'till one whose ball bears life and liberty,
Cuts off the string and sets the captive free.
Loud is the shout and much the noise
Of men, and barking dogs, and running boys,
'till worried out the panting game they take,
And tie the unwilling victim to the stake;
'till some sharp shooter draws the mark so nigh,
They all declare they see the feathers fly!
Again they run and search to find the wound,
Inspect the body, but no blood is found;
Save where some knavish elf with knife or pin,
By one sly scratch cuts through the tender skin,
Then searching closely tells a dozen lies,
And roundly swears his bullet won the prize.
Thus pass their hours as custom leads the way,
'till night brings home the trophies of the day.
Here those are found so scrupulously nice,

Who fly from cards, from billiards and from dice,
Who at this sport their money will advance,
And make no conscience at such games of chance.

Some whom the pleasure of the Chase invite,
Whom woods and fields and mountain-scenes delight,
With eager strides the wonted game in view,
The wily Fox and Turkey now pursue,
O'er hills and vales, through swamps and thickets run,
Nor quit the pastime 'till the setting sun;
'till night returns them in a sober mood,
More tir'd and tamer than the game pursu'd.
Oft times whole troops of chosen hunters make
The *squirrel-hunt* the pleasures they partake;
Some bottled bet, to cheer their drooping frames,
Waits 'till the night the victory proclaims;
Arm'd with their guns, with axes, dogs and poles,
To rout their game and drive from their holes,
At early dawn they to the woodland stray.
Eager to win the honors of the day,
Round hills and plains they spread the parish o'er,
Search every wood and every swamp explore,
As if (their feats so eager to display)
Their Country's fate depended on the day!
Loud is the noise of many a dog and gun,
And great exploits by many a marksman's done,
Squirrels and birds now fall like setting bees,
As if they hail'd by hundreds from the trees;
Or if by dealing death in every place,
They now resolv'd t' exterminate their race;
So fast the guns keep up th' incessant roar,
This way and that way and a hundred more,
From every copse and hedge, both near and far,
As though th' woods sustain'd an Indian War.
No stop, no stay, they have no time to make,
Nor food nor rest but few afford to take,
Through cold and wet, through frost and miry bogs,
Through brush and brambles, over rocks and logs,
Some run, some creep, some skulk behind the stumps,
Some fire erect, some sitting on their rumps,
And many an eager youth with erring eye,
Fires as he runs and helps his game to fly;
And many a hasty hunter through mistakes,
Squirrels of limbs and birds of brushwood makes;
Claps up his gun, lets fly a thundering shot,

Yet sees his game unrouted from the spot;
Again he loads, resolved to do his best,
Aims with precision at the victim's breast,
Who still unhurt, nor lead can kill or scare,
Nor legs nor wings are seen to move a hair;
Surprise and wonder now the hunters seize,
Some think 'tis witchcraft got among the trees!
'till one who looks with less deceitful eyes.
Finds out the cheat and points them where it lies.
Thus they go on and spend the sportive day,
And many a worthless beast and bird they slay,
'till night's dark shades spread wide the woodland o'er,
And bids them now pursue the chase no more,
While to the appointed place they all repair,
To know their luck and find refreshments there;
Some chosen hands now counts the piles of game,
And oft, while counting, find both *wild* and *tame*,
Which makes the talk and clamor run so high,
All peace and concord for a season fly!
Now round the clutter'd hall huge piles display
The various feats and trophies of the day!
There birds and quadrupeds of every kind,
With which our native fields and woods are lin'd,
Squirrels and hares, with land and water fowls,
Woodcocks and ducks, and partridges and owls!
A motley groupe, all clotted with their gore,
In mingled heaps lie rang'd along the floor;
Now round the merry hall the liquor plies,
And many a jest and many a banter flies,
And many a tale too big to be believ'd,
Of wondrous feats by guns and dogs achiev'd,
And oft the sprightly dance or social play,
Concludes the fond diversions of the day.

But this is far more honorable sport,
Than that display'd where gambling sots resort;
They who their time, their money and their fame,
Their neighbor's interest, and their friend's good name,
All in one frantic hour advanc'd at stake,
The bane of families and fortune's wreck,
Or when vile Tipplers midnight homeward drives,
Reeling to curse their suppers and their wives;
Or when unblest with charity and love,
Sectarians loud each others creed disprove,
Making Religion run such wild extremes,

Their zeal a burlesque on the Gospel seems;
While far from such the Gospel spirit flies,
And Love, and Charity, and Union dies.
Or when associate Infidels combine
To spurn all subjects sacred and divine;
When to break loose from prejudices strong,
And systems which have fool'd mankind so long.
All sense and reason they calmly quit,
And scoffs and censures substitute for wit,
God's holy word deriding but to show
What more by reason's purer light they know,
As if their doctrine more of comfort spread,
Or claim'd a patent for the light it shed!
Or man could better read his Maker's will,
In the loud tempest or the murm'ring rill,
Or searching nature find through all her reign,
How he was born to die and live again.

Or when more sober, yet disgraceful scene,
For evening plays when children oft convene,
And some old woman superstition nursed
With wonders loaded and strange horrors curs'd
Tells any a bloody tale of other times,
Of murders, goblins, ghosts and smother'd crimes!
Of haunted woods and houses, horrid sights,
Of headless bodies and village frights;
Or while their hair with terror stands upright,
And every child begins to hate the night,
Changes the theme which equal horrors cause,
To tales of *witch-craft* and its secret laws;
Tells how in days of yore strange pranks were play'd,
Which men transformed and parishes dismay'd,
How many miles beneath a pond'rous load,
Chang'd to a Horse, a neighbor had been rode;
How Imps at night, through key-holes us'd to glide,
When barns were burnt and neighbors cattle died,
How lights on masts or trees was seen to glare,
How Cats and Partridges by silver bled,
In the same hour old women were found dead.

Or thence descending to more modern days,
With Goblin tales her auditors dismays;
How Maids bewitch'd, and claw'd by tooth and nail,
Frightened whole towns and made the doctors pale;
When stubborn spinning wheels refus'd to go,

In spite of all that human strength could do;
Or how when charms were us'd to lay the gloom,
Good books and bibles flew about the room.
Such are the frightful tales too often told,
Which children hear 'till ev'n their blood runs cold;
Ev'n in this friendly age of boasted light,
That long has been beam'd o'er superstition's night,
Ev'n on this soil that boasts of cultur'd minds,
Where no *Magnalia* modern reason binds,
By far too oft some village wonder flies,
Which reason combats and truth denies.

O! were the Day to its just ends appli'd,
And sober reason left to be our guide,
Were Heaven's high King the object we ador'd,
His gifts acknowledg'd and his grace implor'd,
Soon would the Pulpit cease its factious roar,
And party rage His altars stain no more,
Nor would the time its thoughtless crowds decoy,
In custom's road to catch the sensual joy.
Then would the Muse with rapture and delight,
Hail the glad day and in its work unite,
While solemn anthems of resounding praise
Tun'd her fond lyre a nobler song to raise.

O! could she now on More's exalted wing,
In loftier strains a worthier tribute bring,
Here chosen numbers while they flow'd along,
Her God and Country should inspire here song.
Nor would she stoop, tho' fortune led the way,
To flatter knaves, or Freedom's cause betray;
Fearless alike of censure or applause,
She scorns to fly her bleeding country's cause;
Nor on the wings of fancy will she rove
Beyond the bounds which justice must approve.

O! while here western sons Columbia sees
With active zeal obey here prompt decrees,
While fearless now to quell here haughty foes,
Here bravest blood a holy offering flows!
Shall this extraneous soil our sires disgrace,
While its *peace parties* nurse a traitorous race!
Combine to lay their country's freedom low,
Ev'n at her vitals aim the deadly blow!
League to dissolve her Union's sacred chain,

Pollute with impious hands her hallowed fane,
And while they spurn their country's righteous laws,
Cherish her foes and aid the Briton's cause,
Or 'gainst the patriot who obeys her call,
With frenzied zeal prolong th' cleric brawl!
Here on these once regenerate climes
The Priest absolves the venal *Briton's* crimes,
Defiles the altar where sedition's fires
With pious rage he kindles and inspires!
Hears, while regardless of his country's moans,
The savage war song and the ocean's groans!
Ev'n while the hall of legislation shows
Hate to her cause and friendship to her foes;
War's crimson wave thro' western climes that roars,
Beats soft and harmless round these eastern shores.

But He who first ordain'd Columbia's laws
Will still support and aid her righteous cause;
'twas then our fathers, fearless in the field,
Knew how to die but knew not how to yield,
'till all was gain'd their country's cause requir'd,
'till Freedom triumph'd and the world admir'd
'tis the same cause, as glorious and as just,
in the same arm with confidence we trust;
'twas God himself, omnipotent and kind,
Our favor's land for Liberty design'd,
Here taught each patriot sage the liberal plan,
Here wak'd the noblest energies of man!
Here far from all the empty pride of kings,
Open'd a new and happier scene of things!
Bade the red sea of tyranny retreat
To distant regions where its bounds were set;
Gave to the view a paradise regain'd,
A world of treasures in itself contain'd,
Where favor'd man no proud distinction knows,
Save what on merit or on virtue grows;
Lo! free as light its common blessing sheds,
Nor claims protection from vain man to draw,
Nor props from erring codes of human law,
Shedding its influence like the gentle dew,
God its great author and protector too.

Let not the Christian build his faith so low
As that foundation pride and avarice show,
Nor think whatever hypocrites pretend,

Vile man the great JEHOVAH's works can mend;
Tho' kings and states too often interfere,
Mark Heav'n's own lines and legal barriers rear,
HE who maintains his own Almighty cause,
Confounds the builders and rejects their laws!
Sees His own kingdom thro' the nations shine,
Its honors, laws and precepts all divine,
His gospel opening all its boundless springs,
Seeks not the aid of cabinets nor kings,
To man no pow'r to legislate is given,
It flows in living streams direct from Heaven,
Spreads thro' the world wide as its gifts unfold,
Its hopes immortal and its joys untold!
From time's sad brow dispels th' involving gloom,
Its brighter splendors dawning o'er the tomb;
Gives wand'ring man on faith's bold wings to rise
O'er nature's clogs and hail his kindred skies!
Or while it guides him to the blest abode,
Marks his mild way thro' virtue's sacred road,
Embracing in his comprehensive view,
His God, his neighbor, and his country too.

Yes, let the deist argue all he can,
The christian only is the happy man,
Not he who impiously assumes the name
But he whose heart that character can claim,
Who builds no hopes of Heav'n's eternal joys,
On that which reason or which truth destroys,
Nor thinks his duty to God is shown
In the dull round of modes and forms alone,
Or that his neighbor's creed, while bound to hate,
Deserves the exploding thunders of the state;
Nor he the mask of piety that feigns,
For worldly honors or for worldly gains,
The meek-eyed christian, who pursues the road
To peace and joy, to glory and to God,
With honest aim and nobler motives flies
The worldling's views and hypocrite's disguise,
Feels Heaven's own breath his constant bosom fan,
Which glows with love to God and love to man.

Some Early Thanksgiving Recipes

Here are some examples of New England recipes from the time of the early Republic. The first, for roast turkey (turkeys were also boiled), is from Amelia Simmons' *American Cookery* (1796), the country's first indigenous cookbook. Previously, only English or European cookbooks, including American reprints, were available.

To Stuff & Roast a Turkey, or Fowl.

One pound soft wheat bread, 3 ounces beef suet, 3 eggs, a little sweet thyme, sweet marjoram, pepper and salt, and some add a gill of wine; fill the bird therewith and sew up, hang down to a steady solid fire, basting frequently with salt and water, and roast until a steam emits from the breast, put one third of a pound of butter into the gravy, dust flour over the bird and baste with the gravey; serve up with boiled onions and cramberry [*sic*]-sauce, mangoes, pickles or celery.

2. Others omit the sweet herbs, and add parsley done with potatoes.

3. Boil and mash 3 pints potatoes, wet them with butter, add sweet herbs, pepper, salt, fill and roast as above.

Another turkey recipe is from Lydia Maria Child's *American Frugal Housewife* (1833). Mrs. Child also wrote the famous "over the river and through the woods" Thanksgiving poem with its wintry scenes, which was eventually shifted in popular culture to become a Christmas song.

A good-sized turkey should be roasted two hours and a half, or three hours; very slowly at first. If you wish to make a fine stuffing, pound a cracker, or crumble some bread very fine, chop some raw salt pork, very fine, sift some sage, (and summer-savory, or sweet-marjoram, if you have them in the house and fancy them,) and mould them all together, seasoned with a little pepper. An egg worked in makes the stuffing cut better; but it is not worth while eggs are dear. About the same length of time is required for boiling and roasting.

Another recipe is from *The New England Economical Housekeeper*, by Mrs. E. A. Howland (1848).

Roast Turkey

Let your turkey be picked clean, and washed and wiped dry, inside and out. Have your stuffing, No 2, prepared, fill the crop and then the body full, sew it up, put it on a spit, and roast it, before a moderate fire, three hours. If more convenient, it is equally good when baked.

Serve up with cranberry or applesauce, turnip sauce, squash, and a small Indian pudding; or dumplings boiled hard is a good substitute for bread.

Stuffing "No 2"

Take dry pieces of bread or crackers, chop them fine, put in a small piece of butter or a little cream, with sage, pepper, and salt, one egg, and a small quantity of flour, moistened with milk.

This chicken pie is also from Amelia Simmons. It calls for six chickens and about ten pounds of crust, which indicates the size of the pie. The author notes that Mrs. Ballard "Brougt home Six fowls" from which "Hannah & Dolly md Pies" in preparation for Thanksgiving in 1785.

A Chicken Pie.

Pick and clean six chickens, (without scalding) take out their inwards, and wash the birds, while whole, then joint the birds, salt and pepper the pieces and inwards. Roll one inch thick paste No. 8 and cover a deep dish, and double at the rim or edge of the dish, put thereto a layer of chickens and a layer of thin slices of butter, till the chickens and one and a half pound of butter are expended, which cover with a thick paste; bake one hour and a half.

Or if your oven be poor, parboil the chickens with a half pound of butter, and put the pieces with the remaining pound of butter, and half the gravy into the paste, and while boiling, thicken the residue of the gravy, and when the pie is drawn, open the crust and add the butter.

No. 8 paste: Rub in one and half pound of suet to six pounds of flour, and a spoonfull of salt, wet with cream, roll in, in six or eight times, two and half pounds of butter — good for a chicken or meat pie.[1]

Cranberries, like many New World foods, were adapted to European tastes by following precedents for more familiar Old World ingredients. Thomas Dawson gives a recipe for barberry conserve or sauce in his *Second part of the good Huswives Iewell* (London, 1597) that would be familiar to the Pilgrims:

To make a conserve of Barberies

Take your Barberies and picke them cleare, and set them over a soft fire, and put to them Rosewater as much as you thinke good, then when you thinke it be sodde enough, straine that, and then seeth it againe, and to every pound of Barberies, one pound of suger, and meat your conserve.[2]

Mrs. Child also provides a good, detailed Yankee recipe for mincemeat:

> Boil a tender, nice piece of beef—any piece that is clear from sinews and gristle;
> boil it till it is perfectly tender. When it is cold, chop it very fine, and be very
> careful to get out every particle of bone and gristle. The suet is sweeter and
> better to boil half an hour or more in the liquor the beef has been boiled in; but
> few people do this. Pare, core, and chop the apples fine. If you use raisins, stone
> them. If you use currants, wash and dry them at the fire. Two pounds of beef,
> after it is chopped; three quarters of a pound of suet; one pound and a quarter
> of sugar; three pounds of apples; two pounds of currants, or raisins. Put in a
> gill of brandy; lemon-brandy is better, if you have any prepared. Make it quite
> moist with new cider. I should not think a quart would be too much; the more
> moist the better, if it does not spill out into the oven. A very little pepper. If you
> use corn [salted] meat, or tongue, for pies, it should be well soaked, and boiled
> very tender. If you use fresh beef, salt is necessary in the seasoning. One ounce
> of cinnamon, one ounce of cloves. Two nutmegs add to the pleasantness of the
> flavor; and a bit of sweet butter, put upon the top of each pie, makes them rich,
> but these are not necessary. Baked three quarters of an hour. If your apples are
> rather sweet, grate in a whole lemon.[3]

Catherine Beecher (Harriet Beecher Stowe's sister) offers a recipe for Marlborough
pudding to be used as a pie filling:

Marlborough Pudding

Six tart apples.
Six ounces of sifted sugar.
Six ounces of butter, or a pint of thick cream.
Six eggs.
The grated peel of one lemon, and half the juice.

> Grate the apples after paring and coring them. Stir together the butter and
> sugar as for cake. Then add the other ingredients, and bake in a rich paste.
> Some persons grate in crackers, and add rosewater and nutmeg. It is much
> better to grate than to stew the apples, for this and all pies.[4]

A recipe for a small pudding of the type from *The Cook's Own Book* (1832), "Pudding—Plum (3)," is as follows:

> One pound of the best raisins stoned, half a pound of currants well cleaned,
> one pound of fresh beef suet finely minced, five table-spoons of grated bread,
> three of flour, two of brown sugar, one tea-spoon of pounded ginger, one of
> cinnamon, and one of salt, six well-beaten eggs, and three wine-glasses ful of
> rum, all to be mixed thoroughly together the day before it is to be boiled. Boil
> it in a cloth or mould for four or five hours.[5]

United American Indians of New England Press Release (11 December 1997)

Plymouth rocked by police riot

Cops brutally assault Native people & supporters at Nat'l Day of Mourning

By Moonanum James & Mahtowin Munro
Co-leaders, United American Indians of New England

Police attacked a peaceful march of several hundred Native people and our sup-porters in Plymouth, Mass., on "Thanksgiving" day. More than 150 cops—latter-day descendants of Custer and the U.S. Cavalry—descended on women, children, elders and men who were merely attempting to march on a side street of Plymouth. The cops attacked without warning and with no provocation. Those of us at the front of the march tried to avert trouble. We sent negotiators to speak to them to explain where we were marching. The cops refused to negotiate. As the sea of blue uniforms approached us, we yelled to them: "Look! You can see we don't want any trouble! We have all women and children up here at the front!" The police response was to knock two men down to the ground and grab a leader of United American Indians of New England—Mahtowin Munro. Mahtowin says: "They handcuffed me and dragged me off. As the cops grabbed me, I could feel several people behind me grabbing me around the waist and trying to pull me away." One woman yelled, "You are not taking my sister!" But there were too many cops. Some of the cops were dressed in full riot gear. A few were on horseback. Some were dressed in plain clothes and did not even identify themselves. They used pepper spray and mace. They sprayed the eyes and mouths of people who were already down on the ground and handcuffed. They gassed two children—one an 8-year-old Black child from Providence, R.I., and the other a 10-year-old Latino boy from New York. Some Plymouth residents came out of their houses to offer water to those who had been gassed. The cops knocked people to the ground and arrested people who had stepped aside to get out of the way.

Carefully planned cop attack

When the police assault began, supporters whisked another UAINE leader—Moonanum James—to the sidewalk "so I would not be arrested," Moonanum says. "This made no difference. The cops swept down on me anyway." It was clear that the combined forces of the Plymouth Police Department, the county sheriff's office, and the Massachusetts state troopers had planned and rehearsed this assault for some time. This was a carefully orchestrated police assault. Cops pointed at the march's leaders and peace keepers and said: "Get that one! That one! A Chilean who was one of those arrested said he had not seen anything like it since Chile under the fascist military junta. . . . Those who were not arrested pressed forward, chanting against police brutality and declaring that "the whole world is watching." In fact, many cameras and video cameras recorded the police violence. . . . In all, 25 people were arrested. Those arrested included not only several Native people but also Black, Latino and white supporters. The ages of those arrested range from 18 to 67. . . . The cops were particularly brutal to the Black people arrested. They ripped out dreadlocks from the scalp of Kazi Toure, a Black former political prisoner. They refused to take the handcuffs off the two Black women who were arrested, Imani Henry and Nicole Wood, until an hour after all the other women's handcuffs had been removed. Imani Henry said: "This shows the importance of multinational and multi-gender solidarity. There were a lot of lesbian and gay people there, and a lot of people of color there who were arrested." . . . "The cops pepper-sprayed people who were standing on the sidewalks trying to get out of the way," [John Perry Ryan] said. "I got jumped from behind, grabbed around the neck, and tackled onto the ground."

The charges ranged from disorderly conduct and unlawful assembly to assault and battery on a police officer. The latter charge usually means police have assaulted someone, whom they then charge with assault. . . . And sure enough, we have videotapes showing the people charged with assault and battery being tackled to the ground and slammed up against walls by cops. . . . Many of those who were not arrested rallied at the Plymouth police headquarters. They raised money for bail and cheered as those who had been arrested came outside after being freed hours later. . . . Several hundred Native people and their supporters had gathered in Plymouth for the 28th Annual National Day of Mourning. Since 1970, UAINE has organized the National Day of Mourning, a protest against the U.S. celebration of the mythology of Thanksgiving and against the racist "Pilgrim Progress Parade." Before the police assault on the attempted march, there was a speak-out on Cole's Hill. Native people representing the Maya, Yaqui, Inuit, Wampanoag, Lakota and other nations spoke. UAINE chose not to disrupt the parade this year [It was not there to be attacked, this time]. The police attacked anyway. Why? Because the government is afraid of the people's movement we have been building at the National Day of Mourning. We have been able to bring people of all races and ages and genders and sexual orientations, together like one fist. This is the oppressors' worst nightmare. . . . Those arrested were arraigned Nov. 28 and Dec. 2. Many supporters turned out at court. . . . In fact, support has been pouring in to UAINE. We have been receiving about 150 email messages a day. Expressions of solidarity have come not only from this country, but from Latin America and Europe.

Notes

Introduction: A Thanksgiving Detective Story (pp. 1–13)

1 The occasional difference in the cited dates for these events, which has led to much confusion, arises from the divergence between the old Julian calendar and our modern Gregorian calendar. Many countries switched to the new calendar soon after its introduction in 1582, but Britain did not do so until 1752. The dates found in *Mourt's Relation* or Bradford's *Of Plymouth Plantation* are "Old Style" or Julian calendar dates, while those found in later sources are often "New Style" or Gregorian dates. The confusion occurs when a writer uses both—for example, citing the departure from Plymouth, England, as September 6 (Old Style), but giving the signing of the Mayflower Compact as November 21 (New Style), that being the accepted anniversary date.

2 Michael Kammen, *Mystic Chords of Memory: The Transformation of Tradition in American Culture* (New York: Knopf, 1991), p. 386.

3 I wish now I had never done so. After I concluded that Forefathers' Day was historically unrelated to the evolution of Thanksgiving, I was never able to convince some of my colleagues of the fact, and my initial assumption kept coming back to haunt me.

4 There have been recent exceptions to this assumption, in particular Elizabeth Pleck's excellent chapter "Family, Feast and Football" in *Celebrating the Family: Ethnicity, Consumer Culture, and Family Rituals* (Cambridge, Mass.: Harvard University Press, 2000), pp. 21–42; Janet Siskind, "The Invention of Thanksgiving: A Ritual of American Nationality," *Critique of Anthropology* 12 (1992); and Penny Coleman, *Thanksgiving: The True Story* (New York: Henry Holt and Company), 2008. I should mention that I talked to Ms. Siskind at length about my discovery and its ramifications while she was researching this article, and that Ms. Coleman utilized the material available on the Pilgrim Hall website, http://www.pilgrimhall.org, which is the work of my wife, Peggy M. Baker.

5 *A Journal of the Pilgrims at Plymouth*, Dwight B. Heath, ed. (New York: Corinth Books, 1963), p. 60–61.

6 Samuel Purchas, *Hakluytus Posthumus or Purchas His Pilgrimes. Contayning a History of the World in Sea Voyages and Lande Travells by Englishmen and others* (London: Imprinted for H. Fetherston, 1625).

7 Alexander Young, *Chronicles of the Pilgrim Fathers of the Colony of Plymouth* (Boston: Charles C. Little and James Brown, 1841), p. 231.

Chapter 1. New England's Puritan Holy Days (pp. 14–30)

1 Coincidentally, another similar "First Thanksgiving" article was published in the *Illustrated American* (November 20, 1897) by a Henry Austin, with a large illustration of outdoor cooking, if not dining, by C. D. Graves. Jane Goodwin Austin's husband was named Loring Henry Austin and apparently known as "Henry," but he died in 1892, and they had no son named "Henry."

2 Horton Davies, *The Worship of the American Puritans, 1629–1730* (New York: Peter Lang, 1990), p. 51.

3 Ibid., p. 246.

4 Edward Winslow, "Good News from New England," in *A Library of American Puritan Writings: The Seventeenth Century, Volume 9, Histories and Narratives* (New York: AMS Press, 1986), p. 577.

5 William Bradford, *Of Plymouth Plantation*, S. E. Morison, ed. (New York: Knopf, 1984), p. 47. It is in describing this event that Bradford quotes from Hebrews 11:13–16, "they knew they were pilgrims," which may have led to their being called so by posterity.

6 William DeLoss Love, *Fast and Thanksgiving Days of New England* (Boston: Houghton, Mifflin, 1895), p. 69.

7 Isaac Allerton was the Pilgrims' chief agent in trans-Atlantic negotiations with the English merchants who underwrote the colonial effort. Although he apparently began with honest intentions, Allerton became entangled in a serious conflict of interest in which his own ambitions as a merchant worked to the financial detriment of the Pilgrim community, and he was eventually "fired." *Mayflower* passenger John Billington, described by William Bradford as "one of the profanest" of the colonists, had a long history of dissent against the powers that be, but they were appalled by his fatal shooting of John Newcomen and sought reassurances from the Massachusetts Bay authorities before he was hanged in 1630.

8 Alexander Young, *Chronicles of the First Planters of the Colony of Massachusetts Bay, from 1623 to 1636* (Boston: Charles C. Little and James Brown, 1846), p. 224.

9 "Scituate and Barnstable Church Records," in *The New England Historical and Genealogical Register* (Boston, 1856), vol. 10, p. 38.

10 Ibid., p. 39.

11 *The Compact with the Charter and Laws of the Colony of New Plymouth*, William Brigham, ed. (Boston: Dutton and Wentworth for the State of Massachusetts, 1836), p. 48, p. 199.

12 Richard P. Gildrie, "Ceremonial Puritan Days of Humiliation and Thanksgiving," *New England Quarterly* 136 (January 1982), p. 10.

13 John F. Wilson, *Pulpit in Parliament* (Princeton, N.J.: Princeton University Press, 1969), chapter 3.

14 Quoted in Love, *Fast and Thanksgiving Days*, p. 247.

Chapter 2. *The Traditional New England Thanksgiving (pp. 31–45)*

1 Thomas Hutchinson, *The History of the Colony and Province of Massachusetts-Bay* (Cambridge, Mass.: Harvard University Press, 1936), vol. 1, p. 362. Quoted in Love, *Fast and Thanksgiving Days*, p. 240, who notes that Hutchinson was wrong about the interruptions and that he had not carefully examined the evidence.

2 There were twelve national providential holidays declared by the Continental Congress in addition to those mentioned: Wednesday, April 22, 1778 (Fast); Wednesday, December 30, 1778 (Thanksgiving); Thursday, May 6, 1779 (Fast); Thursday, December 9, 1779 (Thanksgiving); Thursday, December 7, 1780 (Thanksgiving); Thursday, May 3, 1781 (Fast); Thursday, December 18, 1781 (Thanksgiving); Thursday, April 25, 1782 (Fast); Thursday, November 28, 1782 (Thanksgiving); Thursday, December 11, 1783 (Thanksgiving); Tuesday, October 19, 1784 (Thanksgiving); and Wednesday, April 26, 1789 (Fast); See Love, *Fast and Thanksgiving Days*, pp. 502–506.

3 James Truslow Adams, *New England in the Republic* (Boston: Little, Brown, and Company, 1926), p. 187.

4 William Bentley, D.D., *Diary of William Bentley, Vol. III, 1803–1810* (Salem, Mass.: Essex Institute, 1911), p. 124.

5 Thomas Lackland, *Homespun; or, Five and Twenty Years Ago* (New York: Hurd & Houghton, 1867), p. 126.

6 George Lunt, *Old New England Traits* (New York: Hurd & Houghton, 1873), p. 166; Caroline Howard King, *When I Lived in Salem, 1822–1866* (Brattleboro, Vt.: Stephen Daye Press, 1937), p. 111.

7 Susan I. Lesley, *Recollections of My Mother, Mrs. Anne Jean Lyman of Northampton* (Boston: Houghton, Mifflin, 1899), p. 368.

8 Ann Douglas, *The Feminization of American Culture* (New York: Anchor Books, 1988), p. 22.

9 John R. Gillis, *A World of Their Own Making* (New York: Basic Books, 1996), p. 6.

10 Love, *Fast and Thanksgiving Days*, pp. 438–445.

11 De Witt Clinton, "Proclamation" (1820), in [Franklin B. Hough], *Proclamations for Thanksgiving Issued by the Continental Congress, Pres't Washington, by the National and State Governments on the Peace of 1815, and by the Governors of New York, &c.* (Albany: Munsell & Rowland, 1858), p. 56.

12 Samuel Bell (Governor of New Hampshire), "A PROCLAMATION FOR A DAY OF THANKSGIVING, Given at the Council Chamber at Concord, the tenth day of October, in the year of our Lord one thousand eight hundred and twenty-one, and of the Independence of the United States the forty-sixth" (in ibid.).

13 Online document: http://www.acacia.pair.com/Acacia.Vignettes/Proclamation.Thanksgiving.html (accessed December 12, 2006).

14 "On the Sundays of two or three weeks before the appointed day, the minister would unfold a large printed document . . . which was read to the Congregation. It concluded, as did also the Fast Day proclamation, with these words: 'all servile labor and vain recreation are by law forbidden on the said day.'" Edmund Delaney, *Life in the Connecticut River Valley, 1800–1840, from the Recollections of John Howard Redfield* (Essex, Conn.: Connecticut River Museum, 1988), p. 36, quoted in Sandra Oliver, *Saltwater Foodways* (Mystic, Conn.: Mystic Seaport Museum, 1995); John Carver [Theodore A. Dodge], *Sketches of New England; or, Memories of the Country* (New York: E. French, 1842), p. 26.

15 Laurel Thatcher Ulrich, *A Midwife's Tale: The Life of Martha Ballard, Based on Her Diary, 1785–1812* (New York: Random House, 1991); Martha Ballard, *The Diary of Martha Ballard, 1785–1812*, transcr. Robert R. McCausland and Cynthia MacAlman McCausland, introduction by Laurel Thatcher Ulrich (Maine Genealogical Soc. Special Publication No. 10, 1998).

16 "Martha Ballard's Diary," from the online version at www.dohistory.org. The importance of pies is evident in her Thanksgiving preparations: "Hannah & Dolly md Pies (Sat. 12/10/1785)"; "I have been at home. we Bakt Some Apple pies. (Wed. 11/26/1788)"; "we Baked Some Pumpkin & Apple pies (Tue. 1/18/1794)"; "I have been fixing meat for pies, Sally been Cleaning house (Tue. 11/7/1795)"; "Snowd the most of the Day. I have been makeing Pies & other matters (Wed. 12/14/1796)": "Sally and I have been Bakeing Pies (Wed. 11/28/1798)"; Betsy Cowen helpt me this day, we Bakt mins and Apple pies (Tue. 11/25/1800)"; "Bakt mins Pies (Wed. 11/26/1800)"; "I have been at home. we Bakt some Pies & wheat bread (Tuesday, 11/29/1801). I have washt the Bullery, kitchen & N rooms and helpt make apple pies, and done other things. (Wednesday, 11/30/1801)"; "we have Bakt apple Pies. (Tue 11/29/1803)"; "we Bakt 2 oven fulls Pies, washt the floors &C." Grocery stores included "Dolly went to mr Westons & got 1 lb Butter, 2 oz Ginger, 2 oz. Spice, 1 oz. Pepir (1786)"; "Willms Brot me 5 lb of chocolat this afternn. Cyrus bot 1 [lb] Coffee 2 of Sugar, Pepper. mr B. 1 lb Sugar, Beef 8 lb. (1805)."

17 Charles Dudley Warner, *Being a Boy* (Boston: James R. Osgood, 1878), p. 81.

18 See appendix 1 for the first part of this long poetical complaint on the declension from traditional piety.

19 ". . . notwithstanding the stir about the Proclamation, we had an agreeable Thanksgiving. Mr. Hunt's text was Psa. xxiv.I. The Lord reigneth—let the earth rejoice. Mr. Beacon's text PM Psa. xxiv. I. The earth is the Lord's and the fullness thereof. My unkle & aunt Winslow of Boston, their son & daughter, Master Daniel Mason (Aunt Winslow's nephew from Newport, Rhode Island) & Mrs. Soley spent the evening with us. We young folk had a room with a fire in it to ourselves. Mr. Beacon gave us his company for one hour." Alice Morse Earle, ed., *The Diary of Anna Green Winslow* (Boston: Houghton Mifflin, 1894), p. 4.

"November 29. *Thanksgiving* Day. There was Rain in the Morning, but soon afterwards it cleared off & tho' the walking was wet, yet it was a pleasant day. The fame of our Music attracted the notice of many persons, especially the young, & the house was unusually full, but it did not add to the whole amount of the Poor's Contribution five dollars. The order of service was: Opening with Instrumental Music. Two bass viols, tenour viol, 3 violins, hautboy, 4 G. flutes & voices. Introductory prayer. 42 Hymn, set to Music vocal, accompanied. Lecture. Instrumental music. Prayer. Particular metre, Barbault's Hymn 15th, set to music by Mr. Palfrey. Sermon. Instrumental during the Contributions. Anthem on the occasion. Prayer & Blessing. The Song of the Day, 'Adams & Liberty.'" Bentley, *Diary, Vol. II*, p. 290.

"Thursday. Attended meeting; heard a most excellent sermon by Mr. W., text in Psalms, in which he exhorted us in a most pathetic manner to embrace the Gospel, the true and only certain road to happiness. Mr. R. Porter and Miss A. Root were published and married in the evening. Eve, I was at Mr. Mixes; spent an agreeable eve, saw Mrs. Mix from Middletown." Laura H. Moseley, ed., *The Diaries of Julia Cowles: A Connecticut Record, 1797–1803* (New Haven, Conn.: Yale University Press, 1931), p. 41.

"Cloudy, Snowd Some. mr Ballard and Cyrus went to meeting, it is Thanksgiving day. Revd mr Stone discoarst from Psalm C 7th, 13–14–15 verss. Sons Jona & Lambard to hear mr Roggers, his discoars 116 Psm 12th vers. Son Jona & Lambard to hear mr Roggers his discoars 116 Psm 12th vers." Ballard, *Diary*, entry for December 1, 1808.

20 Sarah Josepha Hale, *Northwood; or, Life North and South*, 2nd edition (New York: H. Long & Brother, 1852), pp. 81–82.

21 "Every human being went to 'meeting' on the morning of Thanksgiving Day, the boy included. At that age he did not know that the sermon was, or might be, political. Still an attentive ear might catch words from the pulpit which would not have been heard on Sunday." Edward Everett Hale, *A New England Boyhood* (New York: Cassell Publishing Co., 1893), p. 141; "the religious service began at 11 a.m. instead of 10:30 as on Sundays, and it rarely finished before 1 p.m. The sermon was long, the meeting-house cold, but boyish hope on exultant wing looked beyond the tedious service to the . . . Thanksgiving supper." Delaney, *Life in the Connecticut River Valley*, quoted in Oliver, *Saltwater Foodways*, p. 238.

22 "The New-England Boy's Song" (1844).

23 The Andrews Sisters, "A Merry Christmas at Grandmother's . . . ," Decca 1950, Patty, Maxene & LaVerne w/ Danny Kaye.

24 For the diversity of guests and visitors, see note 19 above and Martha Ballard's *Diary* for Thanksgiving 1796: "Clear and very pleast for the Season. this day is observd as a Day of thanksgiving to our Great parent for his blesings bestowed the year past. we were favd with the Company of all our Children and the Children of those who reside in this Town. mr Gill and wife and his Sister, our friends (Except son and Dagt Town, Jack Ballard and Rhoda Pollard) retired home by 9h Evn. I was Calld at 10 to See mrss Graves who is in Labour. Shee remaind ill thro the night. my Self nor the women who attinded had no Sleep."

Bentley, *Diary, Vol. IV*, p. 424 (1816): "The day of our annual Thanksgiving. The air was serene tho colder tha for some time past. The Congregation decent [attendance], but our day for children to visit with greater liberty & in which our family makes a visit to their friends in the neighboring towns. Our public Contribution about 80 dollars."

For nocturnal sleigh rides, see Frances Trollope, *Domestic Manners of the Americans* (New York: Knopf, 1949), p. 304; Carver, *Sketches of New England*, p. 39. For weddings, see Moseley, ed., *Diaries of Julia Cowles*, p. 41 (above, note 19); Sarah Josepha Hale, *Northwood*, chapter 7; and banns read for "mr Moses Patridg & Ruth Rockwood" on November 29, 1798, in Ballard, *Diary*.

Chapter 3. *The Classic New England Thanksgiving Dinner (pp. 46–61)*

1 Dorothy Davis, *A History of Shopping* (London: Routledge & Kegan Paul), 1966, p. 86; Young, *Chronicles of the First Planters*, p. 43; Bradford, *Of Plymouth Plantation*, p. 90.
2 John James Audubon, quoted in Henry William Herbert, *Frank Forester's Field Sports of the United States* (New York: Stringer & Townsend, 1848), vol. 2, p. 302; and also quoted in Elisha Lewis, *The American Sportsman* (Philadelphia: J. B. Lippincott, 1863), p. 138; Jean Antheleme Brillat-Savarin, *The Physiology of Taste* (New York: Liveright, 1970), pp. 54–55.
3 *Youth's Companion*, November 24, 1888, p. 605.
4 James Fenimore Cooper, *Works of J. Fenimore Cooper* (New York: P. F. Collier, 1891), vol. 1, pp. 642–648. A facsimile of the first edition may be found online on the University of Virginia website at http://repo.lib.virginia.edu:18080/fedora/get/uva-lib:166617/uva-lib-bdef:103/getDynamicView?behav=getObjectBrowse&id=d25 (accessed October 10, 2008).
5 Thomas Nichols Low, *Forty Years of American Life, 1821–1861* (1864) (New York: Stackpole and Sons, 1937), p. 25.
6 Lackland, *Homespun*, p. 124.
7 John Josselyn, *New-Englands Rarities Discovered* (Boston: Massachusetts Historical Society, 1972), p. 91.
8 J. A. Leo Lemay, *"New England's Annoyances": America's First Folk Song* (Newark: University of Delaware Press, 1985), p. 85; Richard Slotkin and James K. Folsom, *So Dreadful a Judgment* (Middletown, Conn.: Wesleyan University Press, 1978), p. 215. "Pompion" is an early spelling of pumpkin, and "cates" are foodstuffs, as in "catering." It is interesting that "Indian trays" are the most common Indian artifact found in early Plymouth Colony probate inventories.
9 Merriam-Webster's *Word for the Wise* (radio show) script for October 9, 1997. Also see C. Anne Wilson, *Food & Drink in Britain* (London: Constable, 1973), pp. 210ff; Madge Lorwin, *Dining with William Shakespeare* (New York: Athenaeum, 1976), pp. 26 and 76; Richard J. Hooker, *Food and Drink in America* (Indianapolis: Bobbs-Merrill, 1981), p. 48.
10 Harvey Levenstein, *Revolution at the Table* (New York: Oxford University Press, 1988), p. 4
11 Josselyn, *New-Englands Rarities Discovered*, p. 65.

12 Constance Crosby, "The Indians and English use them much . . . ," in *Cranberry Harvest: A History of Cranberry Growing in Massachusetts*, Joseph D. Thomas, ed. (New Bedford, Mass.: Spinner Publications, 1990), p. 19.

13 Amelia Simmons, *American Cookery*, facsimile of 1796 Hartford edition (New York: Oxford University Press, 1958), p. 18. The recipe for cranberry tarts is on page 30, and pickled barberries on page 44.

14 Harriet Beecher Stowe, *Oldtown Folks* (Boston: Fields, Osgood & Co., 1869), p. 340.

15 Abby Morton Diaz, "The Slaves of the Rolling Pin," in *The Schoolmaster's Trunk* (Boston: James R. Osgood & Co., 1875), p. 8; Hooker, *Food and Drink in America*, p. 248; Edwin Valentine Mitchell, "To Have Pie for Breakfast," in *It's an Old New England Custom* (New York: Vanguard, 1947), pp. 3–22.

16 Warner, *Being a Boy*, p. 66.

17 Simmons, *American Cookery*, p. 24.

18 John Josselyn, "An Account of Two Voyages to New England" (1675), in *Collections of the Massachusetts Historical Society*, series 3, vol. 3 (1833), p. 337.

19 Quoted in U. P. Hedrick, ed., *Sturtevant's Edible Plants of the World* (New York: Dover, 1972), p. 477.

20 William T. Davis, *Plymouth Memories of an Octogenarian* (Plymouth, Mass.: Memorial Press, 1907), p. 486.

21 Edward Everett Hale, *New England Boyhood*, p. 139; also see King, *When I Lived in Salem*, p. 109.

22 Sarah Josepha Hale, *Northwood*, p. 90; King, *When I Lived in Salem*, p. 112; Sarah Anna Emery, *Reminiscences of a Nonagenarian* (Newburyport, Mass.: William H. Huse, 1879), p. 12; Louisa Crowinshield Bacon, *Reminiscences* (Salem, Mass.: Privately printed, 1922), p. 4.

23 Bacon, *Reminiscences*, p. 4.

24 J[ohn] E[velyn], *Acetaria: A Discourse of Sallets* (London, 1699), p. 63; C. Anne Wilson. *Food & Drink in Britain*, p. 360; Artemus Ward, *The Grocer's Encyclopedia* (New York: Artemus Ward, 1911), p. 107–108.

25 Mrs. E. A. Howland, *The New England Economical Housekeeper* (New London, Conn.: Bolles & Williams, 1848), p. 72.

26 Alice Morse Earle, *Stage-coach and Tavern Days* (New York: Macmillan, 1900), pp. 125–127. Actually the Washingtonian movement did not begin until 1840.

27 George B. Emerson, ed., *A Report of the Trees and Shrubs Growing Naturally in the Forests of Massachusetts* (Boston: Commonwealth of Massachusetts, 1846), p. 172.

28 Edward Whiting, *Changing New England* (New York: Century Co., 1929), pp. 98–101.

29 Edward Everett Hale, *New England Boyhood*, p. 142.

30 Ibid., p. 147. "There is another board game called, 'The New Game of Human Life.' This game's objective is to become immortal. You jump forward and if you land on squares that are labeled with terms like 'studious boy,' 'ambitious youth,' and 'benevolent man.' You go backwards if you land on squares that are labeled with terms like 'negligent boy,' 'complacent man,' and 'drunkard.'

The 'New Game of Human Life's' ultimate goal was to become the immortal man. It was described in the rules as, 'A model for the course of life which can end only in eternity.' It is interesting to note that the 'New Game of Human Life' was one that was played in the United States in the 1790s when George Washington was President." H. James Harrington, "Quality of Life," *Quality Digest*, August 1998; available online: http://www.jhpin.com/home.htm.

31 [Jacob Abbott], *New England and Her Institutions by "One of Her Sons"* (Boston: John Allen & Co., 1835), p. 148.

32 Lackland, *Homespun*, p. 133.

33 Carver, *Sketches of New England*, pp. 37–40.

34 Abby Morton Diaz, "A Plymouth Pilgrimage," *New England Magazine*, September 1889, p. 16.

Chapter 4. *The Nation Embraces Thanksgiving, 1780–1880 (pp. 62–77)*

1 Adams, *New England in the Republic*, p. 116.

2 *Columbian Centinel*, December 4, 1816, p. 2, quoted in Pershing Vartanian, "The Puritan as Symbol in American Thought: A Study of the New England Societies" (PhD dissertation, University of Michigan, 1971), p. 19.

3 *Columbian Centinel*, January 7, 1807, p. 2, quoted in Vartanian, "Puritan as Symbol," p. 20.

4 "[E]very new inch of territory strained the fabric of American culture more, challenging the cohesiveness of its institutions and its values. In this world of continuous flux, Americans longed for stability." John Mayfield, *The New Nation, 1800–1845* (New York: Hill and Wang, 1982), p. 10.

5 Carl Degler, quoted in Glenna Matthews. *"Just A Housewife": The Rise & Fall of Domesticity in America* (New York: Oxford University Press, 1978), p. 10.

6 Glenna Matthews, *"Just a Housewife,"* pp. 3–7; Douglas, *Feminization*, p. 48.

7 Laurel Thatcher Ulrich, *The Age of Homespun* (New York: Knopf, 2001); Glenna Matthews, *"Just A Housewife,"* pp. 11ff.

8 Jack Larkin, *The Reshaping of Everyday Life, 1790–1840* (New York: Harper & Row, 1988), p. 271; Penny L. Restad, *Christmas in America* (New York: Oxford University Press, 1995), p. 21.

9 Restad, *Christmas in America*, p. 20; J.A.R. Pimlott, *The Englishman's Christmas* (Hassocks, Sussex: Harvester Press, 1978), p. 77.

10 Stephen Nissenbaum, *The Battle for Christmas* (New York: Knopf, 1996), p. 309.

11 William T. Davis, *Memories of an Octogenarian*, p. 491.

12 Diana Appelbaum, *Thanksgiving: An American Holiday, an American History* (New York: Facts on File, 1984), chapter 7, "Old Holiday in a New Home"; Larkin, *Reshaping of Everyday Life*, p. 273.

13 [Hough], *Proclamations for Thanksgiving*, p. xiv.

14 In 1859, these included New York, Ohio, Pennsylvania, Indiana, Massachusetts, Mississippi, Maryland, Illinois, New Hampshire, Alabama, New Jersey,

Maine, North Carolina, Arkansas, South Carolina, Michigan, Georgia, Florida, Connecticut, Texas, Rhode Island, Iowa, Wisconsin, Vermont, California, Kentucky, Minnesota, Louisiana, Tennessee, Minnesota, Kansas Territory, Nebraska Territory, and the District of Columbia. Virginia was notable for Governor Wise's scruples about such holidays.

15 Appelbaum, *Thanksgiving*, pp. 142ff.

16 H.S.J. Sickel, *Thanksgiving: Its Source, Philosophy and History* (Philadelphia: International Printing Company, 1940), p. 164.

17 Union League Club, *Report on the Committee on Providing a Thanksgiving Dinner for the Soldiers and Sailors* (New York: Union League Club House, 1865), pp. 3, 4.

18 Ibid., p. 12.

19 Ibid., "Letter from George F. Noyes to Col. George Bliss, Jr.," New York, November 27, 1864, p. 19.

20 S. W. Pope, *Patriotic Games: Sporting Traditions in the American Imagination, 1876–1926* (New York: Oxford University Press, 1997), p. 87.

21 "Thanksgiving Day in New York Up To Date," *Harper's Weekly*, November 28, 1891, p. 950.

22 [Hough], *Proclamations for Thanksgiving*, p. xv.

Chapter 5. Nineteenth-Century Holiday Imagery in Literature and Art
(pp. 78–97)

1 Lawrence Buell, *New England Literary Culture* (New York: Cambridge University Press, 1986), p. 57.

2 Douglas, *Feminization*, p. 229.

3 Ibid., p. 49.

4 Josie Keen, "Thanksgiving: A Home Scene," *Ladies' Repository*, 2nd series, vol. 14, no. 6, December 1874, pp. 426–430.

5 Nathaniel Hawthorne, "John Inglefield's Thanksgiving," *United States Democratic Review*, vol. 7, no. 27, March 1840, pp. 209–213.

6 Sophie May [Rebecca S. Clarke], *Dotty Dimple at Play* (Boston: Lothrop, Lee & Shepard Co., 1868/1910), pp. 144–145.

7 W.J.T. Mitchell, *Iconology: Image, Text, Ideology* (Chicago: University of Chicago Press, 1986), p. 8.

8 John W. Barber, *American Scenes: A Selection of the Most Interesting Incidents in American History* (Springfield, Mass.: D. E. Fisk, 1868), p. 106 (original edition, 1828); Charles Goodrich, *The Universal Traveler* (Hartford, Conn.: Canfield and Robbins, 1837), opposite p. 36 (original edition, 1836).

9 Benson J. Lossing, *Pictorial History of the Civil War in the United States of America* (Philadelphia: George Childs, 1866), p. 168.

10 An interesting parallel in late Victorian painting, where cloudy or overcast (wintry) scenes denoting seriousness and preindustrial authenticity were superseded by sunny images of leisure and frivolity, has been analyzed by Nina

Lübbren, "North to South: Paradigm Shifts in European Art and Tourism," in *Visual Culture and Tourism*, David Crouch and Nina Lübbren, eds. (Oxford: Berg, 2003), pp. 125–146.

11 [Hough], *Proclamations for Thanksgiving*, p. xvi.

12 Jan Nederveen Pieterse, *White on Black: Images of Africans and Blacks in Western Popular Culture* (New Haven, Conn.: Yale University Press, 1992), pp. 134, 170.

13 Roy Strong, *Recreating the Past* (London: Thames and Hudson, 1978), p. 20.

14 Rodris Roth, "The New England, or 'Olde Tyme,' Kitchen Exhibit at Nineteenth-Century Fairs," in *The Colonial Revival in America*, Alan Axelrod, ed. (New York: W. W. Norton, 1985), pp. 159–183.

15 Karal Ann Marling, *George Washington Slept Here: Colonial Revivals and American Culture, 1876–1986* (Cambridge, Mass.: Harvard University Press, 1988), p. 34.

16 Ibid., p. 40.

Chapter 6. Enter the Pilgrims (pp. 98–114)

1 Love, *Fast and Thanksgiving Days*, p. 416; Restad, *Christmas in America*, p. 21.

2 December 22 was in fact a miscalculation, although this was not recognized until 1850. While it had taken eleven days to adjust the date in 1752, it required only ten days for a date in 1620. In 1870, the Pilgrim Society in Plymouth adopted the revision and has celebrated Forefathers' Day on December 21 ever since. The Old Colony Club, on the other hand, continues to observe the traditional December 22 date.

3 Albert Matthews, "The Term 'Pilgrim Fathers' and Early Celebrations of Forefathers' Day," *Transactions of the Colonial Society of Massachusetts* 17 (1914), p. 317.

4 John Rogers (1829–1904) manufactured a series of plaster sculptures for display in private homes illustrating popular scenes from American history, including "Why Don't You Speak For Yourself, John?" (1885) depicting the famous scene from Longfellow's *Courtship of Myles Standish*.

5 Nathaniel Morton, *New England's Memorial*, ed. John Davis (Boston: Crocker and Brewster, 1826), p. 377.

6 Van Wyck Brooks, *The Flowering of New England* (New York: E. P. Dutton & Co., 1936), p. 509.

7 Peter Gomes, "The Darlings of Heaven," *Harvard Magazine*, November 1976, p. 33.

8 Eric Hobsbawm and Terence Ranger, *The Invention of Tradition* (New York: Cambridge University Press, 1984), p. 2.

9 Ibid., p. 9.

10 Ibid., passim; Rudy Koshar, *From Monuments to Traces* (Berkeley: University of California Press, 2000), pp. 35, 40; Hazel W. Hertzberger, *The Search for an American Indian Identity* (Syracuse, N.Y.: Syracuse University Press, 1971), pp.

308–324; and Francis G. Hutchins, *Mashpee: The Story of Cape Cod's Indian Town* (West Franklin, N.H.: Amarta Press, 1979, pp. 135ff. Also see Elizabeth Hoover, "Arbiters of Authenticity: Living History in Native American Museums," www.gradschool.unc.edu/natam/speakers.html (accessed February 2005 but now removed).

11 Michael Kammen, *A Season of Youth* (New York: Alfred A. Knopf, 1978), p. 11.

12 Wesley Frank Craven, *The Legend of the Founding Fathers* (Westport, Conn.: Greenwood Press, 1983), p. 97.

13 Kammen, *Season of Youth*, pp. 388ff.; Mrs. Rutherford, the historian general of the United Daughters of the Confederacy, published her dissent in the January 1925 issue of her *Scrap Book*, a serial publication of "Valuable Information About the South," as "The True History of the Jamestown Colony and the True History of the Plymouth Rock": "The Plymouth Rock Colony had a Thanksgiving time, just as the Jamestown Colony had eleven years earlier," p. 14.

14 Benjamin Scott, *The Pilgrim Fathers Neither Puritans Nor Persecutors*, 4th edition (London: Elliot Stock, 1891).

15 William Macon Coleman, *The History of the Primitive Yankees; or, The Pilgrim Fathers in England and Holland* (Washington, D.C.: Columbia Publishing Company, 1881), pp. 7–8.

16 William Carlos Williams, *In the American Grain* (New York: New Directions, 1956), p. 68.

17 Ibid., p. 74.

18 Craven, *Legend of the Founding Fathers*, p. 187.

19 May Miller, "The Great Pilgrimage," *Our Young Folks*, November 1866, pp. 671–672.

20 Charles W. Elliott, *The New England History* (New York: Charles Scribner, 1857), vol. 1, pp. 129–132; *Harper's Weekly*, December 6, 1873, p. 1086.

21 "I, Brigham Young, Governor of the Territory [Utah] aforesaid, in response to the time-honored custom of our forefathers at Plymouth Rock . . . do proclaim . . . a day of Praise and Thanksgiving. . ." Appelbaum, *Thanksgiving*, p. 125.

22 Love, *Fast and Thanksgiving Days*, p. 69. Less reliably, he identifies an alleged thanksgiving recorded in the "Brewster Book" (which on subsequent research can now be dismissed as historically unauthentic) observed following the *Mayflower*'s arrival on December 20, 1620, as the best candidate for the true First New England Thanksgiving (pp. 457ff).

23 "The First Thanksgiving Day," in Kate Douglas Wiggin and Nora A. Smith, *The Story Hour: A Book for The Home and The Kindergarten* (Boston: Houghton, Mifflin, 1890), p. 114.

24 My initial survey of Thanksgiving postcards was done at postcard and ephemera shows over a number of years. Lately I have taken advantage of a valuable new pop-culture research tool, the eBay auctions, to survey postcard images. Several examples appear each evening, and in the past five years of nightly searches I have looked at thousands of images and found no Taylor-style dinners, with the exception of a single 1920s Walkover Shoe example.

25 Reuben Gold Thwaites, *Epochs of American history: The Colonies, 1492–1750*

(New York: Longmans Green, 1894); D. H. Montgomery, *The Beginners American History* (Boston: Ginn & Company, 1894); G. Barnett Smith, *The Romance of Colonization: The United States, from the Earliest Times to the Landing of the Pilgrim Fathers* (New York: Dodd, Mead, 1897); D. H. Montgomery, *The Leading Facts of American History* (Boston: Ginn and Company, 1920); Charles A. Beard and William C. Bagley, *The History of the American People* (New York: Macmillan Company, 1923); Ruth West, *The Story of Our Country* (Boston: Allyn and Bacon, 1935); Leon H. Canfield, *The United States in the Making* (Boston: Houghton Mifflin, 1940).

26 Interestingly, a Thanksgiving sequence had been proposed by Baker in 1917 but was later dropped from the program. The trope was obviously less compelling then than the other elements of the Pilgrim Story. "Episode III. Scene 4 (1621) — The first Thanksgiving Day. Manners and customs. How the Pilgrims went to church. Their games, sports, etc." *Report of the Pilgrim Tercentenary Commission, January 3, 1917* (Boston: Wright & Potter, 1917), p. 27.

27 Samuel Eliot Morison, *The Pilgrim Fathers: Their Significance in History* (Concord, N.H.: Society of Mayflower Descendants in the State of New Hampshire, 1937), p. 6.

28 Jack Santino, *All around the Year: Holidays and Celebrations in American Life* (Urbana: University of Illinois Press, 1995), p. 175.

Chapter 7. Pilgrims Are for Kids: Thanksgiving in the Progressive Classroom
(pp. 115–128)

1 Robert Haven Schauffler, *Thanksgiving: Its Origin, Celebration and Significance as Revealed in Prose and Verse*, Our American Holidays Series (New York: Dodd, Mead and Co., 1907), p. vii.

2 Gail Hamilton [Mary Abigail Dodge], *Red-Letter Days in Applethorpe* (Boston: Tichnor and Fields, 1855). The holiday stories include New Year's, Washington's Birthday, Fast-Day, May-Day, a birthday, Seventeenth of June (not quite Emancipation Day, which is the 19th), Fourth of July, Thanksgiving, Forefathers' Day, and Christmas. Some of the stories have little to do with the date, but the dawning significance of "days" to children is evident.

3 Ellen M. Litwicki, *America's Public Holidays, 1865–1920* (Washington, D.C.: Smithsonian Institution Press, 2000), p. 206.

4 Barbara Miller Solomon, *Ancestors and Immigrants* (Chicago: University of Chicago Press, 1972), p. 163.

5 Robert H. Weibe, *The Search for Order, 1877–1920* (New York: Hill and Wang, 1967), p. 111.

6 Solomon, *Ancestors and Immigrants*, p. 85.

7 "To be English, French, or German is usually taken for granted, but Americans have always been worried about what 'Americanness' is, and whether they have it." Ruth Miller Elson, *Guardians of Tradition* (Lincoln: University of Nebraska Press, 1964), p. 341.

8 Kammen, *Mystic Chords of Memory*, p. 96.

9 "*Whereas*, The President of the United States has issued his annual proclamation, calling upon the people as a whole to give thanks for prosperity, of which
but few of them have a share, and reiterating the lies so often repeated about the
well-being of the nation; and *Whereas*, the existence of a vast army of homeless
wanderers, scarcity of employment, business depression, and the poverty and
wretchedness of a large majority of the people give the lie to the statement
that abundant prosperity prevails. No nation can be prosperous and contented
where, in the banquet of life, a small number monopolize the general product, while the many are denied a place at nature's table; therefore *Resolved*, By
this mass-meeting of all classes of citizens, that we vote our vigorous protest
against the above-named proclamation at this time; that it is a lie—a stupid,
hollow mockery—a sop thrown out by the ruling classes to tickle the palates
of the ignorant dupes and slaves that they may with better security continue
to rob them. We reiterate the statement that only when the people shall come
into their own—when land and the natural resources of the earth shall have
become free; when liberty shall have become a practical reality, and when the
beast of private property in the means of life shall have ceased to sap the energies of the people; when poverty and the fear of want shall have been abolished
from the face of the earth—then, and not until then, shall we have cause as a
people, to give thanks for our abundant prosperity." *Life of Albert R. Parsons,
with Brief History of the Labor Movement in America* (Chicago: L. E. Parsons,
1889), p. 56–57.

10 Litwicki, *America's Public Holidays*, pp. 174ff.

11 Ibid., p. 177.

12 Ibid., p. 180.

13 Publishers of such booklets include Wehman Brothers (New York), I. & M.
Ottenheimer (Baltimore), M. A. Dononue (Chicago), Walter H. Baker (Boston), and David McKay (Philadelphia, New York).

14 Mary L. Hood, *Special Days in the Primary Grades* (Chicago: A. Flanagan Co.,
1897).

15 Marie Irish, *The Days We Celebrate: A Collection of Original Dialogues, Reci-
tations, Entertainments and Other Pieces for Holidays and Special Occasions*
(Chicago: T. S. Denison & Co., 1904); Amos M. Kellogg, *Special Day Exercises:
Special Programs for School Celebrations* (Philadelphia: Penn Publishing, 1911).

16 Stanley Schell, *Thanksgiving Celebrations No. 1* (New York: Edgar S. Werner
Publishing and Supply Co., 1901).

17 Horace G. Brown (Worcester Normal School, 1911), quoted in Litwicki, *America's Public Holidays*, p. 182.

18 Elizabeth H. Pleck, *Celebrating the Family: Ethnicity, Consumer Culture, and
Family Rituals* (Cambridge, Mass.: Harvard University Press, 2000), p. 28.

19 Asa Don Dickinson, *The Children's Book of Thanksgiving Stories* (Garden City,
N.J.: Doubleday, Page & Co., 1916).

20 Effa E. Preston, *The Children's Thanksgiving Book* (Lebanon, Ohio: March
Brothers, 1928), p. 28.

21 Ibid., p. 8.

22 Marie Irish., *Choice Thanksgiving Entertainments* (Dayton, Ohio: Paine Publishing Co., 1923), p. 21.

23 Ibid., pp. 30–31.

24 Louise Miller Novotnoy and Ida Lee Wolfe, *The Standard Thanksgiving Book No. 1* (Cincinnati: Standard Publishing Co., 1937), p. 29.

25 In the G. P. Brown & Co. *Catalogue of School Supplies* (Beverly, Mass., 1909), p. 32, "Thanksgiving pictures," there are twenty-five classic Pilgrim scenes by Boughton, Weir, Lucy, and Cope, and one called *The Hidden Foe* by Pierce (and six for J. G. Whittier), but none depict any actual Thanksgiving activity. Similarly, *The Teacher's Year Book* catalog for 1927–1928 (March Brothers, Lebanon, Ohio) offers an assortment of eighteen Thanksgiving anthologies, booklets, and music books, but the images are mostly of turkeys and fall scenery. There are also Indian and Pilgrim posters and costumes, but no Thanksgiving depictions. The *Teacher's Catalog* of 1945 from the Paine Publishing Co. (Dayton, Ohio)—a major publisher of holiday anthologies and workbooks—on the other hand offers First Thanksgiving posters, cutouts, and pictures to color in addition to an assortment of booklets.

26 *Thanksgiving Souvenir* (New Philadelphia: Ohio Printing Company, 1908). The same booklet is advertised in the *Teachers Magazine*, vol. 28, no. 3, November 1905, p. 261.

27 Robert Hunt, *A Treatise On The Progressive Improvement & Present State Of The Manufactures In Metal*, vol. 2 (London: Longmans, 1853), p. 363.

28 Jackson Lears, *No Place of Grace* (New York: Pantheon Books, 1981), p. 17.

Chapter 8. Imaging the Holiday (pp. 129–144)

1 Carolyn Kitch, *The Girl on the Magazine Cover: The Origins of Visual Stereotypes in American Mass Media* (Chapel Hill: University of North Carolina Press, 2001), p. 3.

2 Jackson Lears, *Fables of Abundance: A Cultural History of Advertising in America* (New York: Basic Books, 1994), p. 54; James B. Twitchell, *Adcult USA: The Triumph of Advertising in American Culture* (New York: Columbia University Press, 1996), p. 78.

3 W.J.T. Mitchell, *Iconology*, p. 41.

4 George and Dorothy Miller, *Picture Postcards in the United States, 1893–1918* (New York: Clarkson N. Potter, 1976), p. 22.

5 "Interpretant: An emotive association which acquires the value of an established connotation: /dog/ signifies <<fidelity>> and vice versa." Umberto Eco, *A Theory of Semiotics* (Bloomington: Indiana University Press, 1979), p. 70.

6 Siegfried Wichmann, *Japonisme: The Japanese Influence on Western Art since 1858* (New York: Thames & Hudson, 1981), p. 224.

7 A facsimile of a 1924–1925 catalog, unfortunately reprinted without any original company attribution (*Wholesale Trade List No. 26 Toys Favors Hallowe'en*

Thanksgiving Christmas [Gas City, Ind.: L-W Book Sales, 1985], pp. 21–25), lists a wide assortment of toy and miniature turkeys and dollhouse foods imported from Germany, as well as wax fruit, fruit baskets, nut cups, and "kewpie" Thanksgiving figures. It also offers "snapping mottos" (a variation of the English Christmas cracker): "In it's [*sic*] simple form a cracker is a small cardboard tube covered in a brightly coloured twist of paper. When the cracker is 'pulled' by two people, each holding one end of the twisted paper, the friction creates a small explosive 'pop' produced by a narrow strip of chemically impregnated paper. The cardboard tube tumbles a bright paper hat, a small gift, a balloon and a motto or joke" (Absolutely Crackers Ltd, PO Box 3147, Milton Keynes, Buckinghamshire MK15 8ZT, England).

8 *Country Life in America*, November 1904, p. 84.

9 *Saturday Evening Post*, November 18, 1922, p. 76.

10 Lears, *Fables of Abundance*, p. 249.

11 This sort of aggressive rustic "make-do" and a fascination with logs (and practical ignorance) are especially well represented in the illustrations to James Otis, *Mary of Plymouth* (New York: American Book Company, 1910). On page 90, Plymouth men are shown building fires with huge logs to immolate both deer and wildfowl.

12 Gabriel Salomon, *Interaction of Media, Cognition, and Learning* (San Francisco: Jossey-Bass Publishers, 1981), p. 60.

Chapter 9. Parades, Patriotism, and Consumption (pp. 145–164)

1 http://seasons.flyingdreams.org/thanksgiving.htm (accessed October 10, 2008). The T. Eaton Department Store in Toronto began a Christmas parade tradition on December 2, 1904, that would have all the characteristics of subsequent American Thanksgiving parades, except that it does not occur on Thanksgiving but a week or so earlier.

2 Nissenbaum, *Battle For Christmas*, 1996, p. 38; Susan G. Davis, *Parades and Power* (Berkeley: University of California Press, 1986), p. 103; Len Travers, *Celebrating the Fourth* (Amherst: University of Massachusetts Press, 1997), pp. 128ff.

3 Pleck, *Celebrating the Family*, p. 33.

4 http://www.memory.loc.gov/learn/features/thanksgiving/timeline/1924.html (accessed March 12, 2005).

5 http://info.detnews.com/redesign/history/story/historytemplate.cfm?id=173 (accessed October 10, 2008).

6 http://www.detroitkidshow.com/Maureen_Bailey.htm (accessed March 12, 2005).

7 http://www.metro.heritage.com/dtw120199/story1.htm (accessed March 12, 2005).

8 http://www.chicagofestivals.org/site/docs/42569_History.pdf (accessed March 12, 2005).

9 Robert Sullivan, ed., *America's Parade: A Celebration of Macy's Thanksgiving Day Parade* (New York: Time-Life, 2001), p. 16.

10 Ibid., p. 17.

11 Ibid., p. 14.

12 Kammen, *Mystic Chords of Memory*, p. 300.

13 Loren Baritz, *The Good Life: The Meaning of Success for the American Middle Class* (New York: Harper & Row, 1990), p. 110.

14 Ibid., p. 105; David M. Kennedy, *Freedom from Fear: The American People in Depression and War, 1929–1945* (New York: Oxford University Press, 1999), p. 306.

15 Kennedy, *Freedom from Fear*, p. 365.

16 Kammen, *Mystic Chords of Memory*, p. 410.

17 *Old Colony Memorial* (Plymouth, Mass.), October 11, 1941.

18 Appelbaum, *Thanksgiving*, pp. 233ff.

19 *Old Colony Memorial*, November 23, 1939, p. 1.

20 Collections of line drawings of the Pilgrims designed for schoolroom use in the mid–twentieth century such as Etta Garson's *Pilgrims*, Around-the-World Drawings series (Dayton, Ohio: Paine Publishing Co., 1924), Leroy Sauer's *Pilgrim Cut-Outs* (Dayton, Ohio: Paine Publishing Co., 1939), or Helen Strimple's *Pilgrim Village Cut Outs* (Springfield, Mass., 1946) all depict—in a serious, traditional style—the colonists and Indians working, cooking out of doors, or harvesting in the fall amid log cabins.

21 *Life*, November 23, 1942, p. 74.

22 Baritz, *The Good Life*, pp. 176, 178.

23 Litwicki, *America's Public Holidays*, p. 242.

24 Peggy Baker, Thanksgiving "Over There" (1998), an exhibit of Thanksgiving in the military from the Civil War through Operation Desert Storm at Pilgrim Hall Museum, Plymouth, Mass. http://www.pilgrimhall.org/thot-pcw .htm (accessed October 10, 2008).

25 "Bill Sykes was in the Combat Engineers and then 1095th Engineer Utility Company, Command SoPac, US Army Engineers 1942–1945. 'The Thanksgiving dinners were served on trays. (My first one, with the Combat Engineers, was served in mess kits. That doesn't work too well.) They had cranberry sauce, stuffing, the whole thing. It was a good meal. But the feeling of Thanksgiving wasn't there. The meal was there, but the feeling of Thanksgiving wasn't. I guess you couldn't have Thanksgiving when you were overseas. There wasn't much to be thankful for. It was sad. Although, I guess there was some thankfulness, at least you were still alive!' Ed Campbell recalled his 1944 Thanksgiving as a Marine: 'The second [Thanksgiving], I was on Maui and I do remember. It was an odd day. You remember all of your early Thanksgivings with the family and a certain feeling of nostalgia sets in. Then you take your mess kit, which is like an oval opened up, and go down to the mess hall and get your Thanksgiving dinner thrown into the mess kit. It ends up with the turkey and carrots all mixed. The cooks do a great job of trying to make it a festive meal but when you mix it all together with the gravy in the mess kit, it's sort of like mush. I

do remember that. Other than that, there was no celebration. There wasn't too much discussion, we just all sort of hunkered into ourselves and thought of earlier days and days to come, hopefully.'" Thanksgiving "Over There" exhibition, Pilgrim Hall Museum, Plymouth, Mass. (1998). The exhibit is available online in part at www.pilgrimhall.org/thanksot.htm.

26 "How Jack and the Gang Spent Thanksgiving Day," *The Jack Benny Show* (November 26, 1944).

27 Bill Shepard, in Thanksgiving "Over There" exhibition, Pilgrim Hall Museum, Plymouth, Mass. (1998), http://www.pilgrimhall.org/thanksot.htm; *Yank*, European edition, November 24, 1944.

28 Kennedy, *Freedom from Fear*, p. 378.

29 "Servicemen for Thanksgiving" (November 16, 1941), *"Thanksgiving Dinner" (November 22, 1942), The Great Gildersleeve;* "Turkey Trouble," *Amos and Andy* (November 19, 1943); "How Jack and the Gang Spent Thanksgiving Day," *The Jack Benny Show* (November 26, 1944).

30 Eatmor Cranberries, *Woman's Day* (November 1942), p. 5; *New Yorker*, November 27, 1943.

31 Kennedy, *Freedom from Fear*, p. 747.

32 *SLATE*, sidebar to "School for Scandal: Revisiting Ambrose, Bellesiles, Ellis, and Goodwin," by David Greenberg, posted Friday, December 10, 2004, at 1:17 pm PT, http://www.slate.msn.com/id/2110907/sidebar/2110916/ (accessed October 10, 2008).

33 "Accentuate the Positive," lyrics by Johnny Mercer, music by Harold Arlen (1944).

Chapter 10. Consensus and Competition: The Postwar Thanksgiving
(pp. 165–182)

1 Imagery of the "good old days" figured largely in advertisements and in folk-art illustrations such as Doris Lee's *Thanksgiving* (1935), but there was also an interesting collection of Thanksgiving preparations in photographs a half-century old or so in the *Boston Sunday Globe Magazine* on November 18, 1951, under the title "Thanksgiving in the Good Old Days."

2 Quoted in the *Old Colony Memorial*, November 20, 1925, p. 6.

3 Copy of letter dated December 3, 1945, in Plimoth Plantation archives.

4 *The Pilgrim Memorial to be erected in The Town of Plymouth, Massachusetts* (Plymouth, Mass.: Plimoth Plantation, Inc., 1948), p. 8.

5 Thanksgiving ad by the United States Brewers' Foundation, 1953; "Why American Families Can Enjoy 'Thanksgiving Eating' All Year Round," The Continental Can Company, 1952.

6 I say "probable" here because we really do not have any evidence that such an event took place, despite the existence of a clause in the Berkeley Plantation proprietors' instructions that the anniversary of the date should be celebrated annually with a Thanksgiving service. "1. Impr.wee ordaine that the day of our

ships arrivall at the place assigned for plantacon in the land of Virginia shall be yearly and perpetually keept holy as a day of thanksgiving to Almighty god." However, it is entirely reasonable to assume that this did occur as planned in 1620 and 1621 — and in 1619 as well, before it was cut short by the massacre of that plantation's inhabitants in 1622.

7 Craven, *Legend of the Founding Fathers*, p. 6.

8 Proclamation 3505: Thanksgiving Day. November 7, 1962.

By the President of the United States of AMERICA a Proclamation:

Over three centuries ago in Plymouth, on Massachusetts Bay, the Pilgrims established the custom of gathering together each year to express their gratitude to God for the preservation of their community and for the harvests their labors brought forth in the new land. Joining with their neighbors, they shared together and worshipped together in a common giving of thanks. Thanksgiving Day has ever since been part of the fabric which has united Americans with their past, with each and with the future of all mankind.

It is fitting that we observe this year our own day of thanksgiving. It is fitting that we give our thanks for the safety of our land, for the fertility of our harvests, for the strength of our liberties, for the health of our people. We do so in no spirit of self-righteousness. We recognize that we are the beneficiaries of the toil and devotion of our fathers and that we can pass their legacy on to our children only by equal toil and equal devotion. We recognize too that we live in a world of peril and change — and in so uncertain a time we are all the more grateful for the indestructible gifts of hope and love, which sustain us in adversity and inspire us to labor unceasingly for a more perfect community within this nation and around the earth.

Now, THEREFORE, I, JOHN F. KENNEDY, President of the United States of America, in accord with the joint resolution of Congress, approved December 26, 1941, which designates the fourth Thursday in November of each year as thanksgiving Day, do hereby proclaim Thursday, the twenty-second day of November of this year, as a day of national thanksgiving.

I urge that all observe this day with reverence and with humility.

Let us renew the spirit of the Pilgrims at the first Thanksgiving, lonely in an inscrutable wilderness, facing the dark unknown with a faith borne of their dedication to God and a fortitude drawn from their sense that all men were brothers.

Let us renew that spirit by offering our thanks for uncovenanted mercies, beyond our desert or merit, and by resolving to meet the responsibilities placed upon us.

Let us renew that spirit by sharing the abundance of this day with those less fortunate, in our own land and abroad. Let us renew that spirit by seeking always to establish larger communities of brotherhood.

Let us renew that spirit by preparing our souls for the incertitudes ahead — by being always ready to confront crisis with steadfastness and achievement with grace and modesty.

Let us renew that spirit by concerting our energy and our hope with men and women everywhere that the world may move more rapidly toward the time when Thanksgiving may be a day of universal celebration.

Let us renew that spirit by expressing our acceptance of the limitations of human striving and by affirming our duty to strive nonetheless, as Providence may direct us, toward a better world for all mankind.

IN WITNESS WHEREOF, I have hereunto set my hand and caused the seal of the United States of America to be affixed.

DONE at the City of Washington this 7th day of November, in the year of our Lord nineteen hundred and sixty-two, and of the Independence of the United States of America the one hundred and eighty-seventh.

JOHN F. KENNEDY

9 "1962 Nov. 9 PM 3:30 The President. The White House. Your Presidential Proclamation erroneously credits Massachusetts Pilgrims with America's First Thanksgiving observance. As we demonstrated a year ago to the Governor of Massachusetts by original historical records of the Congressional Library, America's First Thanksgiving was actually celebrated in Virginia in 1619 more that a year before the Pilgrims ever landed. And nearly two years before the Massachusetts Thanksgiving. Virginia's claim was officially recognized by President Abraham Lincoln nearly a century ago and further substantiated by historian Dabney's comprehensive article in the November 29, 1958 Saturday Evening Post. As a matter of fairness, please issue an appropriate correction. John J. Wicker Jr. Honorary Chairman Richmond Thanksgiving Festival."

10 "Nov. 30, 1962. Dear Mr. Wicker: The President has asked me to reply to your telegram about the Thanksgiving Proclamation statement. You are quite right, and I can only plead an unconquerable New England bias on the part of the White House staff. We are all grateful to you for reminding us of the Berkeley Hundred Thanksgiving: and I can assure you that the error will not be repeated in the future. Sincerely yours, Arthur Schlesinger, Jr. Special Assistant to The President." (Copy to Pierre Salinger.)

11 Letter to Arthur Schlesinger, Jr., from Henry Hornblower, II, January 7, 1963. He cites *Hakluyt's Voyages*, vol. 8, page 458: "'After he had sayled a certain time he crossed over to the other side of the river, and then in the presence of certaine Indians, which of purpose did attend him, he commanded his men to make their prayers, to give thanks to God, for that of his grace he had conducted the French nation unto these strange places without any danger at all.' This you see happened 57 years before anything happened at Berkeley Hundred." Of course the danger came later when the Spanish wiped out the little French Florida settlement, but that does not affect this particular event.

12 The earliest thanksgiving service in what is now the United States was apparently "[o]n April 3, 1513, in the season of 'Pascua Florida'—as Easter Season is known in Spanish (meaning Feast of Flowers)—Ponce de Leon expedition sighted land in the present locality of St. Augustine and named it La Florida. When they landed, the priest who had accompanied the soldiers said a Mass of thanksgiving as the native Timucua Indians looked on. Ponce de Leon took

possession of the continent for Spain, naming it 'La Florida' to commemorate the Easter season and the blossom-filled coastline he encountered" (http://www.fountainofyouthflorida.com/History, accessed 4/3/2005). There is also an alleged Spanish service that is often cited but for which I have been unable to find any primary source justification: "The first recorded Christian thanksgiving in America occurred in Texas on May 23, 1541 when Spanish explorer, Francisco Vasquez de Coronado, and his men held a service of thanksgiving after finding food, water, and pasture for their animals in the Panhandle" (ibid.). The Palo Duro Canyon thanksgiving may be mere legend.

13 Arthur Pyle, *Thanksgiving Day Observance* (Plymouth, Mass.: Plimoth Plantation, n.d., ca. 1962), p. 6; *Pilgrim Times*, vol. 1, no. 1, 1963, p. 63.

14 Robert San Souci, *N. C. Wyeth's Pilgrims* (New York: Chronicle Books, 1991); Richard Scarry, *First Thanksgiving of Low Leaf Worm* (New York: Little Simon [Simon and Schuster], 2003).

15 Elsa Okon Rael, *Rivka's First Thanksgiving*, Maryann Kovalski, illustrator (New York: Athenaeum/Simon & Schuster, 2004); Shana Corey, Milly and the Macy's Parade, *Brett Helquist, illustrator (New York: Scholastic, 2002); Irene Smalls, A Strawbeater's Thanksgiving*, Melodye Benson Rosales, illustrator (Boston: Little Brown & Co, 1998); Emily Arnold McCully, *An Outlaw Thanksgiving* (New York: Puffin Books, 2000); Barbara Cohen, *Molly's Pilgrim*, Daniel Mark Duffy, illustrator. (New York: Lothrop Lee and Shepard Company, 1983).

16 Eve Bunting, *How Many Days to America*, Beth Peck, illustrator (Boston: Clarion Books, 1990); Debbie Atwell, *The Thanksgiving Door* (Boston: Houghton Mifflin/Walter Lorraine Books, 2003); Paula Daniziger, *Amber Brown Is Feeling Blue* (New York: Scholastic Paperbacks, 1999); Ann Rockwell, *Thanksgiving Day*, Lizzy Rockwell, illustrator (New York: Harper Trophy, 2002); Eve Bunting, *A Turkey for Thanksgiving*, Diane de Groat, illustrator (Boston: Clarion Books, 1991); Lillian Hoban, *Silly Tilly's Thanksgiving Dinner* (New York: Harper Trophy, 1991); Suzy-Jane Tanner, *The Tasty Thanksgiving Feast* (New York: Harper Festival, 1998); Joy Cowley, *Gracias, the Thanksgiving Turkey*, Joe Cepeda, illustrator (New York: Scholastic, 1996); Michele Sobel Spirn, *The Know-Nothings Talk Turkey*, R. W. Alley, illustrator (New York: HarperCollins, 2000).

Chapter 11. New Myths for Old—Thanksgiving under Siege
(pp. 183–200)

1 *Springfield Union-News* (Springfield, Mass.), November 28, 1969; *New Haven Journal Courier* (New Haven, Conn.), November 28, 1969. The Plymouth, Massachusetts, *Old Colony Memorial* had little to say about the protest in its coverage of the holiday events, in which 3,997 people attended Plimoth Plantation on Thanksgiving and 5,100 ate dinner in local restaurants (December 4, 1969).

2 Associated Press release from Plymouth, November 26, 1969.

3 *Portland Express* (Maine), November 28, 1969; *Boston Globe*, November 28,

1969. This and the following clippings are in the Plimoth Plantation archives, and unfortunately lack page numbers.

4 Ben Winton, "Alcatraz Indian Land," *Native Peoples Magazine*, Fall 1999, available online: http://www.nativepeoples.com/np_features/np_articles/1999_fall _article/alcatraz-p2.html (accessed March 30, 2005).

5 Ilka Hartmann, "Native Americans Liberate the Rock Celebrating the 35th Anniversary of the Alcatraz Occupation," November 20, 2004, at 10:44 a.m., http://www.indybay.org/news/2004/11/1706264.php (accessed March 30, 2005).

6 "Alcatraz Is Not an Island" (ITVS), http://www.pbs.org/itvs/alcatrazisnotan island/occupation.html (accessed March 31, 2005).

7 *Old Colony Memorial*, December 3, 1970, p. 14.

8 Ibid.

9 Elroy S. Thompson, *History of Plymouth, Norfolk and Barnstable Counties, Massachusetts* (New York: Lewis Historical Publishing Co., 1928), p. 80.

10 http://www.faculty.smu.edu/twalker/protest4.htm (accessed February 3, 2006).

11 See appendix 2.

12 *Times Literary Supplement* (London), July 24, 1998, p. 8.

13 Mitchel Cohen, "Why I Hate Thanksgiving," online document: www.scoop .co.nz/stories/HL0311/S00211.htm#a (accessed November 27, 2003); www .brianwillson.com/awolthanksmyth.html (accessed February 13, 2003); www .nativecircle.com/mlmThanksgivingmyth.html (accessed February 13, 2003); www.danielnpaul.com/TheRealThanksgiving.html (accessed February 13, 2003). Another such site offers this contribution to the myth: "In 1621 the myth of thanksgiving was born. The colonists invited Massasoit, chief of the Wampanoags, to their first feast as a follow up to their recent land deal. Massasoit in turn invited 90 of his men, much to the chagrin of the colonists. Two years later the English invited a number of tribes to a feast 'symbolizing eternal friendship.' The English offered food and drink, and two hundred Indians dropped dead from unknown poison." www.rense.com/general45/thanks.htm (accessed February 14, 2006). Obviously historical truth is not the intent.

14 http://www.sail1620.org/discover_feature_thanksgiving_on_the_net_roast_ bull_with_cranberry_sauce_part_1.shml (accessed February 3, 2003).

15 www.mayflowerhistory.com/Introduction/lessonplandebunk.php (accessed February 3, 2003).

16 Ronald Wright, in a review of Richard Grant's *Ghost Riders: Travels with American Nomads*, in *Times Literary Supplement* (London), March 21, 2003, p. 24.

17 http://www.ewebtribe.com/NACulture/articles/thanksgiving.html (accessed October 10, 2008).

18 http://www.common-place.dreamhost.com/vol-01/no-02/talk/ (accessed February 13, 2003).

19 Much of the new Thanksgiving myth is easily available on the World Wide Web. The identification of the 1636 Thanksgiving following the Pequot War (in which, incidentally, the Plymouth colonists had no role, having postponed their involvement until after the cessation of hostilities) as the

real First Thanksgiving can be found in Moonanum James and Mahtowin Munro, "Thanksgiving: A National Day of Mourning for Indians," at www2 .ios.com/~uaine19/dom.htm. It was proposed earlier in the 1970s by a Native spokesman from Maine. The identification of the 1676 proclamation as the official first proclamation of Thanksgiving (see Julia Armstrong Murphy, "Thanksgiving from an Indigenous Point of View," at www.nativeamculture .about.com/culture/nativeamculture/library/weekly/aa111600a.htm) is perhaps because it is the earliest surviving example of a *printed* proclamation, hence, for some, the first. The actual first (oral) proclamation of Thanksgiving in Plymouth Colony was of course in the summer of 1623, and the first in Massachusetts in 1630 following the arrival of the "Winthrop Fleet." Neither concerned the Native population. The idea that the Wampanoag supplied most of the food can be found in Chuck Larsen and coauthors' bathetic "Teaching about Thanksgiving" (Tacoma Public Schools, 1987, p. 5) at www.ewebtribe .com/NACulture/articles/thanksgiving.html (accessed February 3, 2003).

20 http://www.nativeweb.org/pages/legal/thanksgiving_nelte.html (accessed October 10, 2008).

Chapter 12. Thanksgiving Now, Then, and Forever (pp. 201–217)

1 http://www.thanksgiving.org/about.html (accessed February 17, 2006).

2 http://www.snowgoose.org/about_snowgoose.html (accessed October 10, 2008).

3 Edward Bleier, *The Thanksgiving Ceremony: New Traditions for America's Family Feast* (New York: Crown Publishers, 2003), p. 23.

4 http://amazon.com/gp/product/customer-reviews/1400047870/ref=cm_cr _dp_2_1/103-7480906-1381453?%5Fencoding=UTF8&customer-reviews.sort %5Fby=-SubmissionDate&n=283155 (accessed February 17, 2006).

5 *Gay City News*, November 29, 2002, vol. 1, no. 27.

6 "History of the Parade," http://www.usathanksgiving.com.

7 U.N. Resolution 1997/46 1997/46, "International Year of Thanksgiving, 2000," Economic and Social Council, 37th plenary meeting, July 22, 1997.

8 Pleck, *Celebrating the Family*, pp. 1–3.

9 Leigh Eric Schmidt, *Consumer Rites: The Buying and Selling of American Holidays* (Princeton, N.J.: Princeton University Press, 1993), p. 302.

10 Santino, *All around the Year*, p. xviii.

11 Barry Schwartz, *Abraham Lincoln and the Forge of National Memory* (Chicago: University of Chicago Press, 1992), pp. 310–311.

12 R. I. Moore, review of Chris Wickham, *Framing the Early Middle Ages: Europe and the Mediterranean, 400–800*, and Julia M. H. Smith, *Europe after Rome: A New Cultural History, 500–1000*, in *Times Literary Supplement* (London), February 17, 2006, p. 4.

13 Robert Segal, review of Karen L. King's *What Is Gnosticism?* in *Times Literary Supplement* (London), November 21, 2003, p. 31.

14 From the proclamation of Henry Laurens, president of the Continental Congress, for the first national Thanksgiving on Thursday, December 18, 1777.

15 Schwartz, *Abraham Lincoln and National Memory*, p. 296.

Appendix 2. Some Early Thanksgiving Recipes (pp. 230–232)

1 Simmons, *American Cookery*, p. 18; Mrs. Child, *The American Frugal Housewife* (Boston: Carter, Hendee, and Co., 1833), p. 55; Howland, *New England Economical Housekeeper*, p. 55; Simmons, *American Cookery*, pp. 23, 29.

2 Thomas Dawson, *The Second part of the good Hus-wives Iewell* (Norwood, N.J.: Walter J Johnson, 1977), p. 51.

3 Lydia Maria Child, *The American Frugal Housewife*, 10th edition (Boston: Carter & Hence, 1832), p. 66.

4 Catherine Beecher, *Miss Beecher's Domestic Receipt-Book* (New York: Harper and Brothers, 1846), p. 126, also a variant in H. M. Cornelius, *The Young Housekeeper's Friend* (Boston: Taggard and Thompson, 1863), p. 75. This is essentially the same as the apple pudding in Simmons, *American Cookery*, p. 17.

5 Mrs. N.K.L. Lee ("a Boston Housekeeper"), *The Cook's Own Book* (Boston: Munroe and Francis, 1832), p. 163.

Bibliography

[Abbott, Jacob]. *New England and Her Institutions by "One of Her Sons."* Boston: John Allen & Co., 1835.

Adams, James Truslow. *New England in the Republic.* Boston: Little, Brown, and Company, 1926.

Appelbaum, Diana. *Thanksgiving: An American Holiday, an American History.* New York: Facts on File, 1984.

Atwell, Debbie. *The Thanksgiving Door.* Boston: Houghton Mifflin/Walter Lorraine Books, 2003.

Axelrod, Alan, ed. *The Colonial Revival in America.* New York: W. W. Norton, 1985.

Bacon, Louisa Crowninshield. *Reminiscences.* Salem, Mass.: Privately printed, 1922.

Baker, Peggy M. *Thanksgiving "Over There."* Plymouth, Mass.: Pilgrim Hall Museum, 1998. www.pilgrimhall.org/thanksot.htm.

Ballard, Martha. *The Diary of Martha Ballard, 1785–1812.* Transcr. Robert R. McCausland and Cynthia MacAlman McCausland. Introduction by Laurel Thatcher Ulrich. Maine Genealogical Soc. Special Publication No. 10, 1998.

Barber, John W. *American Scenes: A Selection of the Most Interesting Incidents in American History.* Springfield, Mass.: D. E. Fisk, 1868.

Baritz, Loren. *The Good Life: The Meaning of Success for the American Middle Class.* New York: Harper & Row, 1990.

Bentley, William. *Diary of William Bentley, D.D., Vol. III, 1803–1810.* Salem, Mass.: Essex Institute, 1911.

Bleier, Edward. *The Thanksgiving Ceremony: New Traditions for America's Family Feast.* New York: Crown Publishers, 2003.

Bradford, William. *Of Plymouth Plantation.* S. E. Morison, ed. New York: Knopf, 1984.

Brillat-Savarin, Jean Antheleme. *The Physiology of Taste.* New York: Liveright, 1970.

Brooks, Van Wyck. *The Flowering of New England.* New York: E. P. Dutton & Co., 1936.

Buell, Lawrence. *New England Literary Culture.* New York: Cambridge University Press, 1986.

Bunting, Eve. *How Many Days to America.* Beth Peck, illustrator. Boston: Clarion Books, 1990.

Bunting, Eve. *A Turkey for Thanksgiving.* Diane de Groat, illustrator. Boston: Clarion Books, 1991.

Carver, John [Theodore A. Dodge]. *Sketches of New England; or, Memories of the Country*. New York: E. French, 1842.

Cohen, Barbara. *Molly's Pilgrim*. Daniel Mark Duffy, illustrator. New York: Lothrop Lee and Shepard Company, 1983.

Coleman, William Macon. *The History of the Primitive Yankees; or, The Pilgrim Fathers in England and Holland*. Washington, D.C.: Columbia Publishing Company, 1881.

The Compact with the Charter and Laws of the Colony of New Plymouth. William Brigham, ed. Boston: Dutton and Wentworth for the State of Massachusetts, 1836.

Cooper, James Fenimore. *Works of J. Fenimore Cooper*. New York: P. F. Collier, 1891.

Corey, Shana. *Milly and the Macy's Parade*. Brett Helquist, illustrator. New York: Scholastic, 2002.

Cowley, Joy. *Gracias, the Thanksgiving Turkey*. Joe Cepeda, illustrator. New York: Scholastic, 1996.

Craven, Wesley Frank. *The Legend of the Founding Fathers*. Westport, Conn.: Greenwood Press, 1983.

Crosby, Constance. "The Indians and English use them much...," in *Cranberry Harvest: A History of Cranberry Growing in Massachusetts*, Joseph D. Thomas, ed. New Bedford, Mass.: Spinner Publications, 1990.

Daniziger, Paula. *Amber Brown Is Feeling Blue*. New York: Scholastic Paperbacks, 1999.

Davies, Horton. *The Worship of the American Puritans, 1629–1730*. New York: Peter Lang, 1990.

Davis, Dorothy. *A History of Shopping*. London: Routledge & Kegan Paul, 1966.

Davis, Susan G. *Parades and Power*. Berkeley: University of California Press, 1986.

Davis, William T. *Plymouth Memories of an Octogenarian*. Plymouth, Mass.: Memorial Press, 1907.

Diaz, Abby Morton. "A Plymouth Pilgrimage." *New England Magazine*, September 1889.

Diaz, Abby Morton. *The Schoolmaster's Trunk*. Boston: James R. Osgood & Co., 1875.

Dickinson, Asa Don. *The Children's Book of Thanksgiving Stories*. Garden City, N.J.: Doubleday, Page & Co., 1916.

Douglas, Ann. *The Feminization of American Culture*. New York: Anchor Books, 1988.

Earle, Alice Morse, ed. *The Diary of Anna Green Winslow*. Boston: Houghton Mifflin, 1894.

Earle, Alice Morse. *Stage-coach and Tavern Days*. New York: Macmillan, 1900.

Eco, Umberto. *A Theory of Semiotics*. Bloomington: Indiana University Press, 1979.

Elliott, Charles W. *The New England History*. New York: Charles Scribner, 1857.

Elson, Ruth Miller. *Guardians of Tradition*. Lincoln: University of Nebraska Press, 1964.

Emery, Anna. *Reminiscences of a Nonagenarian*. Newþuryport, Mass.: William H. Huse, 1879.

E[velyn], J[ohn]. *Acetaria: A Discourse of Sallets*. London, 1699.

Gildrie, Richard P. "Ceremonial Puritan Days of Humiliation and Thanksgiving." *New England Quarterly* 136 (January 1982).

Gillis, John R. *A World of Their Own Making*. New York: Basic Books, 1996.

Gomes, Peter. "The Darlings of Heaven." *Harvard Magazine*, November 1976.

Goodrich, Charles. *The Universal Traveler*. Hartford, Conn.: Canfield and Robbins, 1837.

Hale, Edward Everett. *A New England Boyhood*. New York: Cassell Publishing Co., 1893.

Hale, Sarah Josepha. *Northwood; or, Life North and South*, 2nd edition. New York: H. Long & Brother, 1852.

Hamilton, Gail [Mary Abigail Dodge]. *Red-Letter Days in Applethorpe*. Boston: Tichnor and Fields, 1855.

Hawthorne, Nathaniel. "John Inglefield's Thanksgiving." *United States Democratic Review*, vol. 7, no. 27, March 1840.

Hedrick, U. P., ed. *Sturtevant's Edible Plants of the World*. New York: Dover, 1972.

Herbert, Henry William. *Frank Forester's Field Sports of the United States*. New York: Stringer & Townsend, 1848.

Hertzberger, Hazel W. *The Search for an American Indian Identity*. Syracuse, N.Y.: Syracuse University Press, 1971.

Hoban, Lillian. *Silly Tilly's Thanksgiving Dinner*. New York: Harper Trophy, 1991.

Hobsbawm, Eric, and Terence Ranger. *The Invention of Tradition*. New York: Cambridge University Press, 1984.

Hood, Mary L. *Special Days in the Primary Grades*. Chicago: A. Flanagan Co., 1897.

Hooker, Richard J. *Food and Drink in America*. Indianapolis: Bobbs-Merrill, 1981.

[Hough, Franklin B., ed.]. *Proclamations for Thanksgiving Issued by the Continental Congress, Pres't Washington, by the National and State Governments on the Peace of 1815, and by the Governors of New York, &c.* Albany: Munsell & Rowland, 1858.

Howland, Mrs. E. A. *The New England Economical Housekeeper*. New London, Conn.: Bolles & Williams, 1848.

Hutchins, Francis G. *Mashpee: The Story of Cape Cod's Indian Town*. West Franklin, N.H.: Amarta Press, 1979.

Irish, Marie. *Choice Thanksgiving Entertainments*. Dayton, Ohio: Paine Publishing Co., 1923.

Irish, Marie. *The Days We Celebrate: A Collection of Original Dialogues, Recitations, Entertainments and Other Pieces for Holidays and Special Occasions*. Chicago: T. S. Denison & Co., 1904.

Josselyn, John. "An Account of Two Voyages to New England" (1675). In *Collections of the Massachusetts Historical Society*, series 3, vol. 3 (1833).

Josselyn, John. *New-Englands Rarities Discovered*. Boston: Massachusetts Historical Society, 1972.

A Journal of the Pilgrims at Plymouth [*Mourt's Relation*]. Dwight B. Heath, ed. New York: Corinth Books, 1963. See also *Relation or Iournall. . . .*

Kammen, Michael. *Mystic Chords of Memory: The Transformation of Tradition in American Culture*. New York: Knopf, 1991.

Keen, Josie. "Thanksgiving: A Home Scene." *Ladies' Repository*, 2nd series, vol. 14, no. 6, December 1874.

Kellogg, Amos M. *Special Day Exercises: Special Programs for School Celebrations*. Philadelphia: Penn Publishing, 1911.

Kennedy, David M. *Freedom from Fear: The American People in Depression and War, 1929–1945*. New York: Oxford University Press, 1999.

King, Caroline Howard. *When I Lived in Salem, 1822–1866*. Brattleboro, Vt.: Stephen Daye Press, 1937.

Kitch, Carolyn. *The Girl on the Magazine Cover: The Origins of Visual Stereotypes in American Mass Media*. Chapel Hill: University of North Carolina Press, 2001.

Koshar, Rudy. *From Monuments to Traces*. Berkeley: University of California Press, 2000.

Hunt, Robert. *A Treatise On The Progressive Improvement & Present State Of The Manufactures In Metal*, vol. 2. London: Longmans, 1853.

Lackland, Thomas. *Homespun; or, Five and Twenty Years Ago*. New York: Hurd & Houghton, 1867.

Larkin, Jack. *The Reshaping of Everyday Life, 1790–1840*. New York: Harper & Row, 1988.

Lears, Jackson. *Fables of Abundance: A Cultural History of Advertising in America*. New York: Basic Books, 1994.

Lears, Jackson. *No Place of Grace*. New York: Pantheon Books, 1981.

Lemay, J. A. Leo. *"New England's Annoyances": America's First Folk Song*. Newark: University of Delaware Press, 1985.

Lesley, Susan I. *Recollections of My Mother, Mrs. Anne Jean Lyman of Northampton*. Boston: Houghton, Mifflin, 1899.

Levenstein, Harvey. *Revolution at the Table*. New York: Oxford University Press, 1988.

Linton, Ralph and Adelin. *We Gather Together: The Story of Thanksgiving*. New York: Henry Schuman, 1949.

Litwicki, Ellen M. *America's Public Holidays, 1865–1920*. Washington, D.C.: Smithsonian Institution Press, 2000.

Lodge, Henry Cabot. *The Democracy of the Constitution and Other Addresses and Essays*. New York: Charles Scribner's Sons, 1915.

Lorwin, Madge. *Dining with William Shakespeare*. New York: Athenaeum, 1976.

Lossing, Benson J. *Pictorial History of the Civil War in the United States of America*. Philadelphia: George Childs, 1866.

Love, William DeLoss. *Fast and Thanksgiving Days of New England.* Boston: Houghton, Mifflin, 1895.

Lunt, George. *Old New England Traits.* New York: Hurd & Houghton, 1873.

Marling, Karal Ann. *George Washington Slept Here: Colonial Revivals and American Culture, 1876–1986.* Cambridge, Mass.: Harvard University Press, 1988.

Matthews, Albert. "The Term 'Pilgrim Fathers' and Early Celebrations of Forefathers' Day." *Transactions of the Colonial Society of Massachusetts* 17 (1914).

Matthews, Glenna. *"Just A Housewife": The Rise & Fall of Domesticity in America.* New York: Oxford University Press, 1978.

May, Sophie [Rebecca S. Clarke]. *Dotty Dimple at Play.* Boston: Lothrop, Lee & Shepard Co., 1910. Originally published 1868.

Mayfield, John. *The New Nation, 1800–1845.* New York: Hill and Wang, 1982.

McCully, Emily Arnold. *An Outlaw Thanksgiving.* New York: Puffin Books, 2000.

Miller, George and Dorothy. *Picture Postcards in the United States, 1893–1918.* New York: Clarkson N. Potter, 1976.

Miller, May. "The Great Pilgrimage." *Our Young Folks,* November 1866.

Mitchell, Edwin Valentine. *It's an Old New England Custom.* New York: Vanguard, 1947.

Mitchell, W.J.T. *Iconology: Image, Text, Ideology.* Chicago: University of Chicago Press, 1986.

Morison, Samuel Eliot. *The Pilgrim Fathers: Their Significance in History.* Concord, N.H.: Society of Mayflower Descendants in the State of New Hampshire, 1937.

Morton, Nathaniel. *New England's Memorial.* John Davis, ed. Boston: Crocker and Brewster, 1826.

Moseley, Laura H., ed. *The Diaries of Julia Cowles: A Connecticut Record, 1797–1803.* New Haven, Conn.: Yale University Press, 1931.

Mourt's Relation. See *Relation or Iournall....* See also *Journal of the Pilgrims at Plymouth.*

Nichols, Thomas. *Forty Years of American Life, 1821–1861* (1864). New York: Stackpole and Sons, 1937.

Nissenbaum, Stephen. *The Battle for Christmas.* New York: Knopf, 1996.

Novotnoy, Louise Miller, and Ida Lee Wolfe. *The Standard Thanksgiving Book No. 1.* Cincinnati: Standard Publishing Co., 1937.

Oliver, Sandra. *Saltwater Foodways.* Mystic, Conn.: Mystic Seaport Museum, 1995.

Pieterse, Jan Nederveen. *White on Black: Images of Africans and Blacks in Western Popular Culture.* New Haven, Conn.: Yale University Press, 1992.

The Pilgrim Memorial to be erected in The Town of Plymouth, Massachusetts. Plymouth: Plimoth Plantation, Inc., 1948.

Pimlott, J.A.R. *The Englishman's Christmas.* Hassocks, Sussex: Harvester Press, 1978.

Pleck, Elizabeth H. *Celebrating the Family: Ethnicity, Consumer Culture, and Family Rituals.* Cambridge, Mass.: Harvard University Press, 2000.

Pope, S. W. *Patriotic Games: Sporting Traditions in the American Imagination, 1876–1926.* New York: Oxford University Press, 1997.

Preston, Effa E. *The Children's Thanksgiving Book.* Lebanon, Ohio: March Brothers, 1928.

Purchas, Samuel. *Hakluytus Posthumus or Purchas His Pilgrimes. Contayning a History of the World in Sea Voyages and Lande Travells by Englishmen and others.* London: Imprinted for H. Fetherston, 1625.

Pyle, Arthur. *Thanksgiving Day Observance.* Plymouth, Mass.: Plimoth Plantation, n.d. (ca. 1962).

Rael, Elsa Okon. *Rivka's First Thanksgiving.* Maryann Kovalski, illustrator. New York: Athenaeum/Simon & Schuster, 2004.

A Relation or Iournall of the beginning and proceedings of the English Plantation settled at Plimoth in New England, facsimile edition. Chester, Vt.: Readex Microprint, 1966. See also *Journal of the Pilgrims at Plymouth. . . .*

Report of the Pilgrim Tercentenary Commission, January 3, 1917. Boston: Wright & Potter, 1917.

Restad, Penny L. *Christmas in America.* New York: Oxford University Press, 1995.

Salomon, Gabriel. *Interaction of Media, Cognition, and Learning.* San Francisco: Jossey-Bass Publishers, 1981.

San Souci, Robert. *N. C. Wyeth's Pilgrims.* New York: Chronicle Books, 1991.

Santino, Jack. *All around the Year: Holidays and Celebrations in American Life.* Urbana: University of Illinois Press, 1995.

Scarry, Richard. *First Thanksgiving of Low Leaf Worm.* New York: Little Simon (Simon and Schuster), 2003.

Schauffler, Robert Haven. *Thanksgiving: Its Origin, Celebration and Significance as Revealed in Prose and Verse.* Our American Holidays Series. New York: Dodd, Mead and Co., 1907.

Schell, Stanley. *Thanksgiving Celebrations No. 1.* New York: Edgar S. Werner Publishing and Supply Co., 1901.

Schmidt, Leigh Eric. *Consumer Rites: The Buying and Selling of American Holidays.* Princeton, N.J.: Princeton University Press, 1993.

Schwartz, Barry. *Abraham Lincoln and the Forge of National Memory.* Chicago: University of Chicago Press, 1992.

"Scituate and Barnstable Church Records." In *The New England Historical and Genealogical Register,* vol. 10. Boston, 1856.

Scott, Benjamin. *The Pilgrim Fathers Neither Puritans Nor Persecutors,* 4th edition. London: Elliot Stock, 1891.

Sickel, H.S.J. *Thanksgiving: Its Source, Philosophy and History.* Philadelphia: International Printing Company, 1940.

Simmons, Amelia. *American Cookery,* facsimile of 1796 Hartford edition. New York: Oxford University Press, 1958.

Siskind, Janet. "The Invention of Thanksgiving: A Ritual of American Nationality." *Critique of Anthropology* 12 (1992).

Slotkin, Richard, and James K. Folsom. *So Dreadful a Judgment*. Middletown, Conn.: Wesleyan University Press, 1978.

Smalls, Irene. *A Strawbeater's Thanksgiving*. Melodye Benson Rosales, illustrator. Boston: Little Brown & Co, 1998.

Solomon, Barbara Miller. *Ancestors and Immigrants*. Chicago: University of Chicago Press, 1972.

Spirn, Michele Sobel. *The Know-Nothings Talk Turkey*. R. W. Alley, illustrator. New York: HarperCollins, 2000.

Stowe, Harriet Beecher. *Oldtown Folks*. Boston: Fields, Osgood & Co., 1869.

Strong, Roy. *Recreating the Past*. London: Thames and Hudson, 1978.

Sullivan, Robert, ed. *America's Parade: A Celebration of Macy's Thanksgiving Day Parade*. New York: Time-Life, 2001.

Tanner, Suzy-Jane. *The Tasty Thanksgiving Feast*. New York: Harper Festival, 1998.

"Thanksgiving Day in New York Up To Date." *Harper's Weekly*, November 28, 1891.

Thanksgiving Souvenir. New Philadelphia: Ohio Printing Company, 1908.

Thompson, Elroy S. *History of Plymouth, Norfolk and Barnstable Counties, Massachusetts*. New York: Lewis Historical Publishing Co., 1928.

Trollope, Frances. *Domestic Manners of the Americans*. New York: Knopf, 1949.

Twitchell, James B. *Adcult USA: The Triumph of Advertising in American Culture*. New York: Columbia University Press, 1996.

Ulrich, Laurel Thatcher. *The Age of Homespun*. New York: Knopf, 2001.

Ulrich, Laurel Thatcher. *A Midwife's Tale: The Life of Martha Ballard, Based on Her Diary, 1785–1812*. New York: Random House, 1991.

Union League Club. *Report on the Committee on Providing a Thanksgiving Dinner for the Soldiers and Sailors*. New York: Union League Club House, 1865.

Vartanian, Pershing. "The Puritan as Symbol in American Thought: A Study of the New England Societies." PhD dissertation, University of Michigan, 1971.

Ward, Artemus. *The Grocer's Encyclopedia*. New York: Artemus Ward, 1911.

Warner, Charles Dudley. *Being a Boy*. Boston: James R. Osgood, 1878.

Weibe, Robert H. *The Search for Order, 1877–1920*. New York: Hill and Wang, 1967.

Whiting, Edward. *Changing New England*. New York: Century Co., 1929.

Wichmann, Siegfried. *Japonisme: The Japanese Influence on Western Art since 1858*. New York: Thames & Hudson, 1981.

Wiggin, Kate Douglas, and Nora A. Smith. *The Story Hour: A Book for The Home and The Kindergarten*. Boston: Houghton, Mifflin, 1890.

Williams, William Carlos. *In the American Grain*. New York: New Directions, 1956.

Wilson, C. Anne. *Food & Drink in Britain*. London: Constable, 1973.

Wilson, John F. *Pulpit in Parliament*. Princeton, N.J.: Princeton University Press, 1969.

Winslow, Edward. "Good News from New England." In *A Library of American*

Puritan Writings: The Seventeenth Century, Volume 9, Histories and Narratives. New York: AMS Press, 1986.

Winton, Ben. "Alcatraz Indian Land." *Native Peoples Magazine*, Fall 1999.

Young, Alexander. *Chronicles of the First Planters of the Colony of Massachusetts Bay from 1623 to 1636*. Boston: Charles C. Little and James Brown, 1846.

Young, Alexander. *Chronicles of the Pilgrim Fathers of the Colony of Plymouth*. Boston: Charles C. Little and James Brown, 1841.

Index

Page numbers in italics refer to illustrations.